THOR

The Asgard/Shi'ar War

WRITER: JASON AARON
ARTISTS: STEVE EPTING (issues #13-14)
& RUSSELL DAUTERMAN (issues #15-19)
COLOURS: FRANK MARTIN (issue #13-14)
& MATT WILSON (issues #15-19)
LETTERS: VIRTUAL CALLIGRAPHY'S JOE SABINO

ASSISTANT EDITOR: CHARLES BEACHAM (ISSUES #13-15)
& SARAH BRUNSTAD (ISSUE #16-19)
EDITOR: WIL MOSS
EXECUTIVE EDITOR: TOM BREVOORT
CHIEF CREATIVE OFFICER: JOE QUESADA
EXECUTIVE PRODUCER: ALAN FINE
EDITOR-IN-CHIEF: AXEL ALONSO
PUBLISHER: DAN BUCKLEY

COVER ART: RUSSELL DAUTERMAN & MATT WILSON

THE MIGHTY THOR CREATED BY STAN LEE, LARRY LIEBER & JACK KIRBY

Do you have any comments or queries about Mighty Thor Vol. 3: The Asgard/Shi'ar War?
Email us at graphicnovels@panini.co.uk Join us on Facebook at Panini/Marvel Graphic Novels

TM & © 2017 Marvel & Subs. Licensed by Marvel Characters B.V. through Panini S.p.A., Italy. All Rights Reserved. First printing 2017. Published by Panini Publishing, a division of Panini UK Limited. Mike Riddell, Managing Director. Alan O'Keefe, Managing Editor. Mark Irvine, Production Manager. Marco M. Lupoi, Publishing Director Europe. Brady Webb, Reprint Editor. Charlotte Harvey, Designer. Office of publication: Brockbourne House, 77 Mount Ephraim, Tunbridge Wells, Kent TN4 8BS. This publication may not be sold, except by authorised dealers, and is sold subject to the condition that it shall not be sold or distributed with any part of its cover or markings removed, nor in a mutilated condition. Printed in Italy by Lito Terrazzi. ISBN: 978-1-84653-814-8.

MARVEL
marvel.com
© 2017 Marvel

MIX
Paper from
responsible sources
FSC® C016466

MARVEL GRAPHIC NOVEL

MIGHTY THOR #13

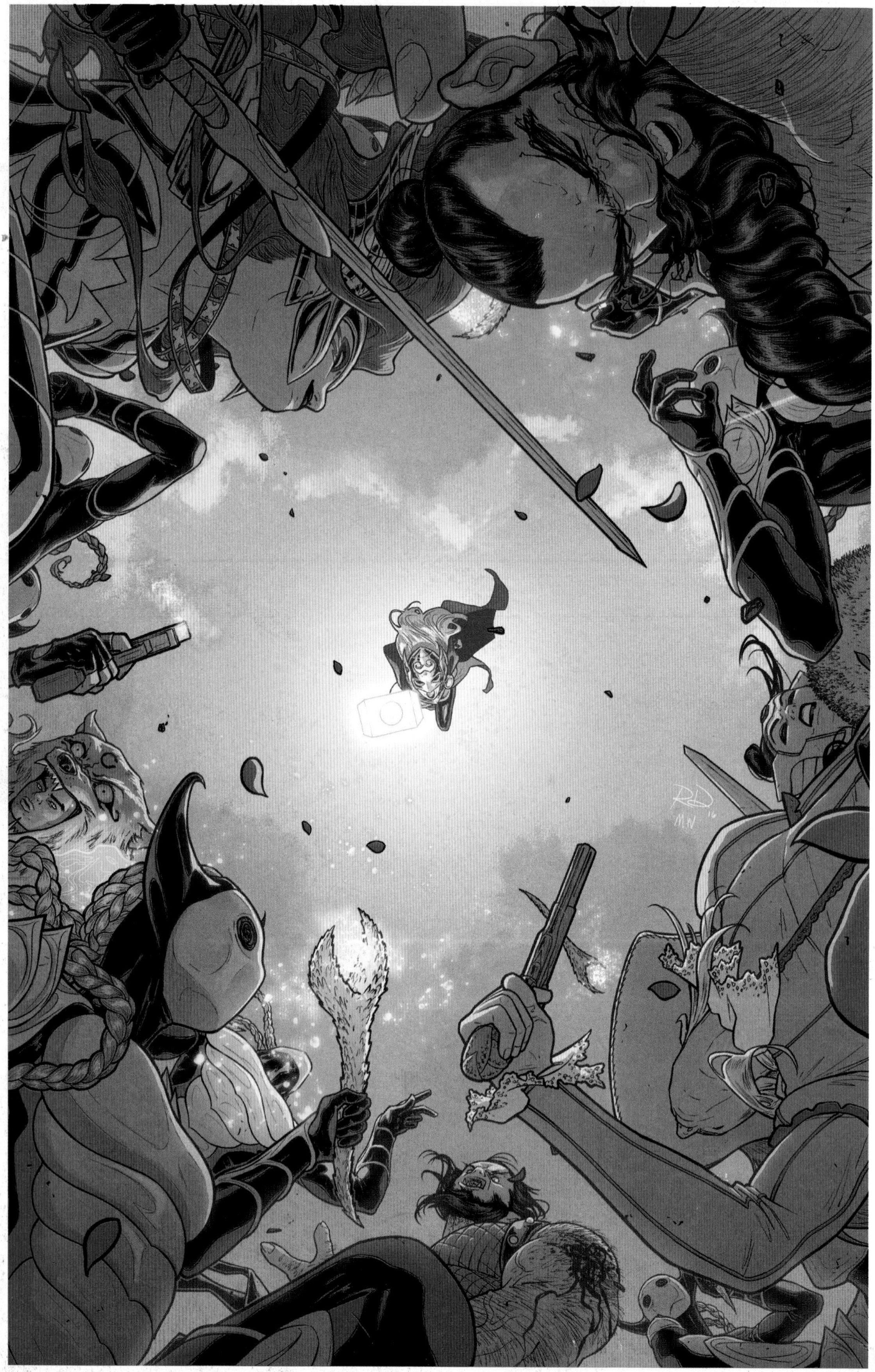

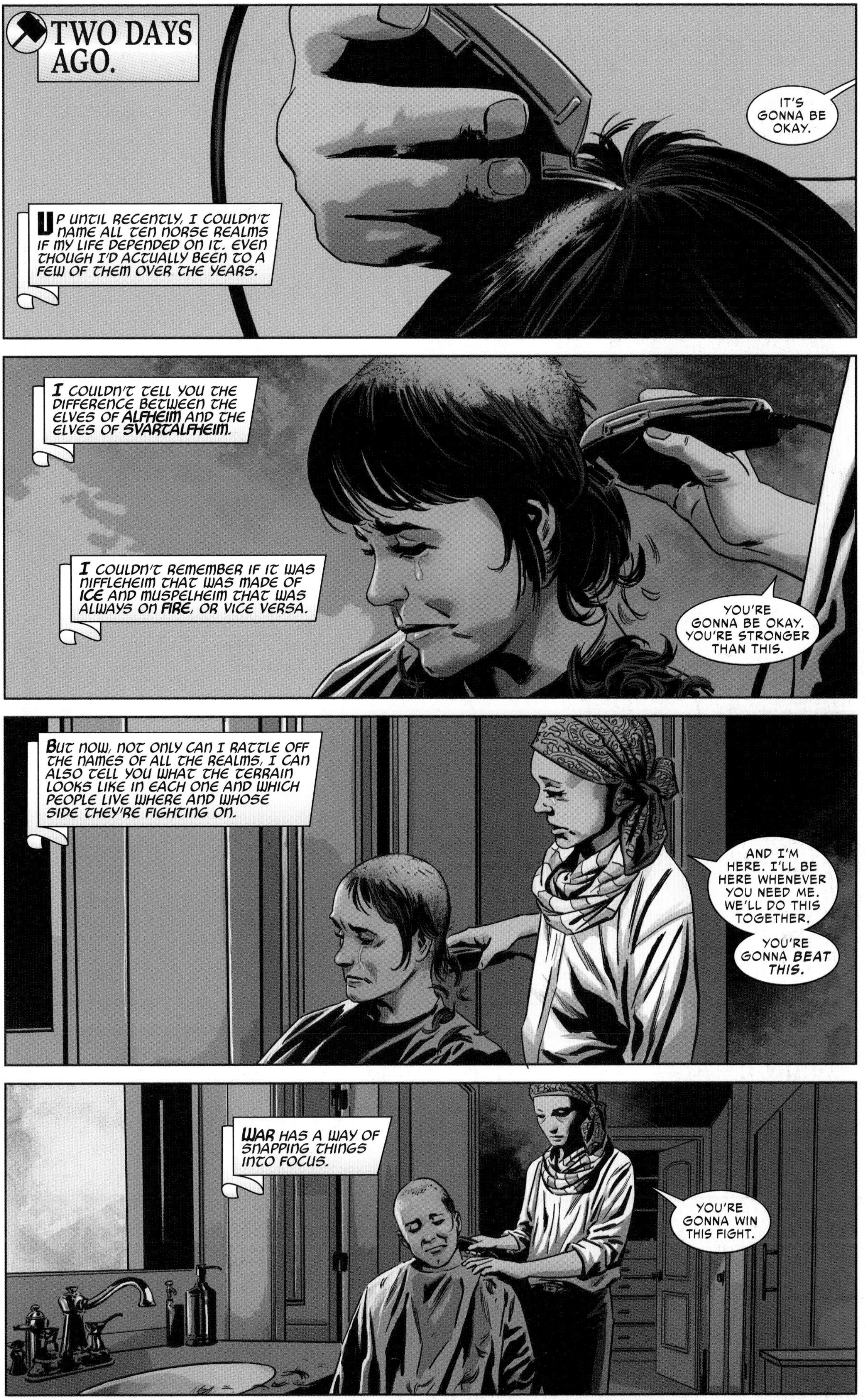
TWO DAYS AGO.
UP UNTIL RECENTLY, I COULDN'T NAME ALL TEN NORSE REALMS IF MY LIFE DEPENDED ON IT. EVEN THOUGH I'D ACTUALLY BEEN TO A FEW OF THEM OVER THE YEARS.
IT'S GONNA BE OKAY.
I COULDN'T TELL YOU THE DIFFERENCE BETWEEN THE ELVES OF ALFHEIM AND THE ELVES OF SVARTALFHEIM.
I COULDN'T REMEMBER IF IT WAS NIFFLEHEIM THAT WAS MADE OF ICE AND MUSPELHEIM THAT WAS ALWAYS ON FIRE, OR VICE VERSA.
YOU'RE GONNA BE OKAY. YOU'RE STRONGER THAN THIS.
BUT NOW, NOT ONLY CAN I RATTLE OFF THE NAMES OF ALL THE REALMS, I CAN ALSO TELL YOU WHAT THE TERRAIN LOOKS LIKE IN EACH ONE AND WHICH PEOPLE LIVE WHERE AND WHOSE SIDE THEY'RE FIGHTING ON.
AND I'M HERE. I'LL BE HERE WHENEVER YOU NEED ME. WE'LL DO THIS TOGETHER.
YOU'RE GONNA BEAT THIS.
WAR HAS A WAY OF SNAPPING THINGS INTO FOCUS.
YOU'RE GONNA WIN THIS FIGHT.

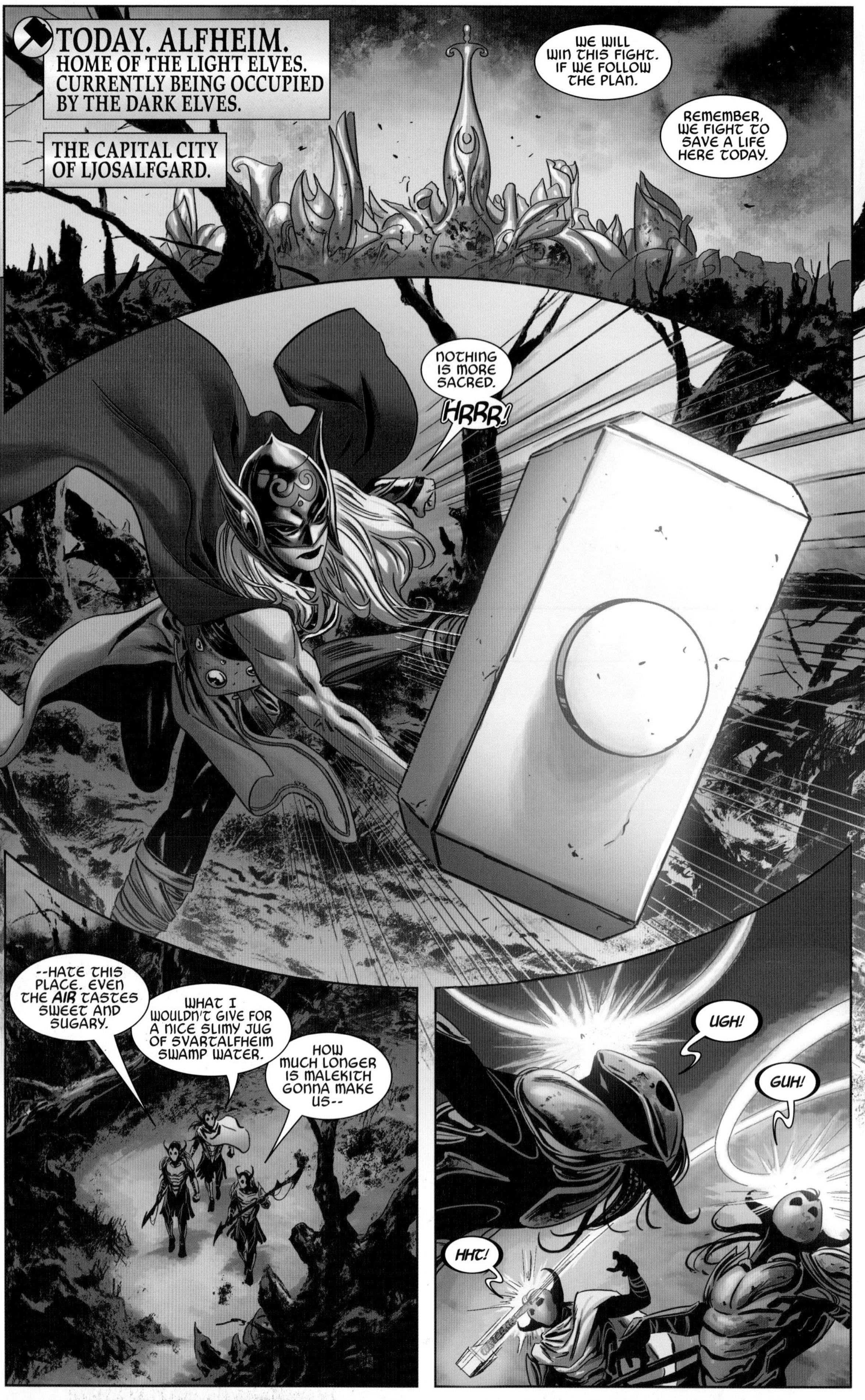
TODAY. ALFHEIM.
HOME OF THE LIGHT ELVES. CURRENTLY BEING OCCUPIED BY THE DARK ELVES.
THE CAPITAL CITY OF LJOSALFGARD.
WE WILL WIN THIS FIGHT. IF WE FOLLOW THE PLAN.
REMEMBER, WE FIGHT TO SAVE A LIFE HERE TODAY.
NOTHING IS MORE SACRED.
HRRR!
--HATE THIS PLACE. EVEN THE AIR TASTES SWEET AND SUGARY.
WHAT I WOULDN'T GIVE FOR A NICE SLIMY JUG OF SVARTALFHEIM SWAMP WATER.
HOW MUCH LONGER IS MALEKITH GONNA MAKE US--
UGH!
GUH!
HHT!

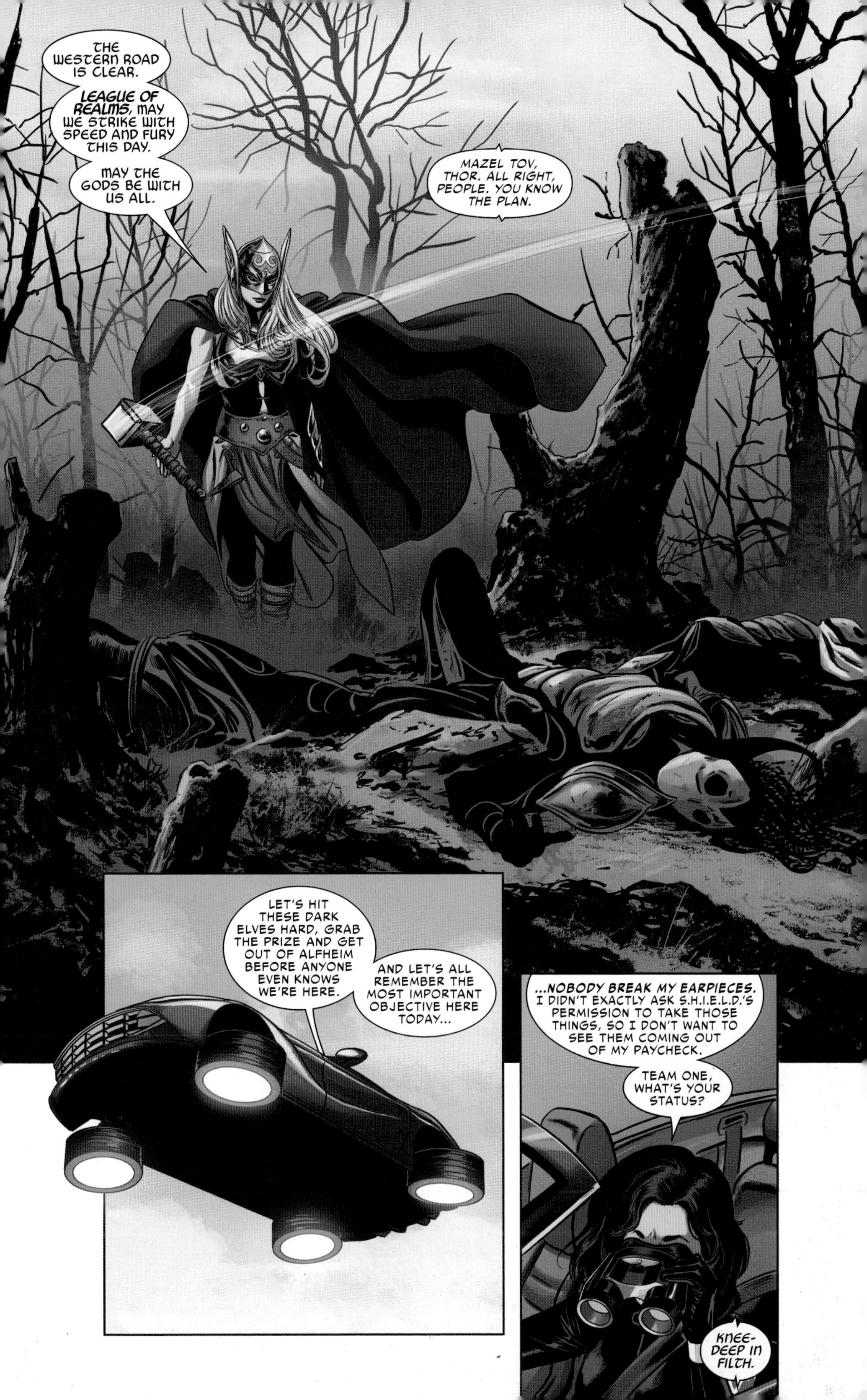
THE WESTERN ROAD IS CLEAR.
LEAGUE OF REALMS, MAY WE STRIKE WITH SPEED AND FURY THIS DAY.
MAY THE GODS BE WITH US ALL.
MAZEL TOV, THOR. ALL RIGHT, PEOPLE. YOU KNOW THE PLAN.
LET'S HIT THESE DARK ELVES HARD, GRAB THE PRIZE AND GET OUT OF ALFHEIM BEFORE ANYONE EVEN KNOWS WE'RE HERE.
AND LET'S ALL REMEMBER THE MOST IMPORTANT OBJECTIVE HERE TODAY...
...NOBODY BREAK MY EARPIECES. I DIDN'T EXACTLY ASK S.H.I.E.L.D.'S PERMISSION TO TAKE THOSE THINGS, SO I DON'T WANT TO SEE THEM COMING OUT OF MY PAYCHECK.
TEAM ONE, WHAT'S YOUR STATUS?
KNEE-DEEP IN FILTH.

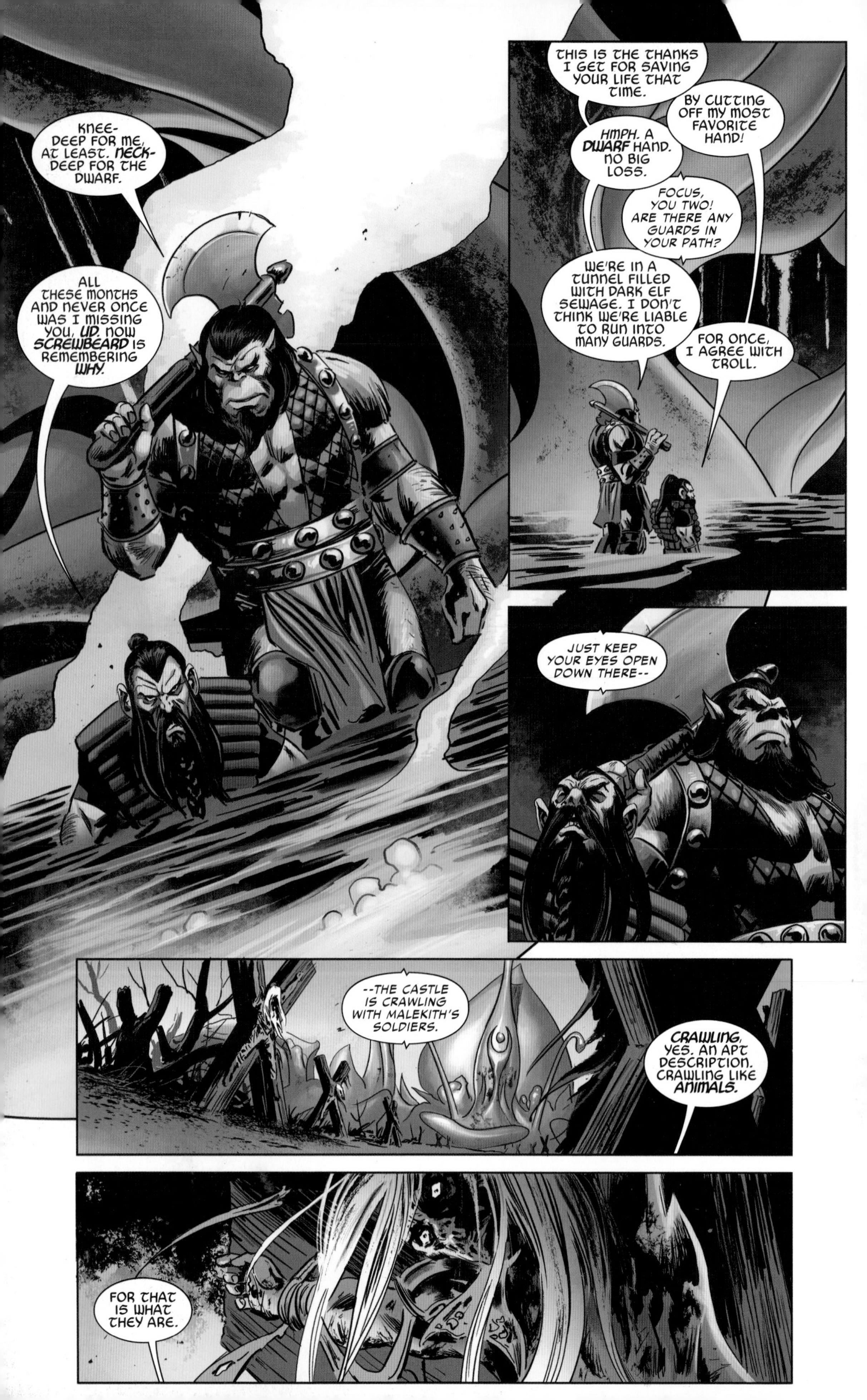
KNEE-DEEP FOR ME, AT LEAST. NECK-DEEP FOR THE DWARF.
ALL THESE MONTHS AND NEVER ONCE WAS I MISSING YOU, UD. NOW SCREWBEARD IS REMEMBERING WHY.
THIS IS THE THANKS I GET FOR SAVING YOUR LIFE THAT TIME.
BY CUTTING OFF MY MOST FAVORITE HAND!
HMPH. A DWARF HAND. NO BIG LOSS.
FOCUS, YOU TWO! ARE THERE ANY GUARDS IN YOUR PATH?
WE'RE IN A TUNNEL FILLED WITH DARK ELF SEWAGE. I DON'T THINK WE'RE LIABLE TO RUN INTO MANY GUARDS.
FOR ONCE, I AGREE WITH TROLL.
JUST KEEP YOUR EYES OPEN DOWN THERE--
--THE CASTLE IS CRAWLING WITH MALEKITH'S SOLDIERS.
CRAWLING, YES. AN APT DESCRIPTION. CRAWLING LIKE ANIMALS.
FOR THAT IS WHAT THEY ARE.

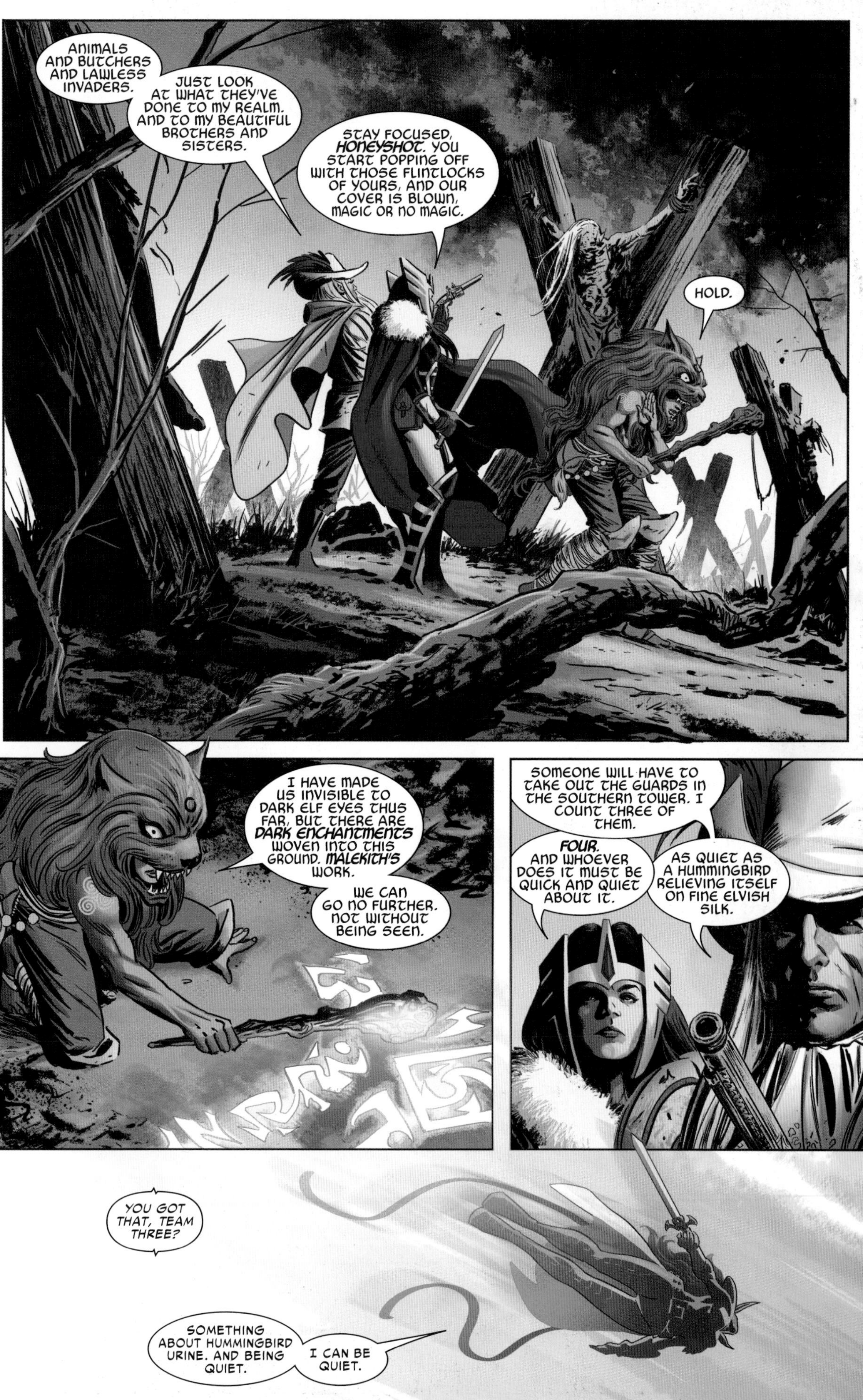

ANIMALS AND BUTCHERS AND LAWLESS INVADERS.
JUST LOOK AT WHAT THEY'VE DONE TO MY REALM. AND TO MY BEAUTIFUL BROTHERS AND SISTERS.
STAY FOCUSED, HONEYSHOT. YOU START POPPING OFF WITH THOSE FLINTLOCKS OF YOURS, AND OUR COVER IS BLOWN, MAGIC OR NO MAGIC.
HOLD.
I HAVE MADE US INVISIBLE TO DARK ELF EYES THUS FAR, BUT THERE ARE DARK ENCHANTMENTS WOVEN INTO THIS GROUND. MALEKITH'S WORK.
WE CAN GO NO FURTHER. NOT WITHOUT BEING SEEN.
SOMEONE WILL HAVE TO TAKE OUT THE GUARDS IN THE SOUTHERN TOWER. I COUNT THREE OF THEM.
FOUR. AND WHOEVER DOES IT MUST BE QUICK AND QUIET ABOUT IT.
AS QUIET AS A HUMMINGBIRD RELIEVING ITSELF ON FINE ELVISH SILK.
YOU GOT THAT, TEAM THREE?
SOMETHING ABOUT HUMMINGBIRD URINE. AND BEING QUIET.
I CAN BE QUIET.

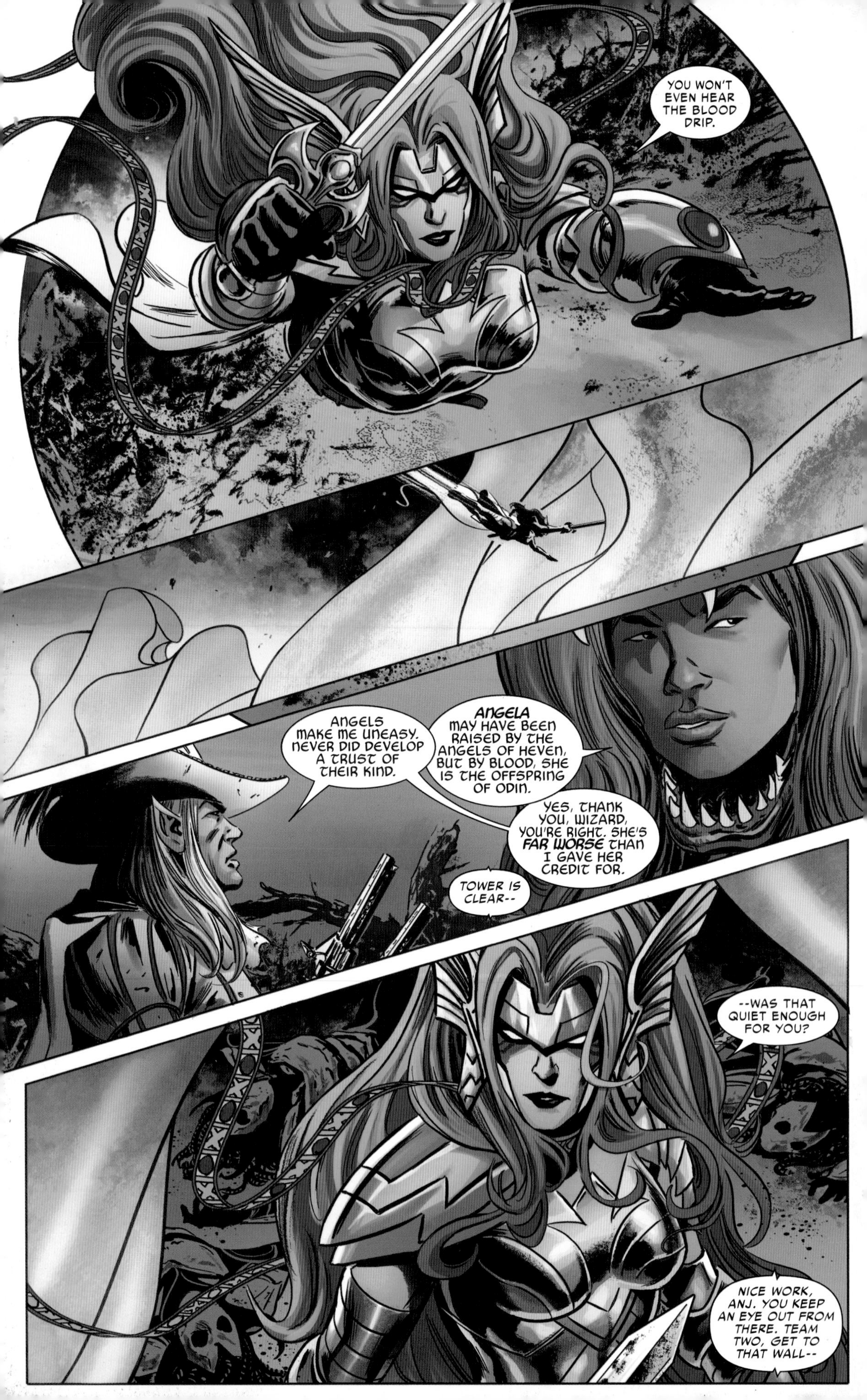
YOU WON'T EVEN HEAR THE BLOOD DRIP.
ANGELS MAKE ME UNEASY. NEVER DID DEVELOP A TRUST OF THEIR KIND.
ANGELA MAY HAVE BEEN RAISED BY THE ANGELS OF HEVEN, BUT BY BLOOD, SHE IS THE OFFSPRING OF ODIN.
YES, THANK YOU, WIZARD, YOU'RE RIGHT. SHE'S FAR WORSE THAN I GAVE HER CREDIT FOR.
TOWER IS CLEAR--
--WAS THAT QUIET ENOUGH FOR YOU?
NICE WORK, ANJ. YOU KEEP AN EYE OUT FROM THERE. TEAM TWO, GET TO THAT WALL--

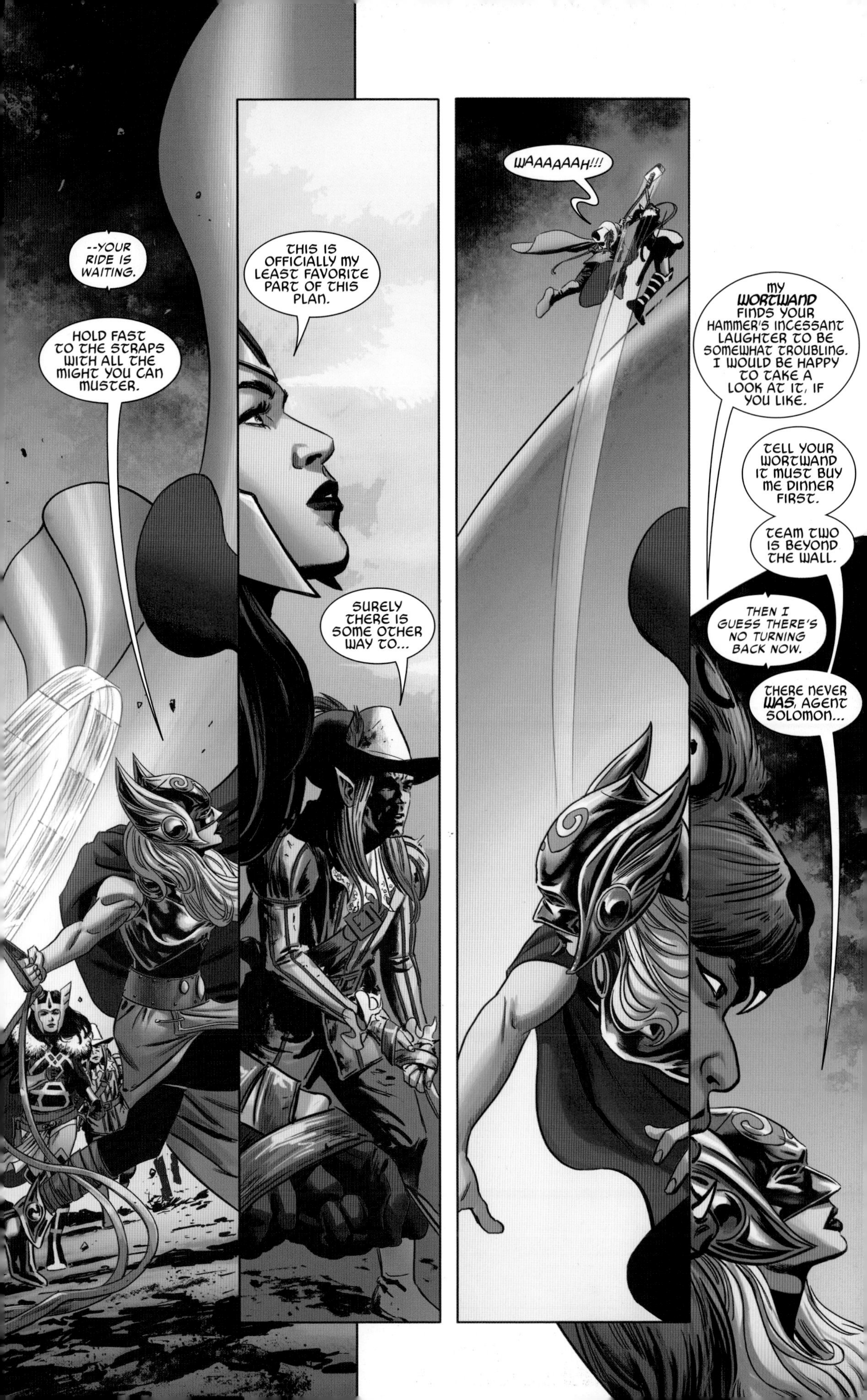
--YOUR RIDE IS WAITING.
HOLD FAST TO THE STRAPS WITH ALL THE MIGHT YOU CAN MUSTER.
THIS IS OFFICIALLY MY LEAST FAVORITE PART OF THIS PLAN.
SURELY THERE IS SOME OTHER WAY TO...
WAAAAAAH!!!
MY WORTWAND FINDS YOUR HAMMER'S INCESSANT LAUGHTER TO BE SOMEWHAT TROUBLING. I WOULD BE HAPPY TO TAKE A LOOK AT IT, IF YOU LIKE.
TELL YOUR WORTWAND IT MUST BUY ME DINNER FIRST.
TEAM TWO IS BEYOND THE WALL.
THEN I GUESS THERE'S NO TURNING BACK NOW.
THERE NEVER WAS, AGENT SOLOMON...

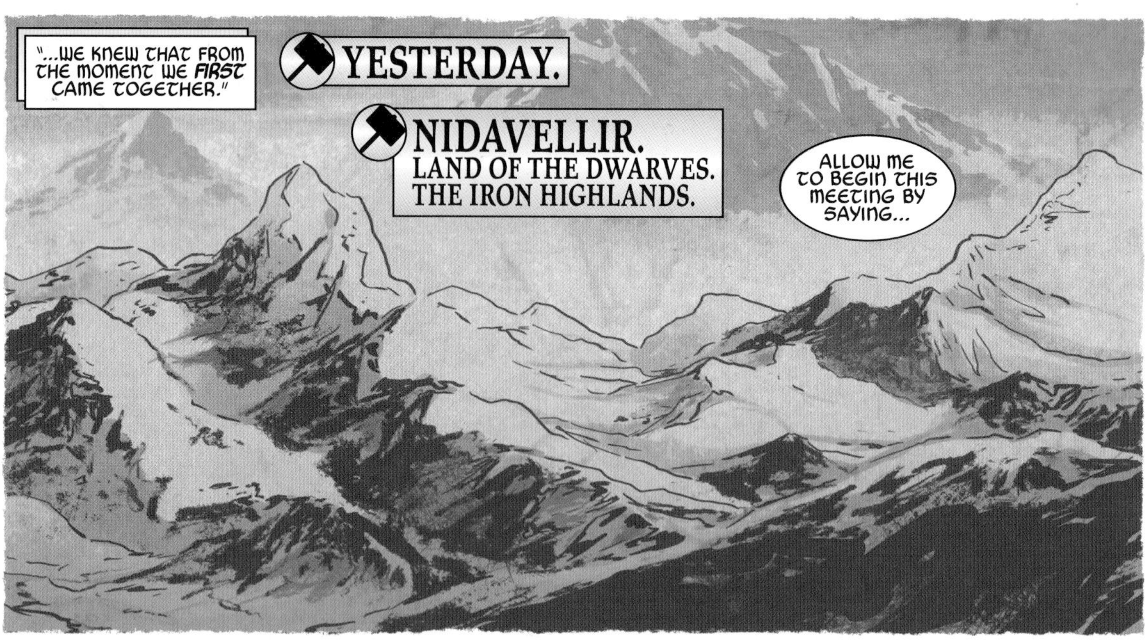
"...WE KNEW THAT FROM THE MOMENT WE FIRST CAME TOGETHER."
YESTERDAY.
NIDAVELLIR. LAND OF THE DWARVES. THE IRON HIGHLANDS.
ALLOW ME TO BEGIN THIS MEETING BY SAYING...

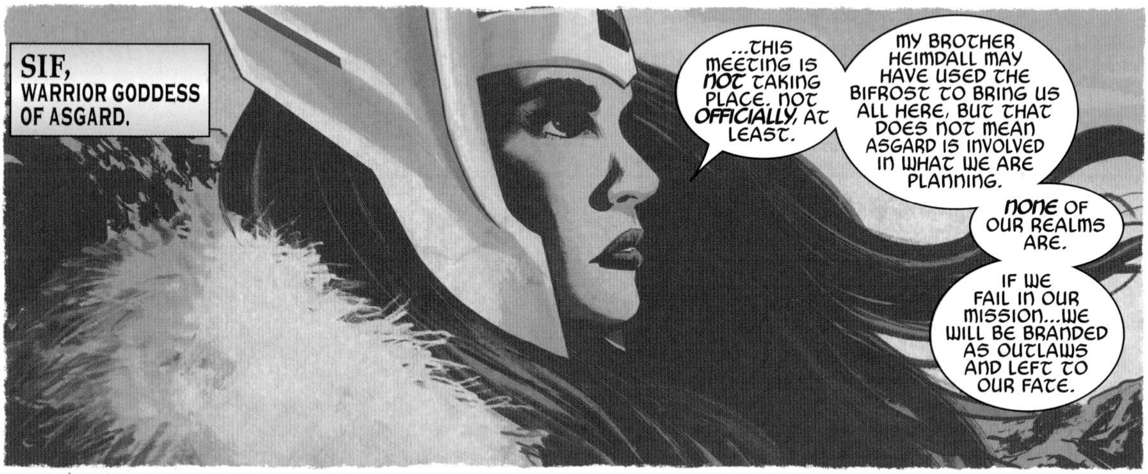
SIF, WARRIOR GODDESS OF ASGARD.
...THIS MEETING IS NOT TAKING PLACE. NOT OFFICIALLY, AT LEAST.
MY BROTHER HEIMDALL MAY HAVE USED THE BIFROST TO BRING US ALL HERE, BUT THAT DOES NOT MEAN ASGARD IS INVOLVED IN WHAT WE ARE PLANNING.
NONE OF OUR REALMS ARE.
IF WE FAIL IN OUR MISSION...WE WILL BE BRANDED AS OUTLAWS AND LEFT TO OUR FATE.

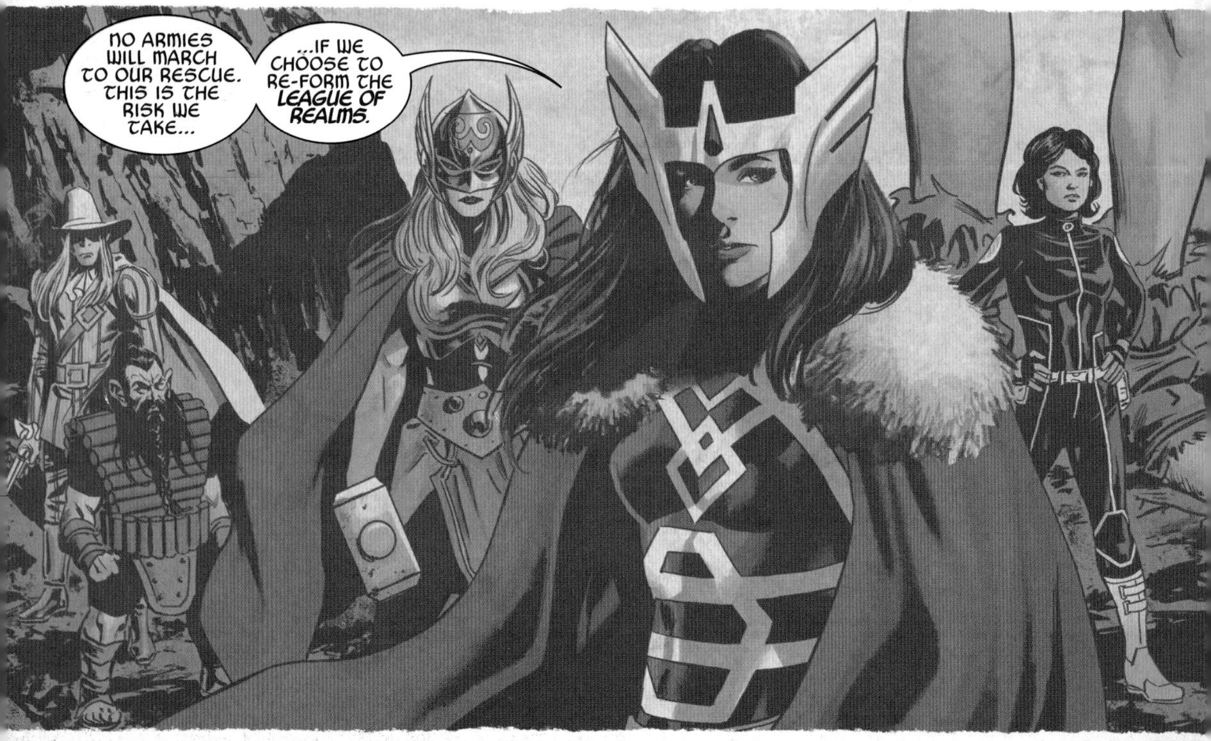
NO ARMIES WILL MARCH TO OUR RESCUE. THIS IS THE RISK WE TAKE...
...IF WE CHOOSE TO RE-FORM THE LEAGUE OF REALMS.

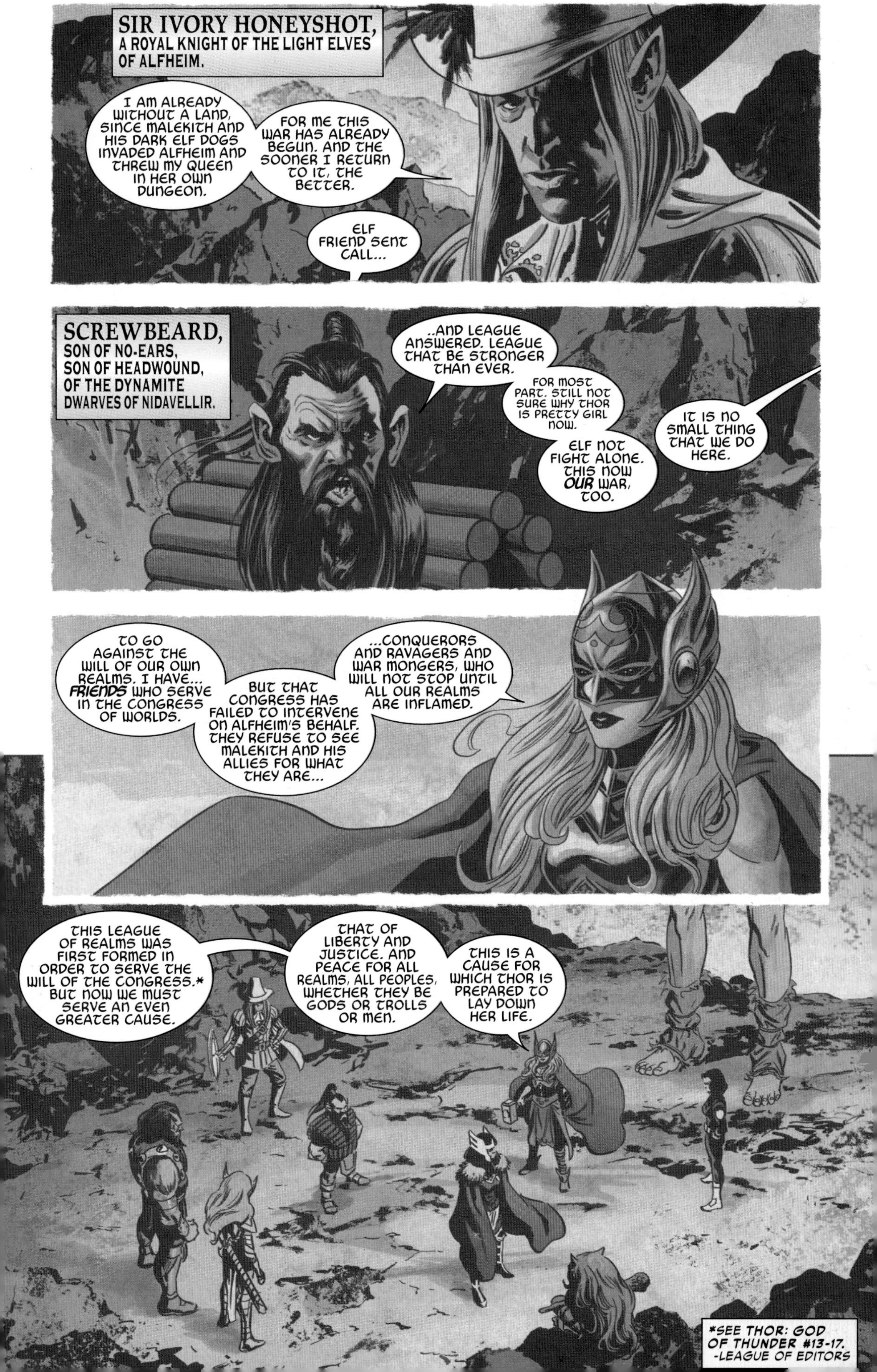
SIR IVORY HONEYSHOT, A ROYAL KNIGHT OF THE LIGHT ELVES OF ALFHEIM.
I AM ALREADY WITHOUT A LAND, SINCE MALEKITH AND HIS DARK ELF DOGS INVADED ALFHEIM AND THREW MY QUEEN IN HER OWN DUNGEON.
FOR ME THIS WAR HAS ALREADY BEGUN. AND THE SOONER I RETURN TO IT, THE BETTER.
ELF FRIEND SENT CALL...
SCREWBEARD, SON OF NO-EARS, SON OF HEADWOUND, OF THE DYNAMITE DWARVES OF NIDAVELLIR.
..AND LEAGUE ANSWERED. LEAGUE THAT BE STRONGER THAN EVER.
FOR MOST PART. STILL NOT SURE WHY THOR IS PRETTY GIRL NOW.
ELF NOT FIGHT ALONE. THIS NOW OUR WAR, TOO.
IT IS NO SMALL THING THAT WE DO HERE.
TO GO AGAINST THE WILL OF OUR OWN REALMS. I HAVE... FRIENDS WHO SERVE IN THE CONGRESS OF WORLDS.
BUT THAT CONGRESS HAS FAILED TO INTERVENE ON ALFHEIM'S BEHALF. THEY REFUSE TO SEE MALEKITH AND HIS ALLIES FOR WHAT THEY ARE...
...CONQUERORS AND RAVAGERS AND WAR MONGERS, WHO WILL NOT STOP UNTIL ALL OUR REALMS ARE INFLAMED.
THIS LEAGUE OF REALMS WAS FIRST FORMED IN ORDER TO SERVE THE WILL OF THE CONGRESS.* BUT NOW WE MUST SERVE AN EVEN GREATER CAUSE.
THAT OF LIBERTY AND JUSTICE. AND PEACE FOR ALL REALMS, ALL PEOPLES, WHETHER THEY BE GODS OR TROLLS OR MEN.
THIS IS A CAUSE FOR WHICH THOR IS PREPARED TO LAY DOWN HER LIFE.
*SEE THOR: GOD OF THUNDER #13-17. -LEAGUE OF EDITORS

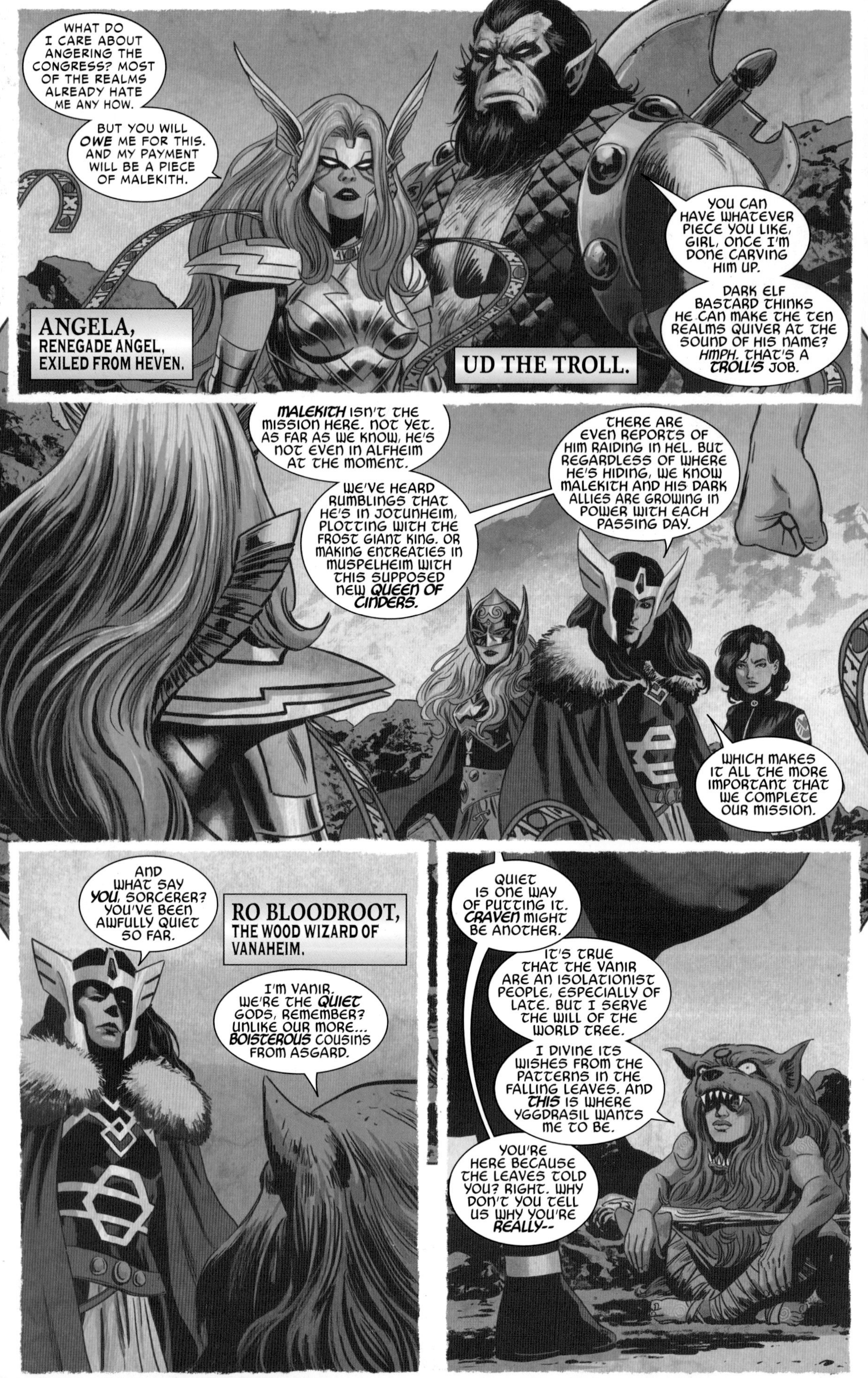

WHAT DO I CARE ABOUT ANGERING THE CONGRESS? MOST OF THE REALMS ALREADY HATE ME ANY HOW.
BUT YOU WILL OWE ME FOR THIS. AND MY PAYMENT WILL BE A PIECE OF MALEKITH.
YOU CAN HAVE WHATEVER PIECE YOU LIKE, GIRL, ONCE I'M DONE CARVING HIM UP.
DARK ELF BASTARD THINKS HE CAN MAKE THE TEN REALMS QUIVER AT THE SOUND OF HIS NAME? HMPH. THAT'S A TROLL'S JOB.
ANGELA, RENEGADE ANGEL, EXILED FROM HEVEN.
UD THE TROLL.
MALEKITH ISN'T THE MISSION HERE. NOT YET. AS FAR AS WE KNOW, HE'S NOT EVEN IN ALFHEIM AT THE MOMENT.
WE'VE HEARD RUMBLINGS THAT HE'S IN JOTUNHEIM, PLOTTING WITH THE FROST GIANT KING. OR MAKING ENTREATIES IN MUSPELHEIM WITH THIS SUPPOSED NEW QUEEN OF CINDERS.
THERE ARE EVEN REPORTS OF HIM RAIDING IN HEL. BUT REGARDLESS OF WHERE HE'S HIDING, WE KNOW MALEKITH AND HIS DARK ALLIES ARE GROWING IN POWER WITH EACH PASSING DAY.
WHICH MAKES IT ALL THE MORE IMPORTANT THAT WE COMPLETE OUR MISSION.
AND WHAT SAY YOU, SORCERER? YOU'VE BEEN AWFULLY QUIET SO FAR.
RO BLOODROOT, THE WOOD WIZARD OF VANAHEIM.
I'M VANIR. WE'RE THE QUIET GODS, REMEMBER? UNLIKE OUR MORE... BOISTEROUS COUSINS FROM ASGARD.
QUIET IS ONE WAY OF PUTTING IT. CRAVEN MIGHT BE ANOTHER.
IT'S TRUE THAT THE VANIR ARE AN ISOLATIONIST PEOPLE, ESPECIALLY OF LATE. BUT I SERVE THE WILL OF THE WORLD TREE.
I DIVINE ITS WISHES FROM THE PATTERNS IN THE FALLING LEAVES. AND THIS IS WHERE YGGDRASIL WANTS ME TO BE.
YOU'RE HERE BECAUSE THE LEAVES TOLD YOU? RIGHT. WHY DON'T YOU TELL US WHY YOU'RE REALLY--

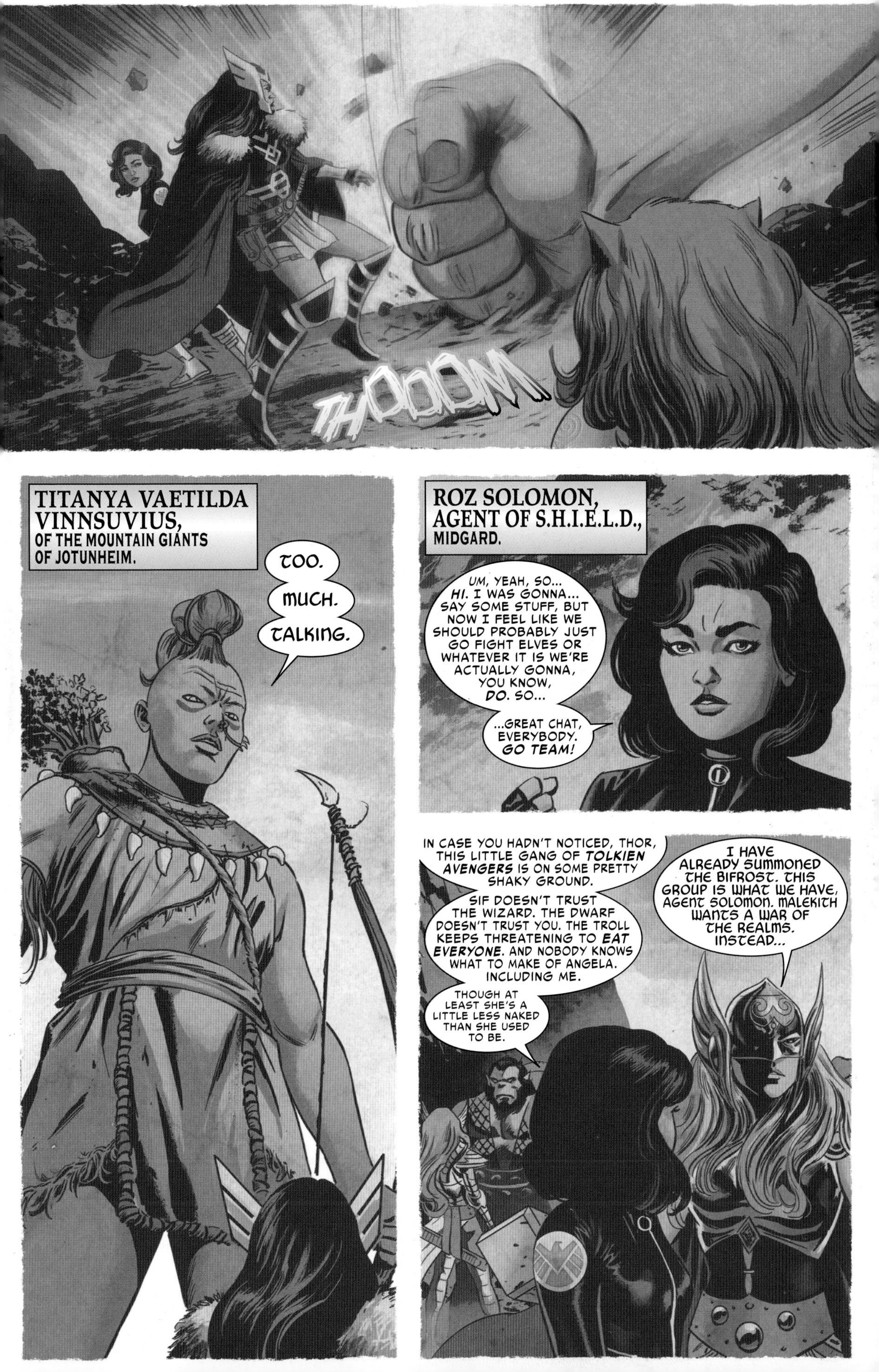
THOOOM
TITANYA VAETILDA VINNSUVIUS, OF THE MOUNTAIN GIANTS OF JOTUNHEIM.
TOO. MUCH. TALKING.
ROZ SOLOMON, AGENT OF S.H.I.E.L.D., MIDGARD.
UM, YEAH, SO... HI. I WAS GONNA... SAY SOME STUFF, BUT NOW I FEEL LIKE WE SHOULD PROBABLY JUST GO FIGHT ELVES OR WHATEVER IT IS WE'RE ACTUALLY GONNA, YOU KNOW, DO. SO...
...GREAT CHAT, EVERYBODY. GO TEAM!
IN CASE YOU HADN'T NOTICED, THOR, THIS LITTLE GANG OF TOLKIEN AVENGERS IS ON SOME PRETTY SHAKY GROUND.
SIF DOESN'T TRUST THE WIZARD. THE DWARF DOESN'T TRUST YOU. THE TROLL KEEPS THREATENING TO EAT EVERYONE. AND NOBODY KNOWS WHAT TO MAKE OF ANGELA. INCLUDING ME.
THOUGH AT LEAST SHE'S A LITTLE LESS NAKED THAN SHE USED TO BE.
I HAVE ALREADY SUMMONED THE BIFROST. THIS GROUP IS WHAT WE HAVE, AGENT SOLOMON. MALEKITH WANTS A WAR OF THE REALMS. INSTEAD...

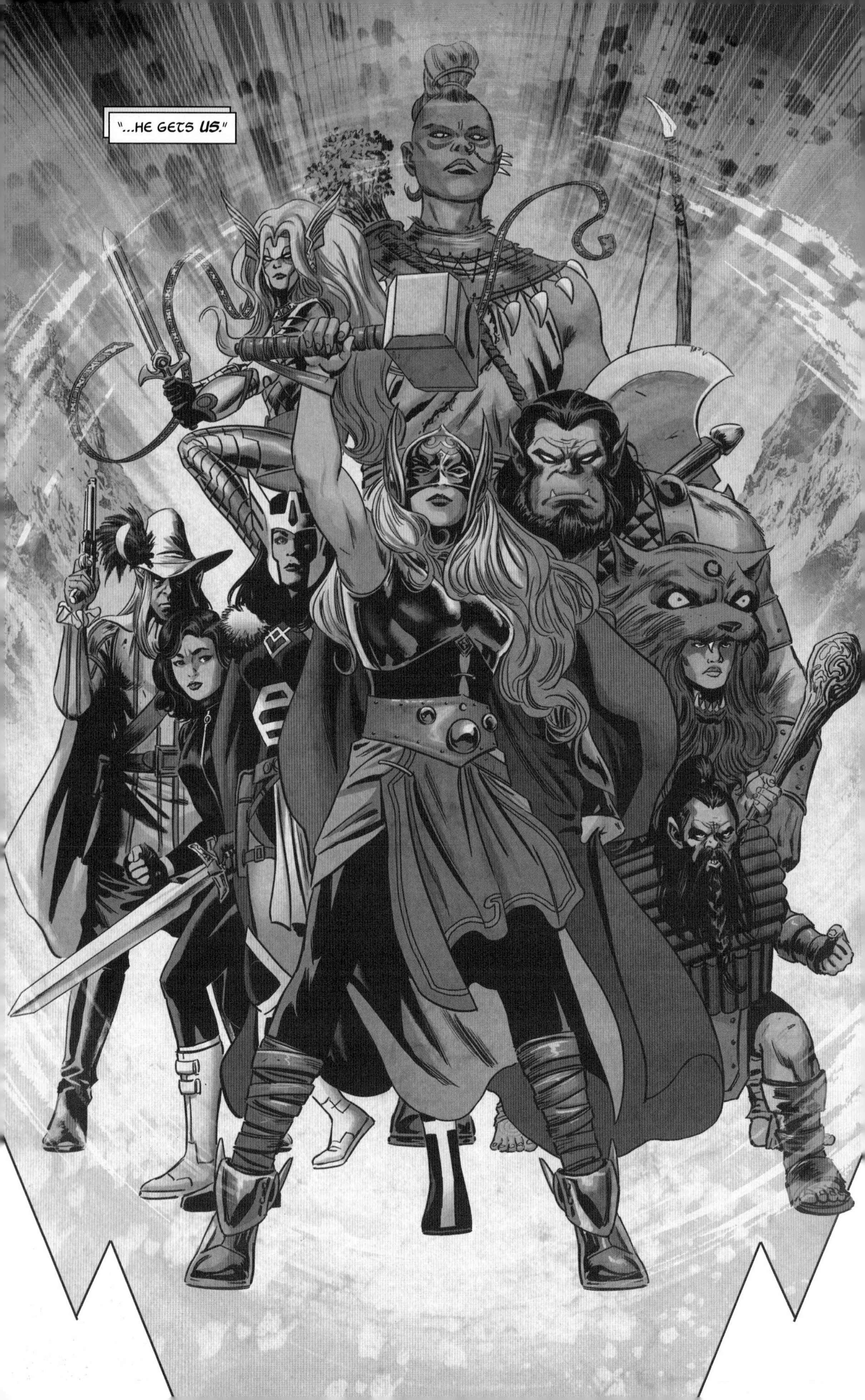
"...HE GETS US."

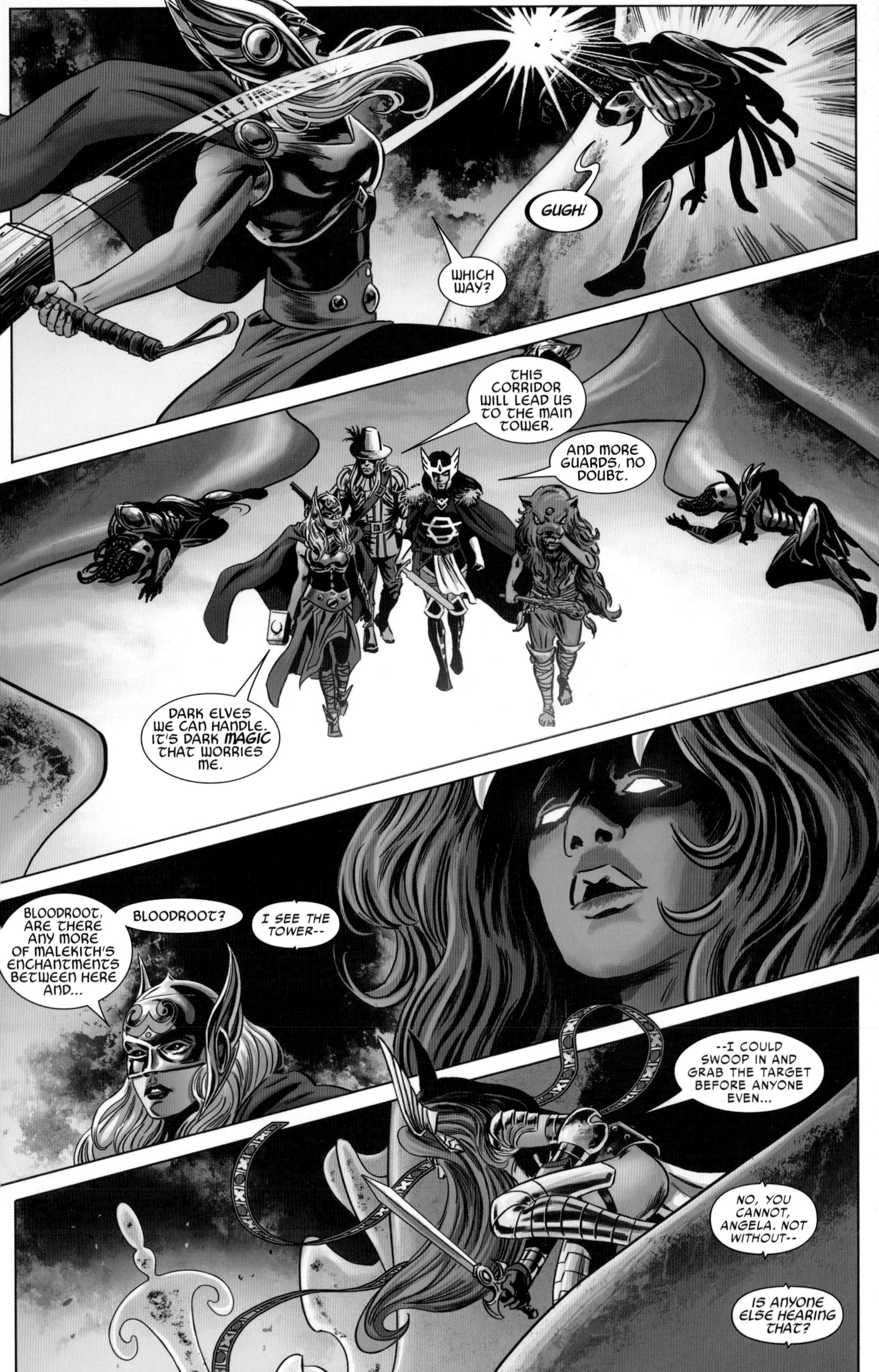
GUGH!
WHICH WAY?
THIS CORRIDOR WILL LEAD US TO THE MAIN TOWER.
AND MORE GUARDS, NO DOUBT.
DARK ELVES WE CAN HANDLE. IT'S DARK MAGIC THAT WORRIES ME.
BLOODROOT, ARE THERE ANY MORE OF MALEKITH'S ENCHANTMENTS BETWEEN HERE AND...
BLOODROOT?
I SEE THE TOWER--
--I COULD SWOOP IN AND GRAB THE TARGET BEFORE ANYONE EVEN...
NO, YOU CANNOT, ANGELA. NOT WITHOUT--
IS ANYONE ELSE HEARING THAT?

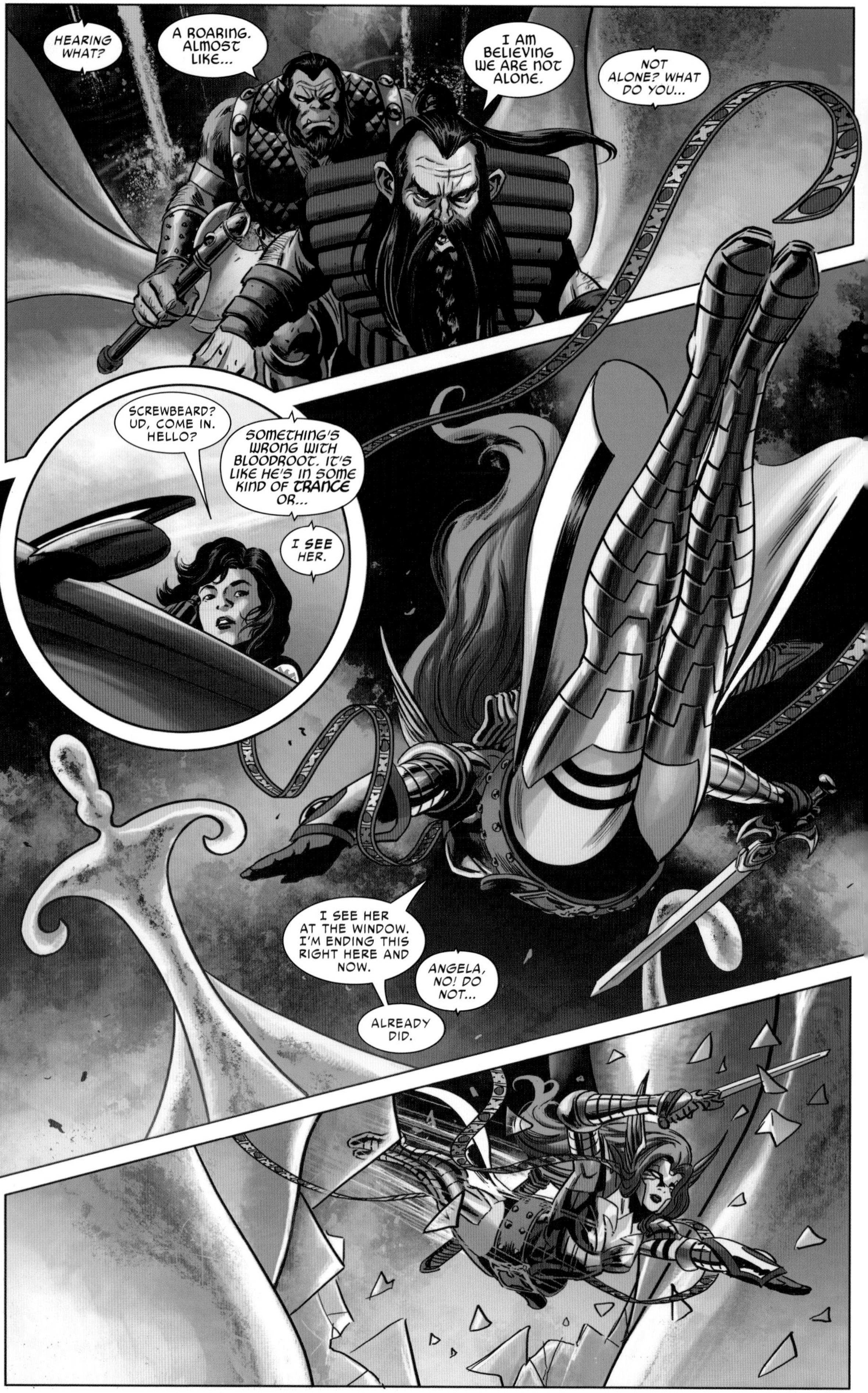
HEARING WHAT?
A ROARING. ALMOST LIKE...
I AM BELIEVING WE ARE NOT ALONE.
NOT ALONE? WHAT DO YOU...
SCREWBEARD? UD, COME IN. HELLO?
SOMETHING'S WRONG WITH BLOODROOT. IT'S LIKE HE'S IN SOME KIND OF TRANCE OR...
I SEE HER.
I SEE HER AT THE WINDOW. I'M ENDING THIS RIGHT HERE AND NOW.
ANGELA, NO! DO NOT...
ALREADY DID.

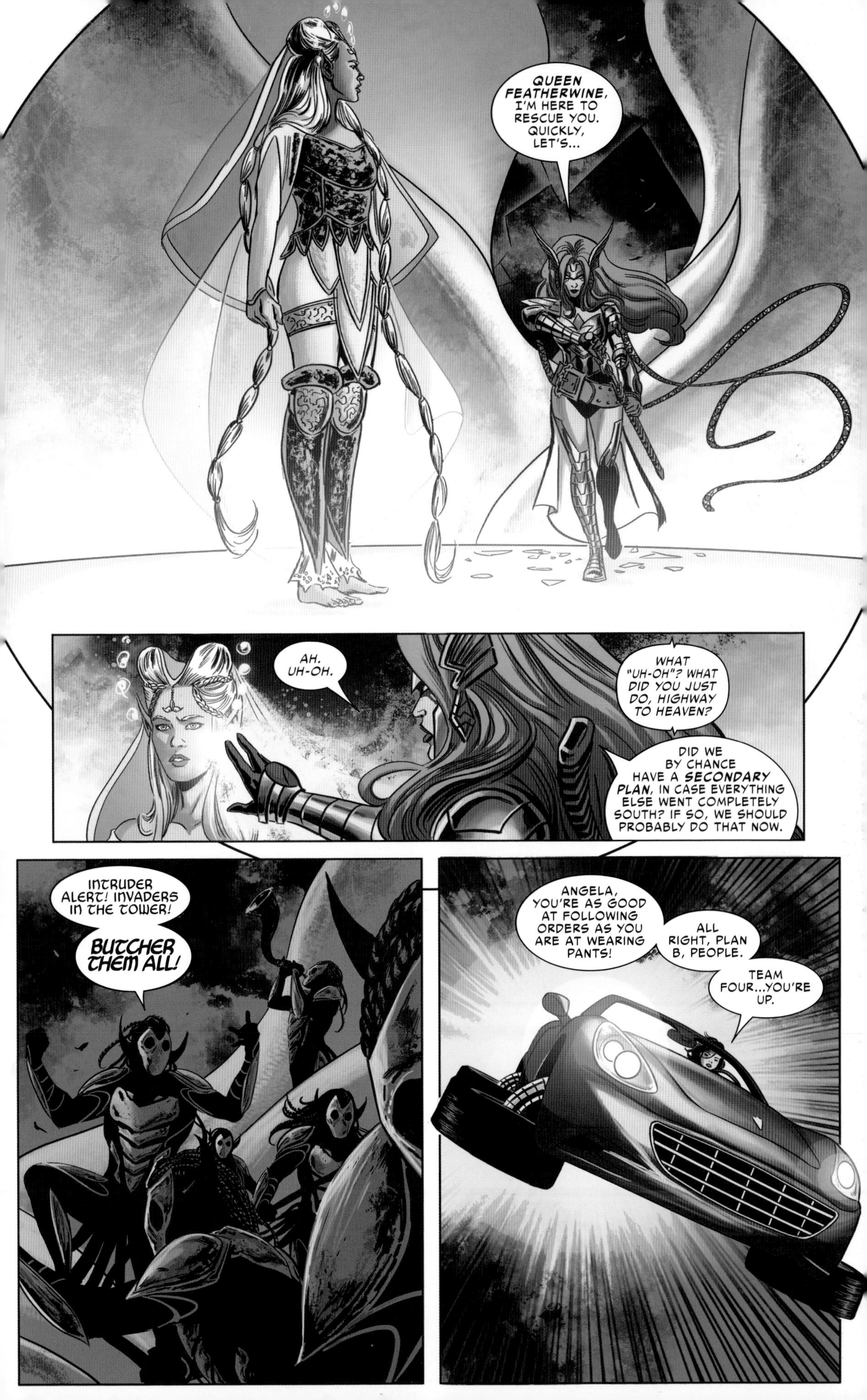
QUEEN FEATHERWINE, I'M HERE TO RESCUE YOU. QUICKLY, LET'S...
AH. UH-OH.
WHAT "UH-OH"? WHAT DID YOU JUST DO, HIGHWAY TO HEAVEN?
DID WE BY CHANCE HAVE A SECONDARY PLAN, IN CASE EVERYTHING ELSE WENT COMPLETELY SOUTH? IF SO, WE SHOULD PROBABLY DO THAT NOW.
INTRUDER ALERT! INVADERS IN THE TOWER!
BUTCHER THEM ALL!
ANGELA, YOU'RE AS GOOD AT FOLLOWING ORDERS AS YOU ARE AT WEARING PANTS!
ALL RIGHT, PLAN B, PEOPLE.
TEAM FOUR...YOU'RE UP.

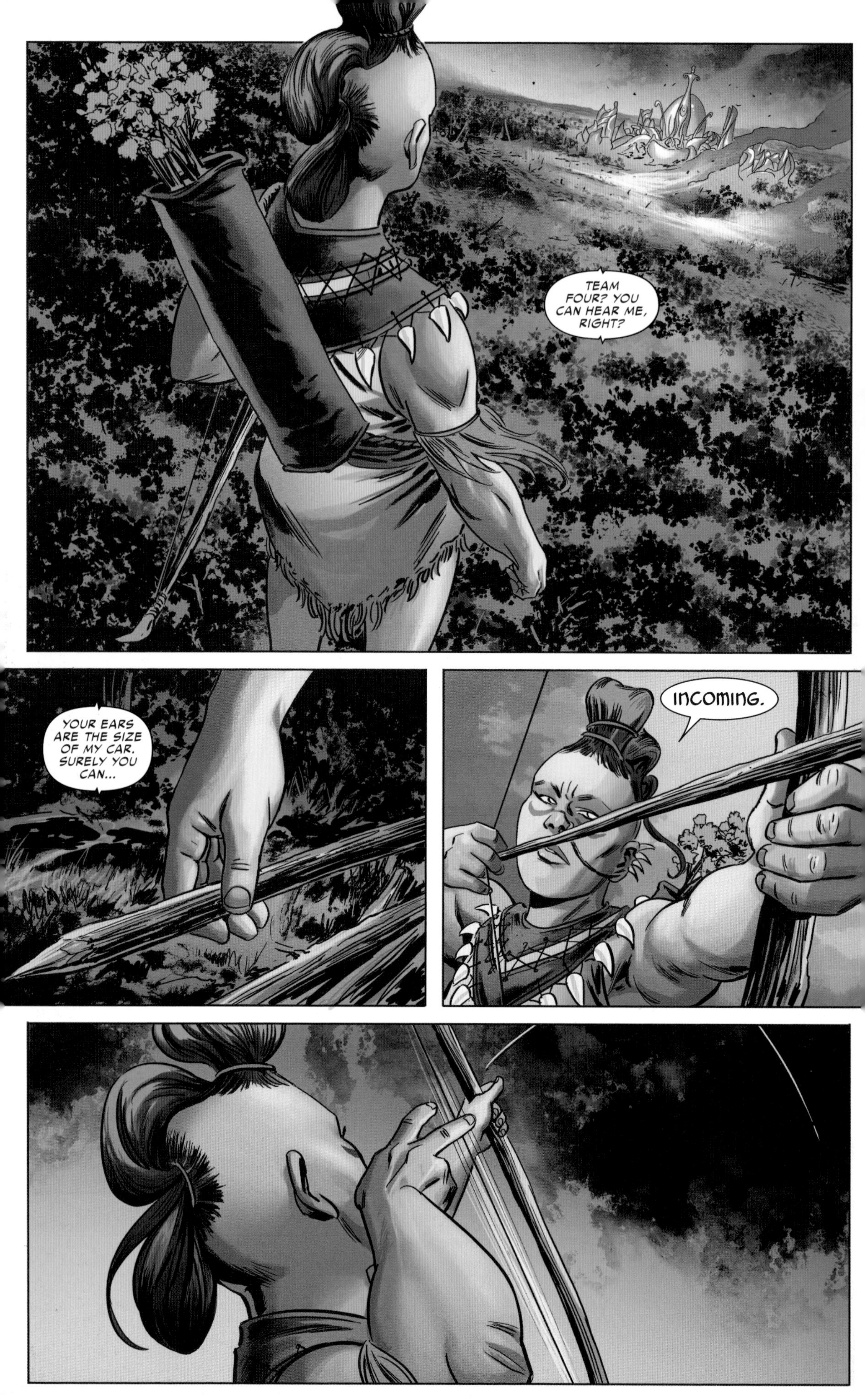
TEAM FOUR? YOU CAN HEAR ME, RIGHT?
YOUR EARS ARE THE SIZE OF MY CAR. SURELY YOU CAN...
INCOMING.

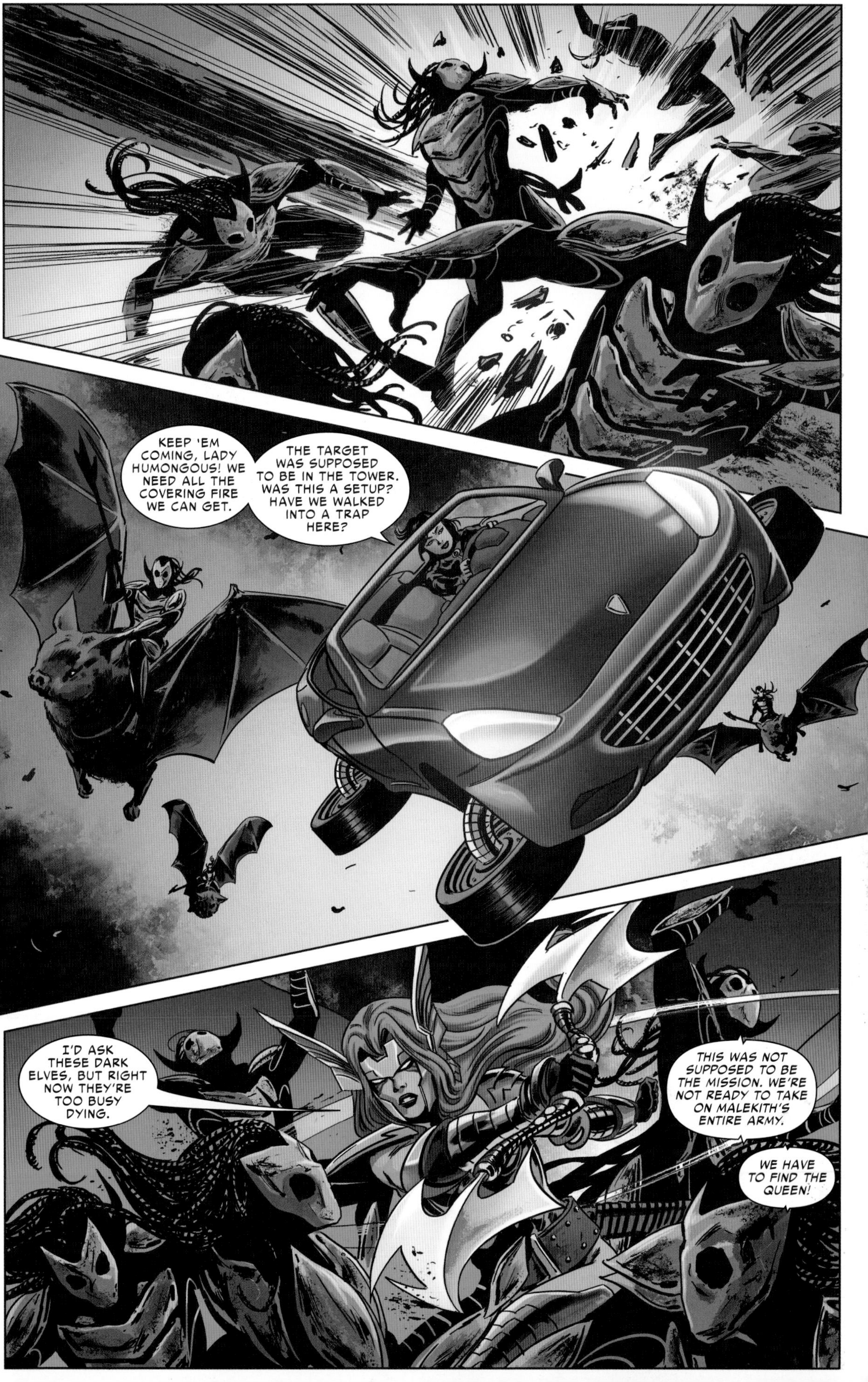
KEEP 'EM COMING, LADY HUMONGOUS! WE NEED ALL THE COVERING FIRE WE CAN GET.
THE TARGET WAS SUPPOSED TO BE IN THE TOWER. WAS THIS A SETUP? HAVE WE WALKED INTO A TRAP HERE?
I'D ASK THESE DARK ELVES, BUT RIGHT NOW THEY'RE TOO BUSY DYING.
THIS WAS NOT SUPPOSED TO BE THE MISSION. WE'RE NOT READY TO TAKE ON MALEKITH'S ENTIRE ARMY.
WE HAVE TO FIND THE QUEEN!

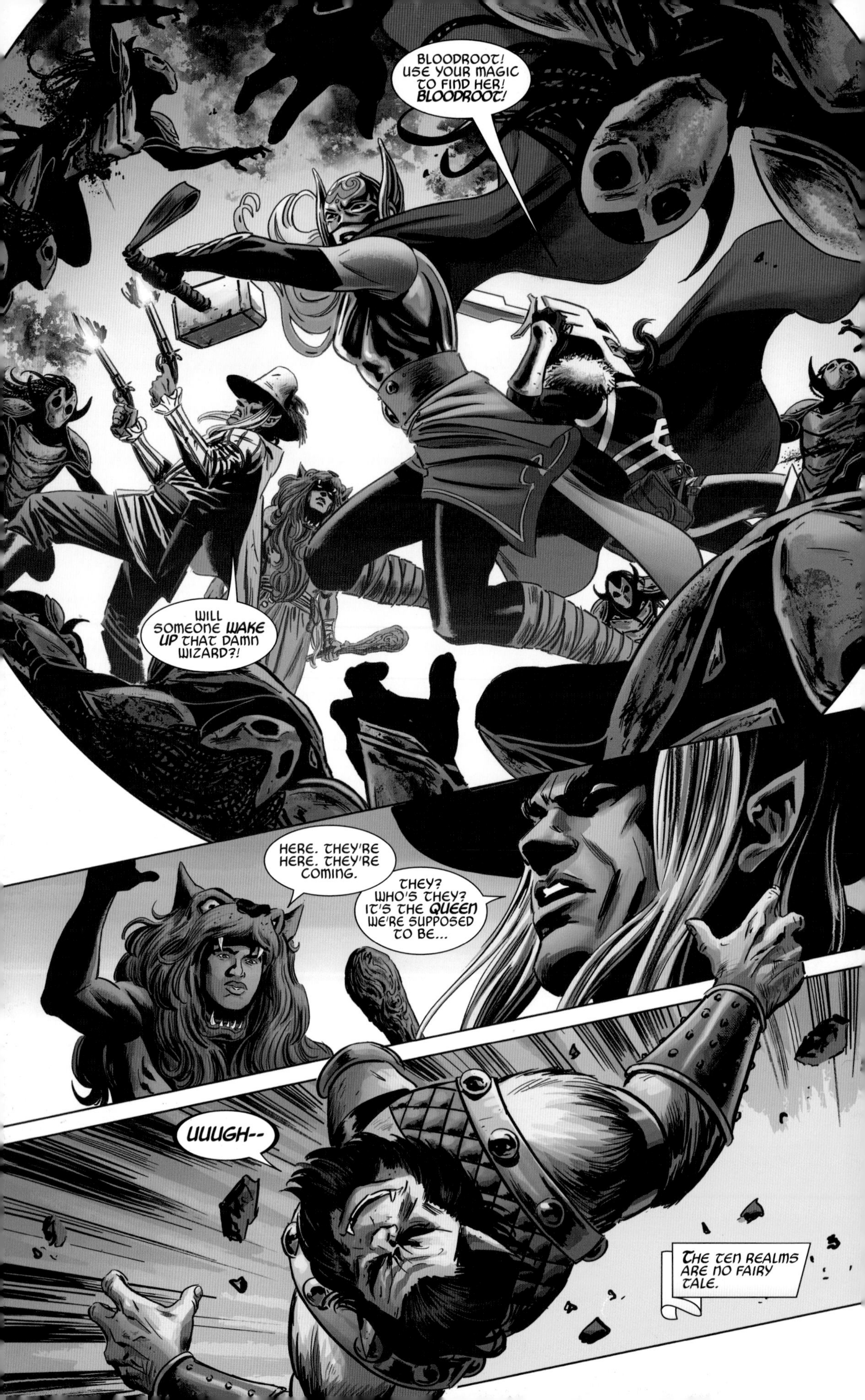
BLOODROOT! USE YOUR MAGIC TO FIND HER! BLOODROOT!
WILL SOMEONE WAKE UP THAT DAMN WIZARD?!
HERE. THEY'RE HERE. THEY'RE COMING.
THEY? WHO'S THEY? IT'S THE QUEEN WE'RE SUPPOSED TO BE...
UUUGH--
THE TEN REALMS ARE NO FAIRY TALE.

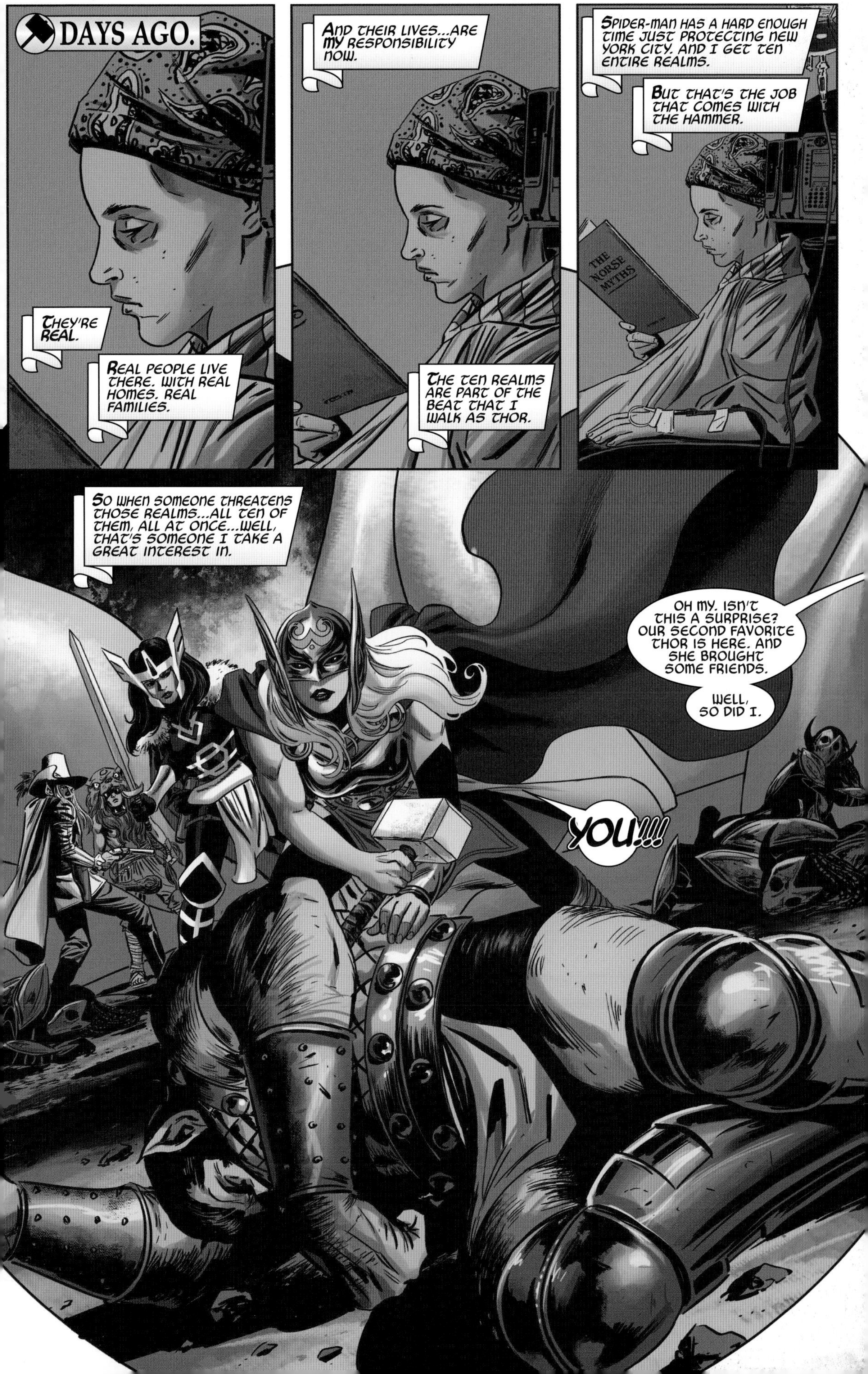
DAYS AGO.
THEY'RE REAL.
REAL PEOPLE LIVE THERE. WITH REAL HOMES. REAL FAMILIES.
AND THEIR LIVES...ARE MY RESPONSIBILITY NOW.
THE TEN REALMS ARE PART OF THE BEAT THAT I WALK AS THOR.
SPIDER-MAN HAS A HARD ENOUGH TIME JUST PROTECTING NEW YORK CITY. AND I GET TEN ENTIRE REALMS.
BUT THAT'S THE JOB THAT COMES WITH THE HAMMER.
THE NORSE MYTHS
SO WHEN SOMEONE THREATENS THOSE REALMS...ALL TEN OF THEM, ALL AT ONCE...WELL, THAT'S SOMEONE I TAKE A GREAT INTEREST IN.
OH MY. ISN'T THIS A SURPRISE? OUR SECOND FAVORITE THOR IS HERE. AND SHE BROUGHT SOME FRIENDS.
WELL, SO DID I.
YOU!!!!

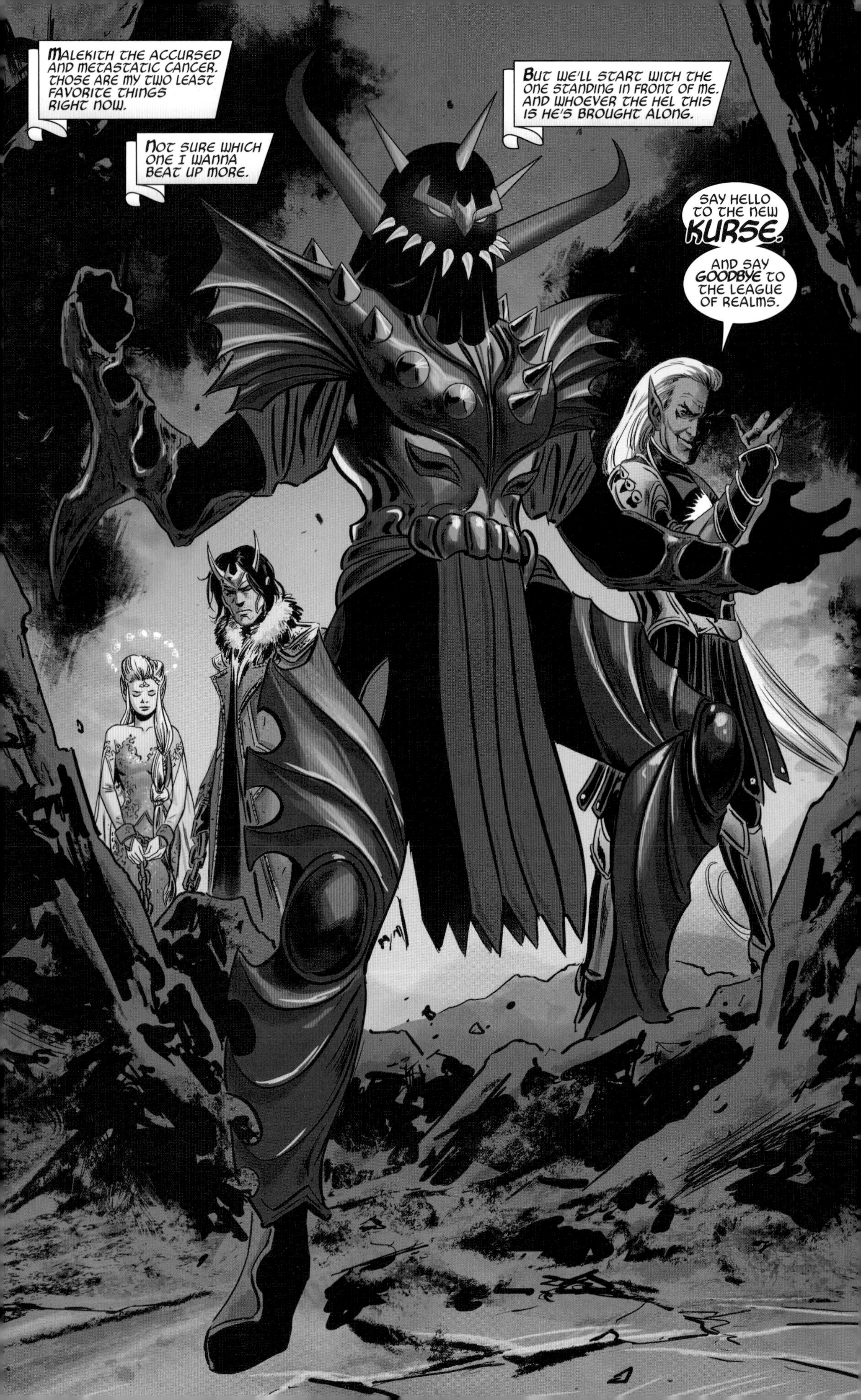
MALEKITH THE ACCURSED AND METASTATIC CANCER. THOSE ARE MY TWO LEAST FAVORITE THINGS RIGHT NOW.
NOT SURE WHICH ONE I WANNA BEAT UP MORE.
BUT WE'LL START WITH THE ONE STANDING IN FRONT OF ME. AND WHOEVER THE HEL THIS IS HE'S BROUGHT ALONG.
SAY HELLO TO THE NEW KURSE.
AND SAY GOODBYE TO THE LEAGUE OF REALMS.

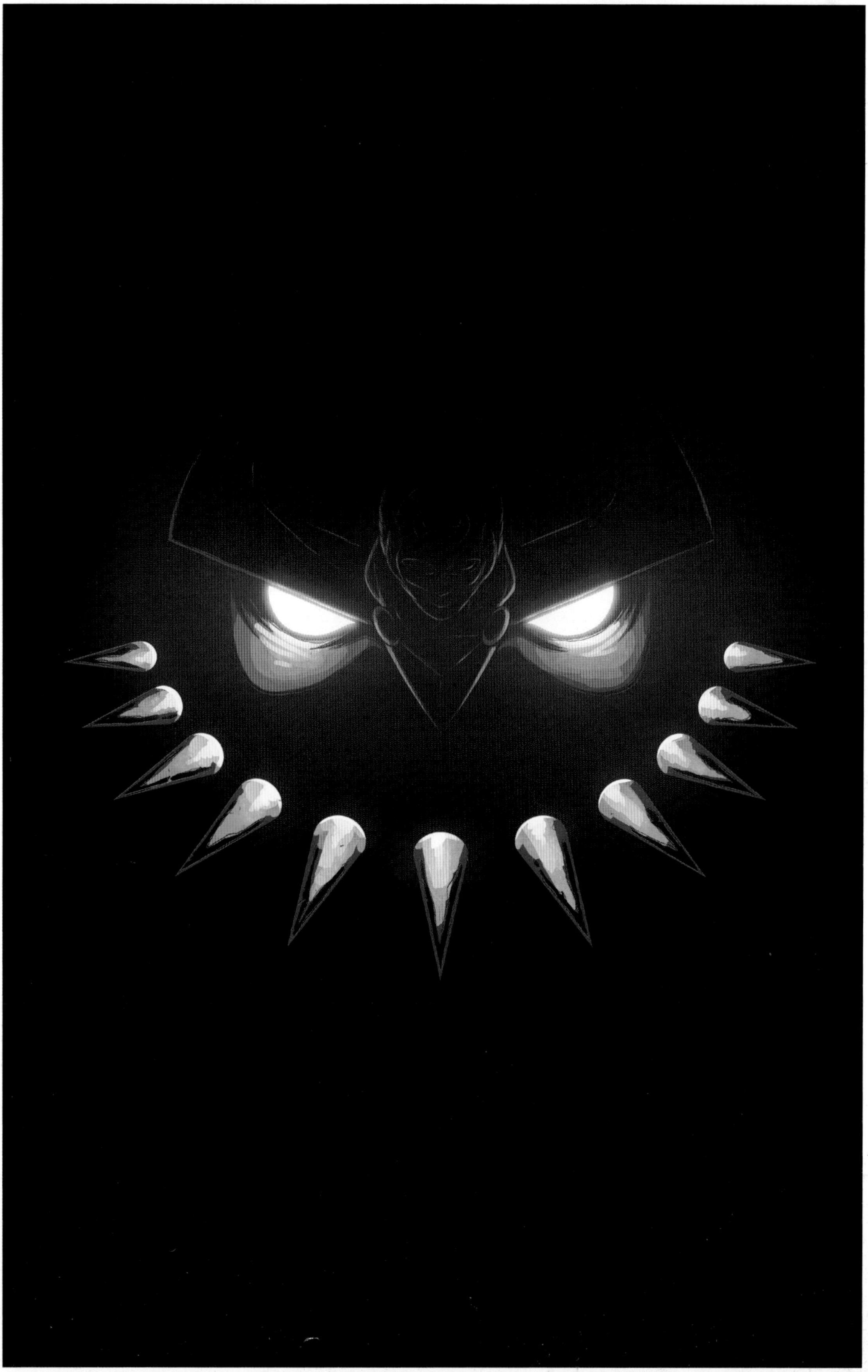

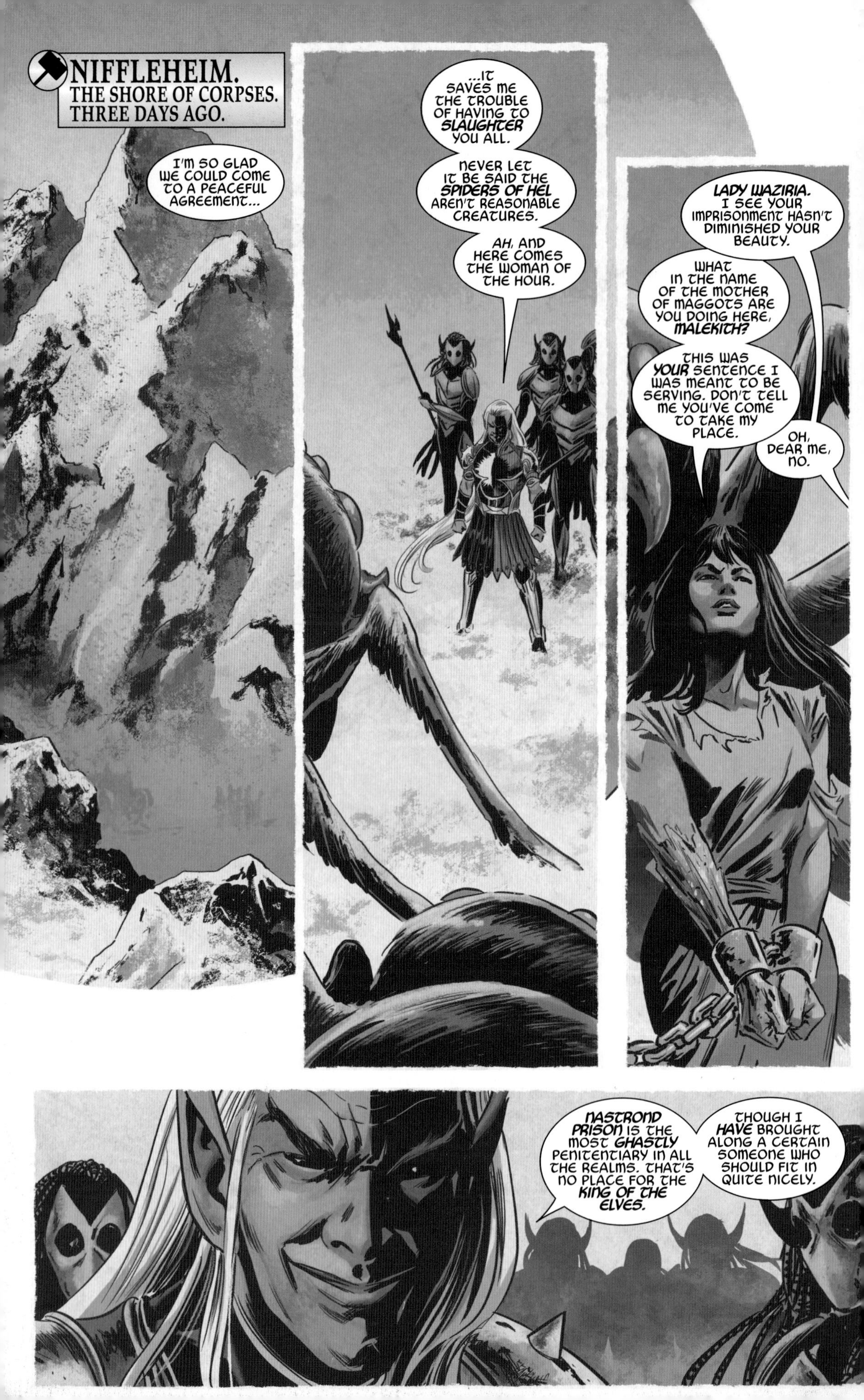
NIFFLEHEIM. THE SHORE OF CORPSES. THREE DAYS AGO.
I'M SO GLAD WE COULD COME TO A PEACEFUL AGREEMENT...
...IT SAVES ME THE TROUBLE OF HAVING TO SLAUGHTER YOU ALL.
NEVER LET IT BE SAID THE SPIDERS OF HEL AREN'T REASONABLE CREATURES.
AH, AND HERE COMES THE WOMAN OF THE HOUR.
LADY WAZIRIA. I SEE YOUR IMPRISONMENT HASN'T DIMINISHED YOUR BEAUTY.
WHAT IN THE NAME OF THE MOTHER OF MAGGOTS ARE YOU DOING HERE, MALEKITH?
THIS WAS YOUR SENTENCE I WAS MEANT TO BE SERVING. DON'T TELL ME YOU'VE COME TO TAKE MY PLACE.
OH, DEAR ME, NO.
NASTROND PRISON IS THE MOST GHASTLY PENITENTIARY IN ALL THE REALMS. THAT'S NO PLACE FOR THE KING OF THE ELVES.
THOUGH I HAVE BROUGHT ALONG A CERTAIN SOMEONE WHO SHOULD FIT IN QUITE NICELY.

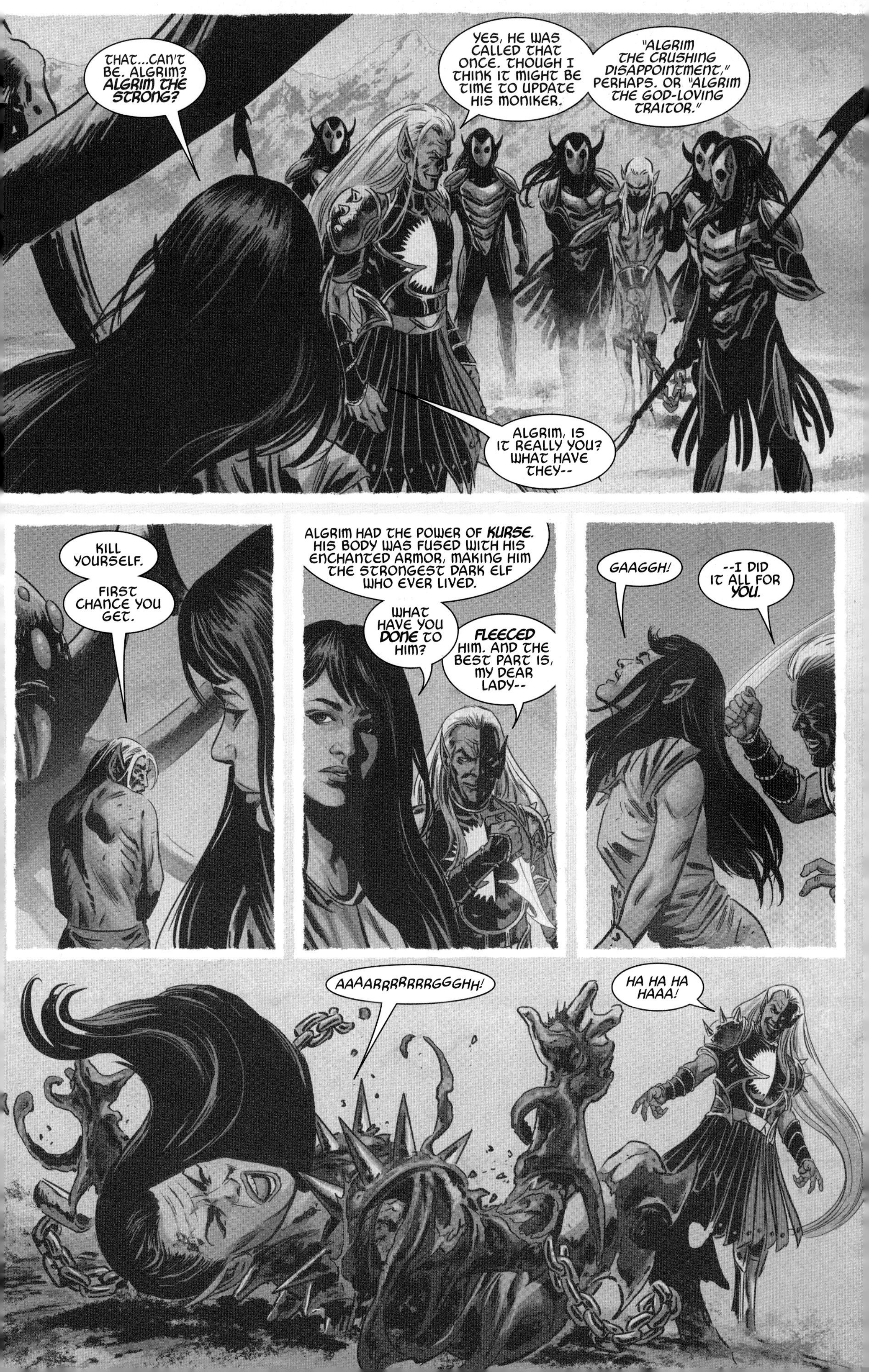
THAT...CAN'T BE. ALGRIM? ALGRIM THE STRONG?
YES, HE WAS CALLED THAT ONCE. THOUGH I THINK IT MIGHT BE TIME TO UPDATE HIS MONIKER.
"ALGRIM THE CRUSHING DISAPPOINTMENT," PERHAPS. OR "ALGRIM THE GOD-LOVING TRAITOR."
ALGRIM, IS IT REALLY YOU? WHAT HAVE THEY--
KILL YOURSELF.
FIRST CHANCE YOU GET.
ALGRIM HAD THE POWER OF KURSE. HIS BODY WAS FUSED WITH HIS ENCHANTED ARMOR, MAKING HIM THE STRONGEST DARK ELF WHO EVER LIVED.
WHAT HAVE YOU DONE TO HIM?
FLEECED HIM. AND THE BEST PART IS, MY DEAR LADY--
GAAGGH!
--I DID IT ALL FOR YOU.
AAAARRRRRRRGGGHH!
HA HA HA HAAA!

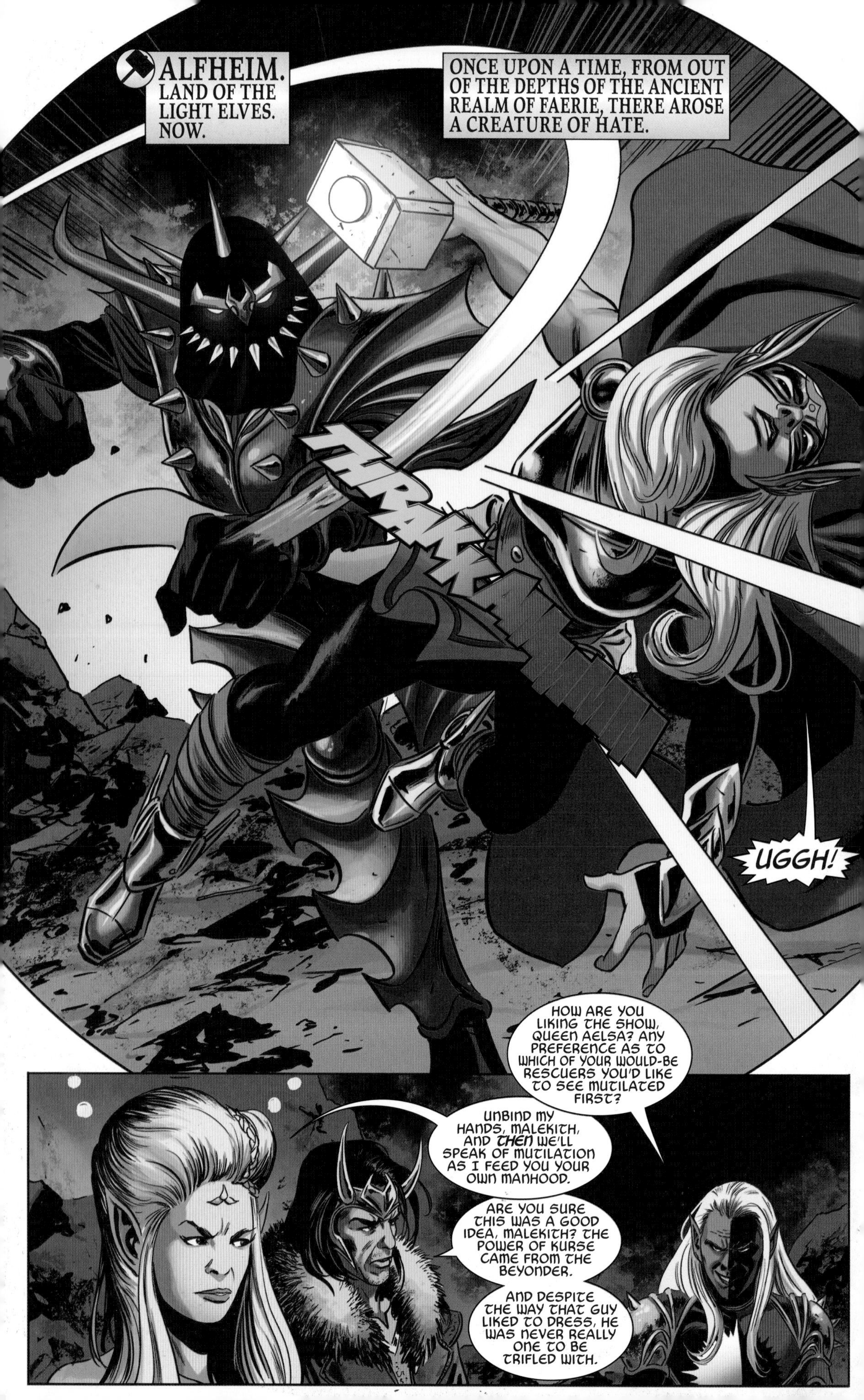
ALFHEIM. LAND OF THE LIGHT ELVES. NOW.
ONCE UPON A TIME, FROM OUT OF THE DEPTHS OF THE ANCIENT REALM OF FAERIE, THERE AROSE A CREATURE OF HATE.
THRAKK
UGGH!
HOW ARE YOU LIKING THE SHOW, QUEEN AELSA? ANY PREFERENCE AS TO WHICH OF YOUR WOULD-BE RESCUERS YOU'D LIKE TO SEE MUTILATED FIRST?
UNBIND MY HANDS, MALEKITH, AND THEN WE'LL SPEAK OF MUTILATION AS I FEED YOU YOUR OWN MANHOOD.
ARE YOU SURE THIS WAS A GOOD IDEA, MALEKITH? THE POWER OF KURSE CAME FROM THE BEYONDER.
AND DESPITE THE WAY THAT GUY LIKED TO DRESS, HE WAS NEVER REALLY ONE TO BE TRIFLED WITH.

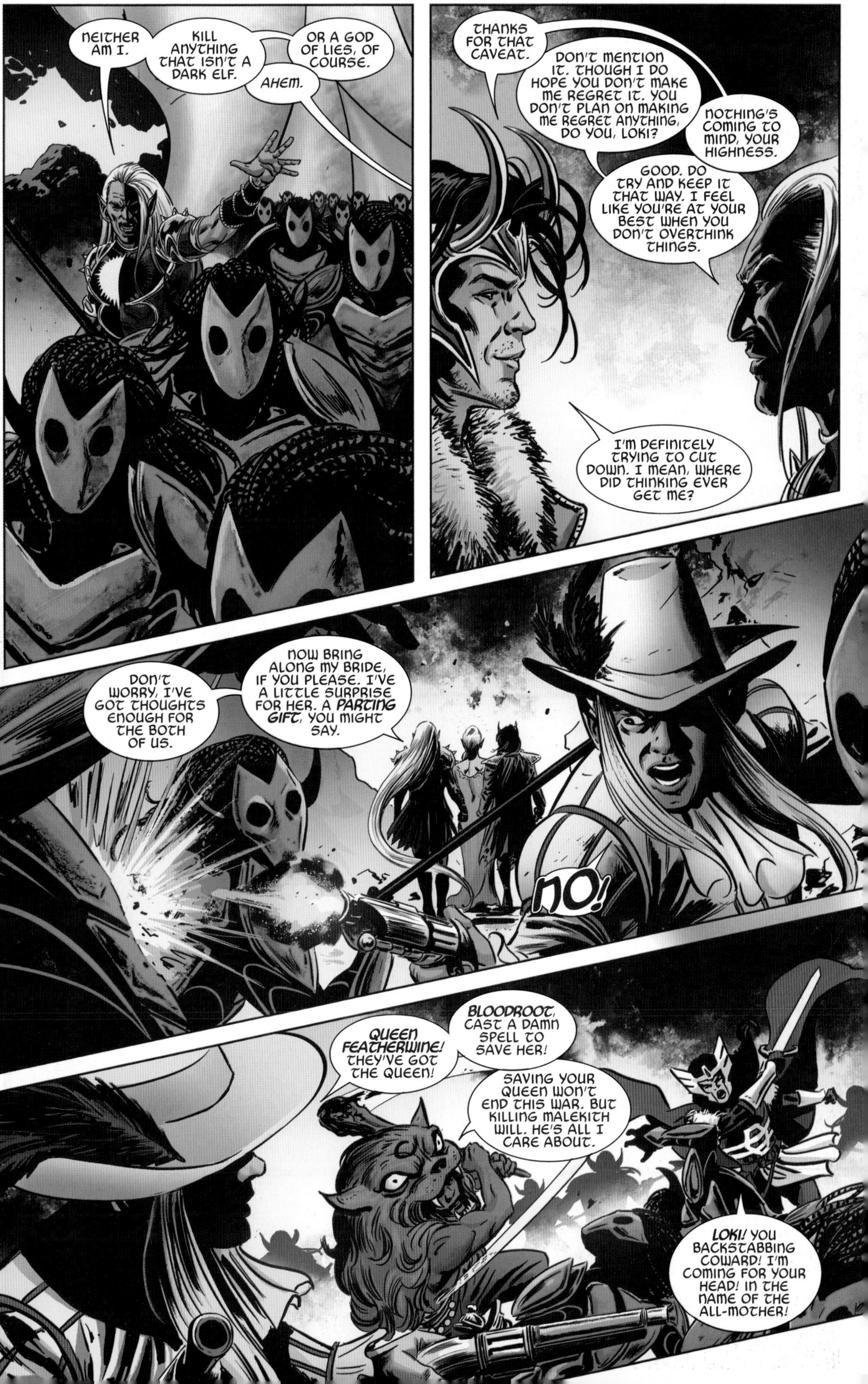
NEITHER AM I.
KILL ANYTHING THAT ISN'T A DARK ELF.
OR A GOD OF LIES, OF COURSE.
AHEM.
THANKS FOR THAT CAVEAT.
DON'T MENTION IT. THOUGH I DO HOPE YOU DON'T MAKE ME REGRET IT. YOU DON'T PLAN ON MAKING ME REGRET ANYTHING, DO YOU, LOKI?
NOTHING'S COMING TO MIND, YOUR HIGHNESS.
GOOD. DO TRY AND KEEP IT THAT WAY. I FEEL LIKE YOU'RE AT YOUR BEST WHEN YOU DON'T OVERTHINK THINGS.
I'M DEFINITELY TRYING TO CUT DOWN. I MEAN, WHERE DID THINKING EVER GET ME?
DON'T WORRY, I'VE GOT THOUGHTS ENOUGH FOR THE BOTH OF US.
NOW BRING ALONG MY BRIDE, IF YOU PLEASE. I'VE A LITTLE SURPRISE FOR HER. A PARTING GIFT, YOU MIGHT SAY.
NO!
QUEEN FEATHERWINE! THEY'VE GOT THE QUEEN!
BLOODROOT, CAST A DAMN SPELL TO SAVE HER!
SAVING YOUR QUEEN WON'T END THIS WAR. BUT KILLING MALEKITH WILL. HE'S ALL I CARE ABOUT.
LOKI! YOU BACKSTABBING COWARD! I'M COMING FOR YOUR HEAD! IN THE NAME OF THE ALL-MOTHER!

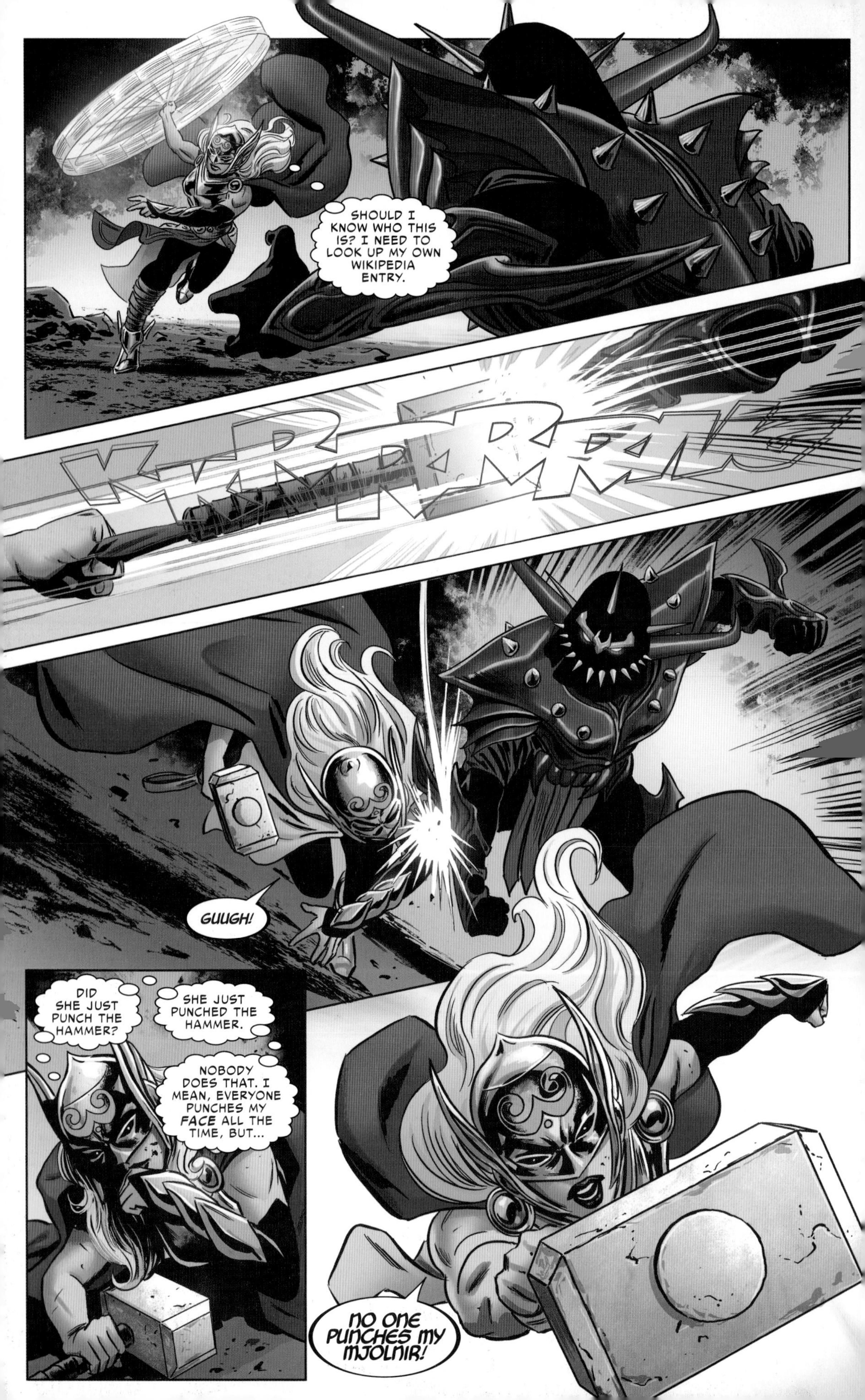
SHOULD I KNOW WHO THIS IS? I NEED TO LOOK UP MY OWN WIKIPEDIA ENTRY.
GUUGH!
DID SHE JUST PUNCH THE HAMMER?
SHE JUST PUNCHED THE HAMMER.
NOBODY DOES THAT. I MEAN, EVERYONE PUNCHES MY FACE ALL THE TIME, BUT...
NO ONE PUNCHES MY MJOLNIR!

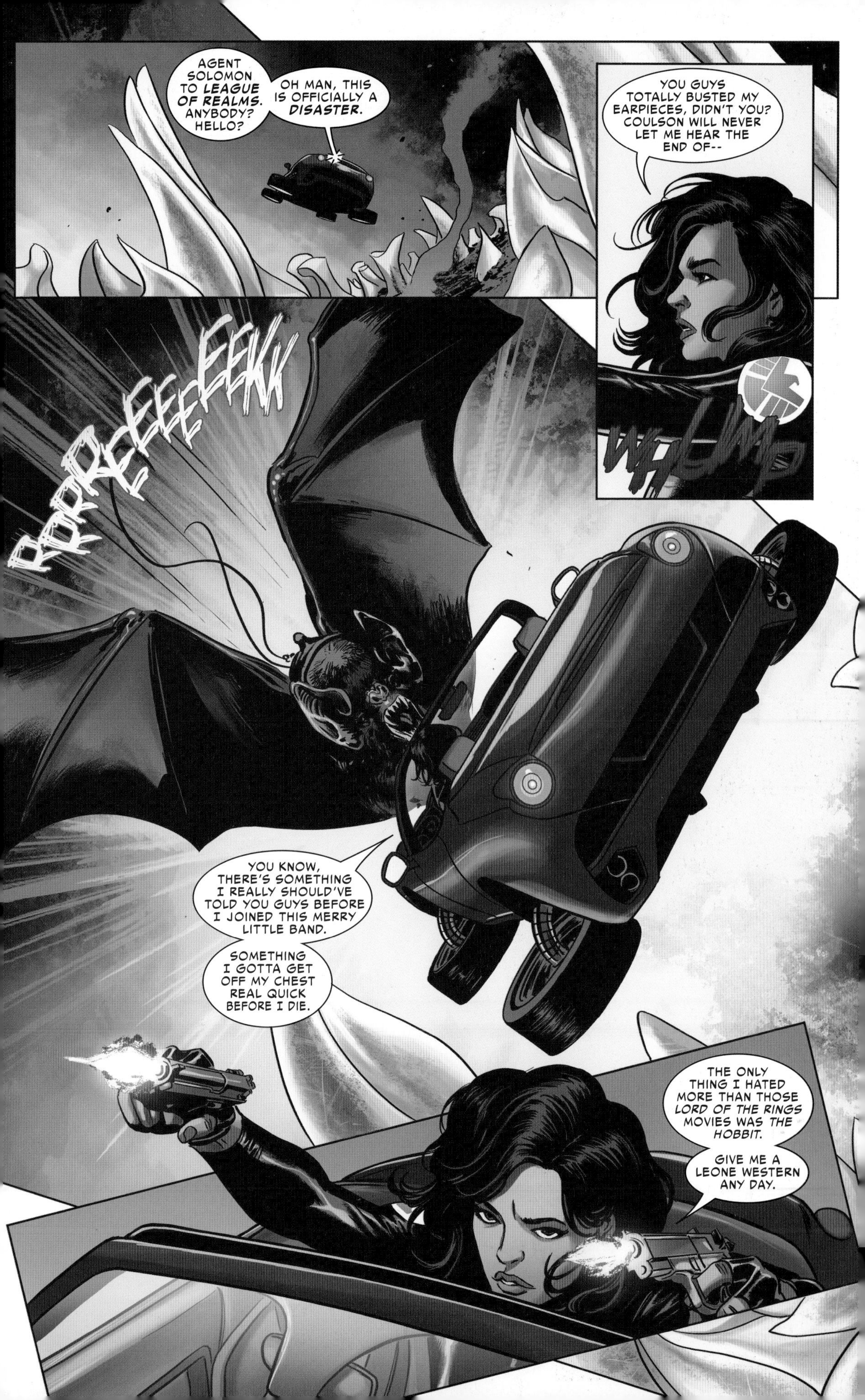

AGENT SOLOMON TO LEAGUE OF REALMS. ANYBODY? HELLO?
OH MAN, THIS IS OFFICIALLY A DISASTER.
YOU GUYS TOTALLY BUSTED MY EARPIECES, DIDN'T YOU? COULSON WILL NEVER LET ME HEAR THE END OF--
WHUMP
RRRREEEEEEEEKK
YOU KNOW, THERE'S SOMETHING I REALLY SHOULD'VE TOLD YOU GUYS BEFORE I JOINED THIS MERRY LITTLE BAND.
SOMETHING I GOTTA GET OFF MY CHEST REAL QUICK BEFORE I DIE.
THE ONLY THING I HATED MORE THAN THOSE LORD OF THE RINGS MOVIES WAS THE HOBBIT.
GIVE ME A LEONE WESTERN ANY DAY.

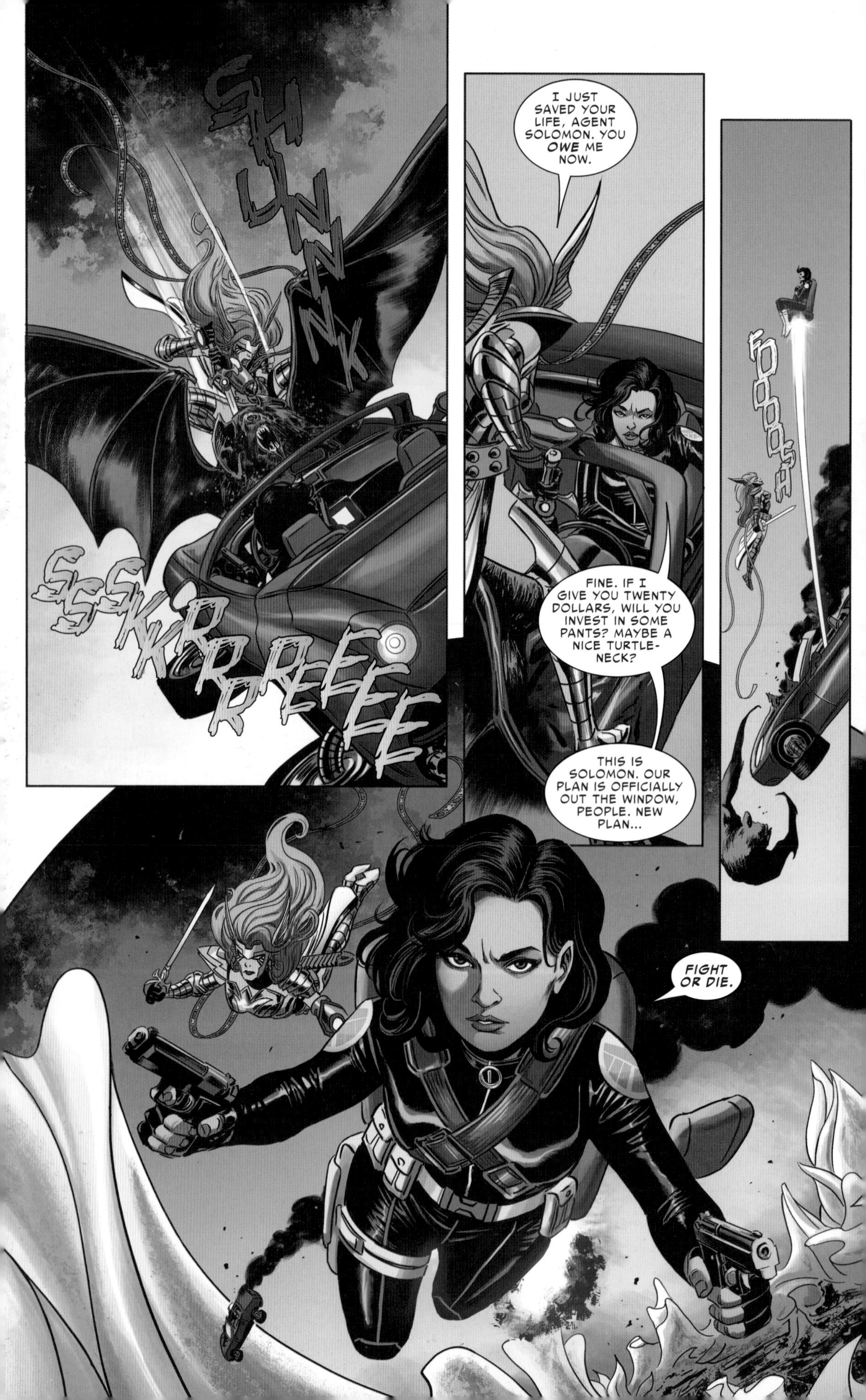
SHHUNNNNK
SSSKRRREEEEE
I JUST SAVED YOUR LIFE, AGENT SOLOMON. YOU OWE ME NOW.
FINE. IF I GIVE YOU TWENTY DOLLARS, WILL YOU INVEST IN SOME PANTS? MAYBE A NICE TURTLE-NECK?
THIS IS SOLOMON. OUR PLAN IS OFFICIALLY OUT THE WINDOW, PEOPLE. NEW PLAN...
FOOOOSH
FIGHT OR DIE.

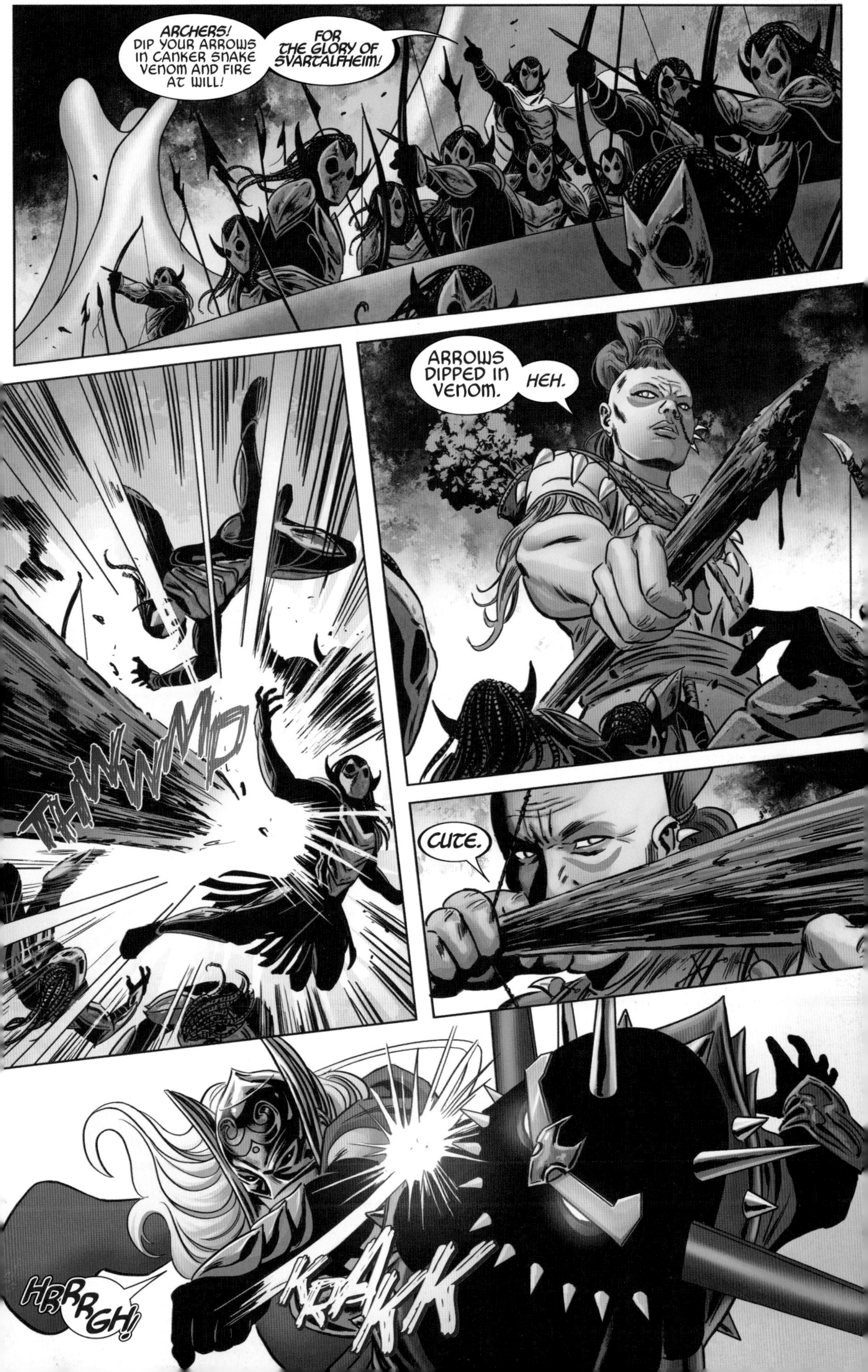
ARCHERS! DIP YOUR ARROWS IN CANKER SNAKE VENOM AND FIRE AT WILL!
FOR THE GLORY OF SVARTALFHEIM!
ARROWS DIPPED IN VENOM.
HEH.
THWWMP
CUTE.
HRRRGH!
KRAKK

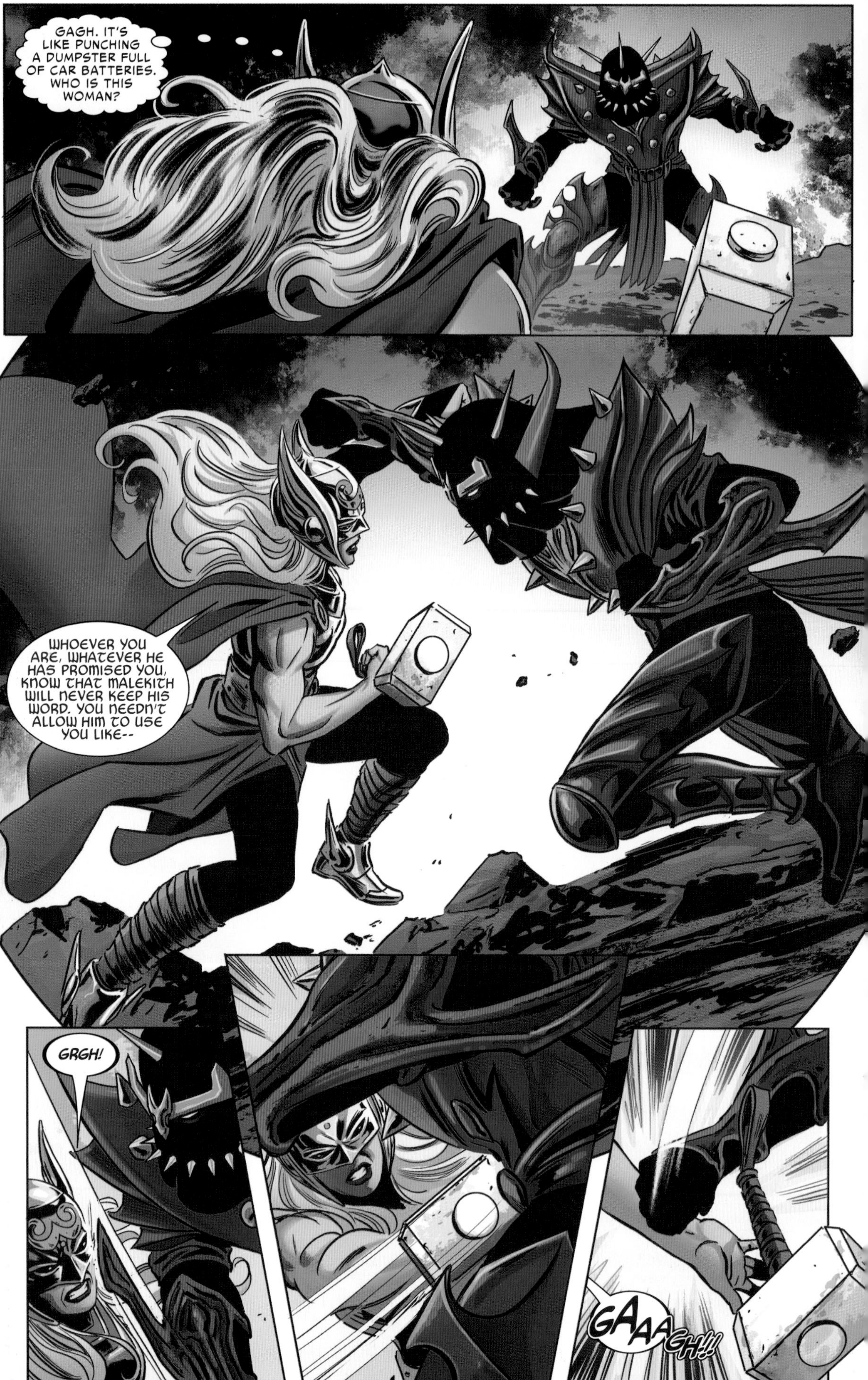
GAGH. IT'S LIKE PUNCHING A DUMPSTER FULL OF CAR BATTERIES. WHO IS THIS WOMAN?
WHOEVER YOU ARE, WHATEVER HE HAS PROMISED YOU, KNOW THAT MALEKITH WILL NEVER KEEP HIS WORD. YOU NEEDN'T ALLOW HIM TO USE YOU LIKE--
GRGH!
GAAAAGH!!

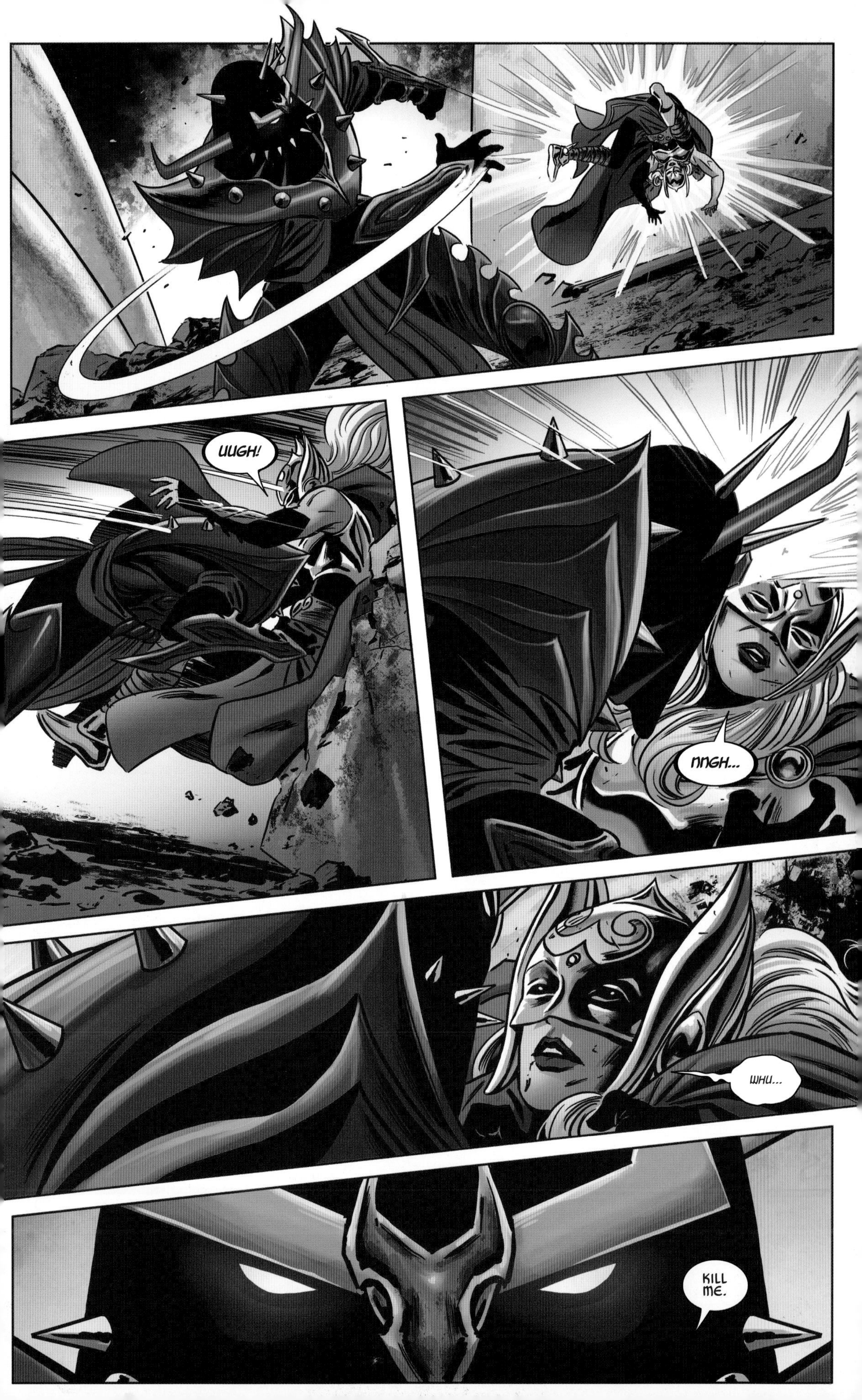
UUGH!
NNGH...
WHU...
KILL ME.

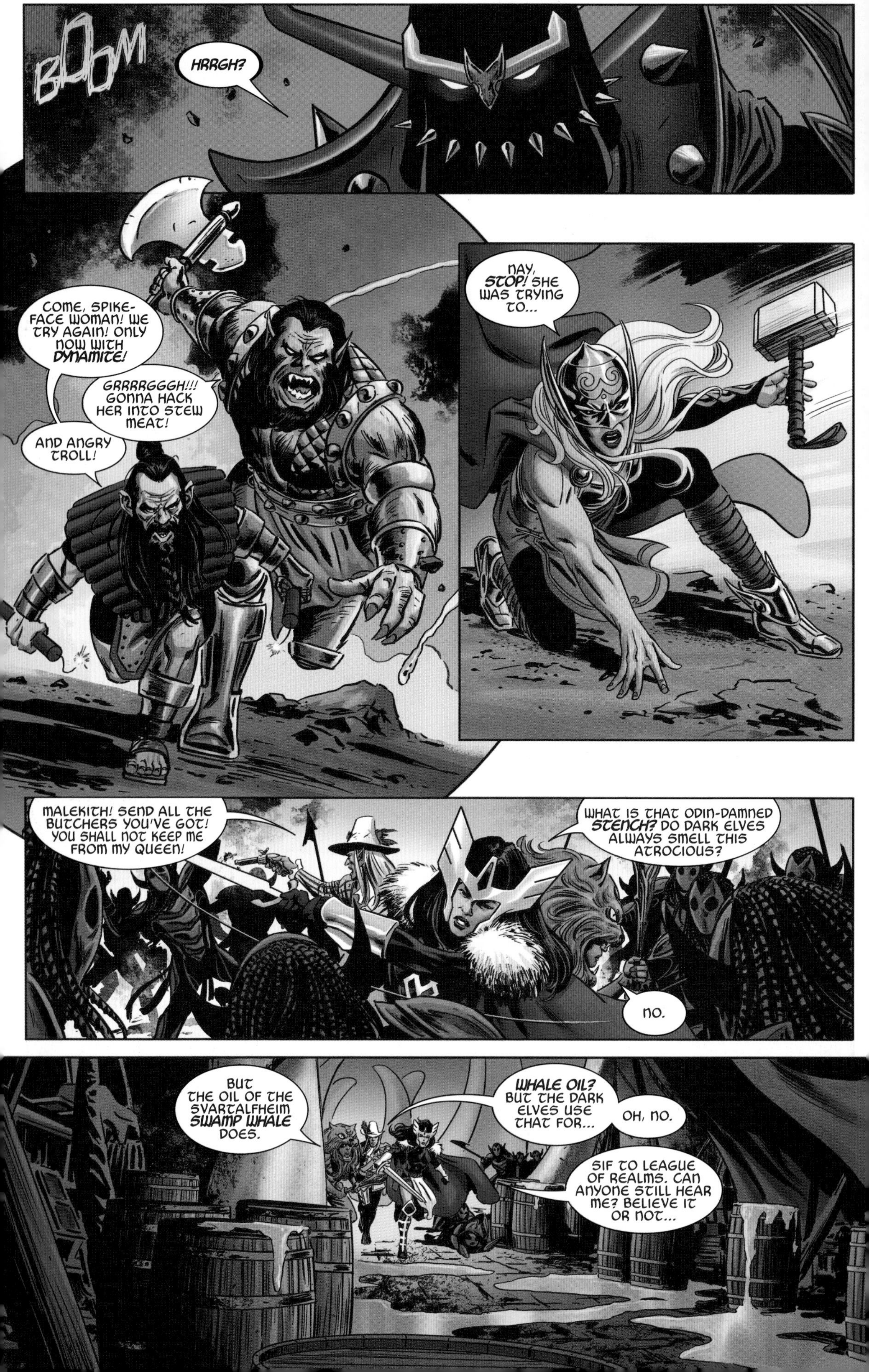
BOOM
HRRGH?
COME, SPIKE-FACE WOMAN! WE TRY AGAIN! ONLY NOW WITH DYNAMITE!
GRRRRGGGH!!! GONNA HACK HER INTO STEW MEAT!
AND ANGRY TROLL!
NAY, STOP! SHE WAS TRYING TO...
MALEKITH! SEND ALL THE BUTCHERS YOU'VE GOT! YOU SHALL NOT KEEP ME FROM MY QUEEN!
WHAT IS THAT ODIN-DAMNED STENCH? DO DARK ELVES ALWAYS SMELL THIS ATROCIOUS?
NO.
BUT THE OIL OF THE SVARTALFHEIM SWAMP WHALE DOES.
WHALE OIL? BUT THE DARK ELVES USE THAT FOR...
OH, NO.
SIF TO LEAGUE OF REALMS. CAN ANYONE STILL HEAR ME? BELIEVE IT OR NOT...

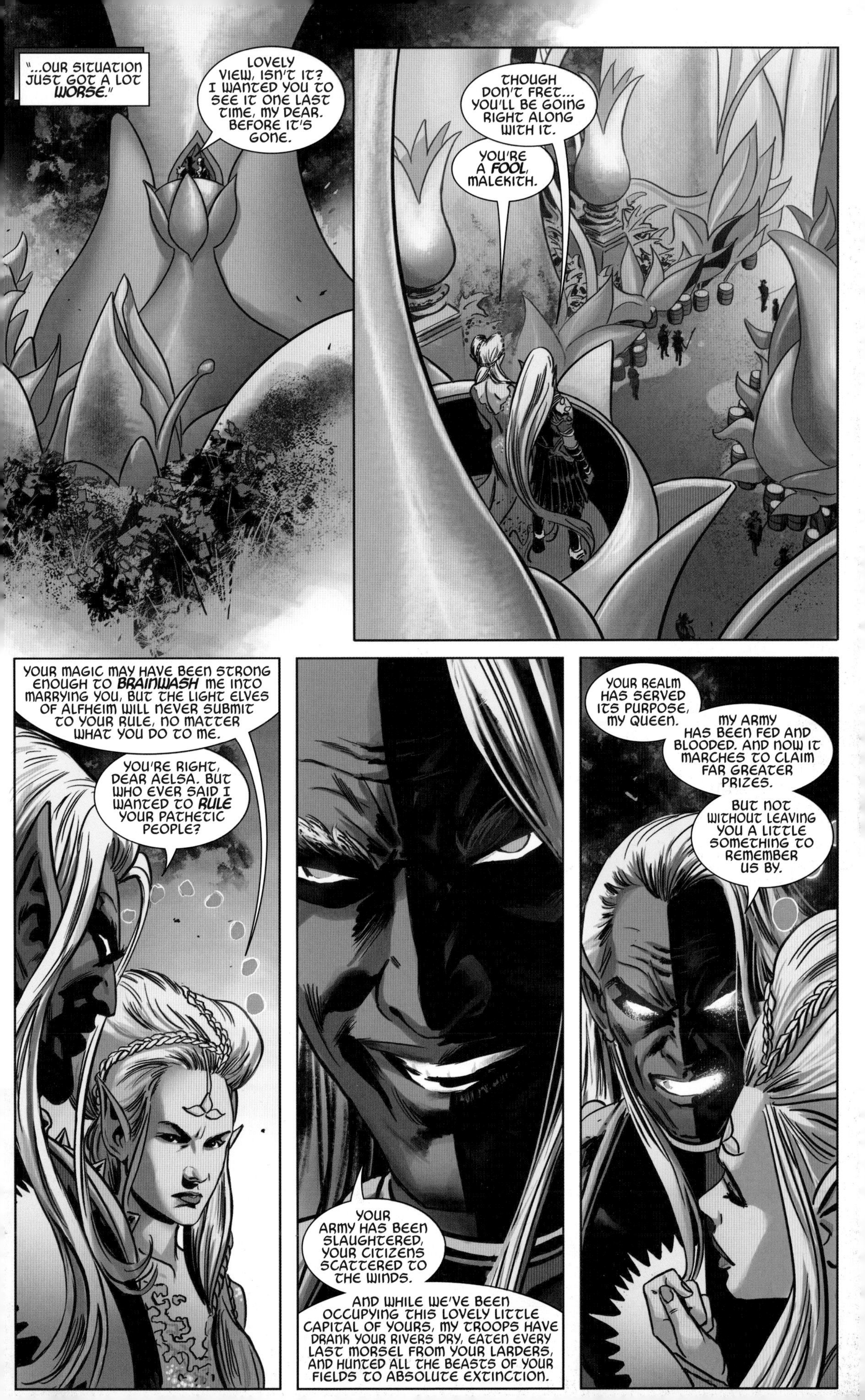
"...OUR SITUATION JUST GOT A LOT WORSE."
LOVELY VIEW, ISN'T IT? I WANTED YOU TO SEE IT ONE LAST TIME, MY DEAR. BEFORE IT'S GONE.
THOUGH DON'T FRET... YOU'LL BE GOING RIGHT ALONG WITH IT.
YOU'RE A FOOL, MALEKITH.
YOUR MAGIC MAY HAVE BEEN STRONG ENOUGH TO BRAINWASH ME INTO MARRYING YOU, BUT THE LIGHT ELVES OF ALFHEIM WILL NEVER SUBMIT TO YOUR RULE, NO MATTER WHAT YOU DO TO ME.
YOU'RE RIGHT, DEAR AELSA. BUT WHO EVER SAID I WANTED TO RULE YOUR PATHETIC PEOPLE?
YOUR ARMY HAS BEEN SLAUGHTERED, YOUR CITIZENS SCATTERED TO THE WINDS.
AND WHILE WE'VE BEEN OCCUPYING THIS LOVELY LITTLE CAPITAL OF YOURS, MY TROOPS HAVE DRANK YOUR RIVERS DRY, EATEN EVERY LAST MORSEL FROM YOUR LARDERS, AND HUNTED ALL THE BEASTS OF YOUR FIELDS TO ABSOLUTE EXTINCTION.
YOUR REALM HAS SERVED ITS PURPOSE, MY QUEEN.
MY ARMY HAS BEEN FED AND BLOODED. AND NOW IT MARCHES TO CLAIM FAR GREATER PRIZES.
BUT NOT WITHOUT LEAVING YOU A LITTLE SOMETHING TO REMEMBER US BY.

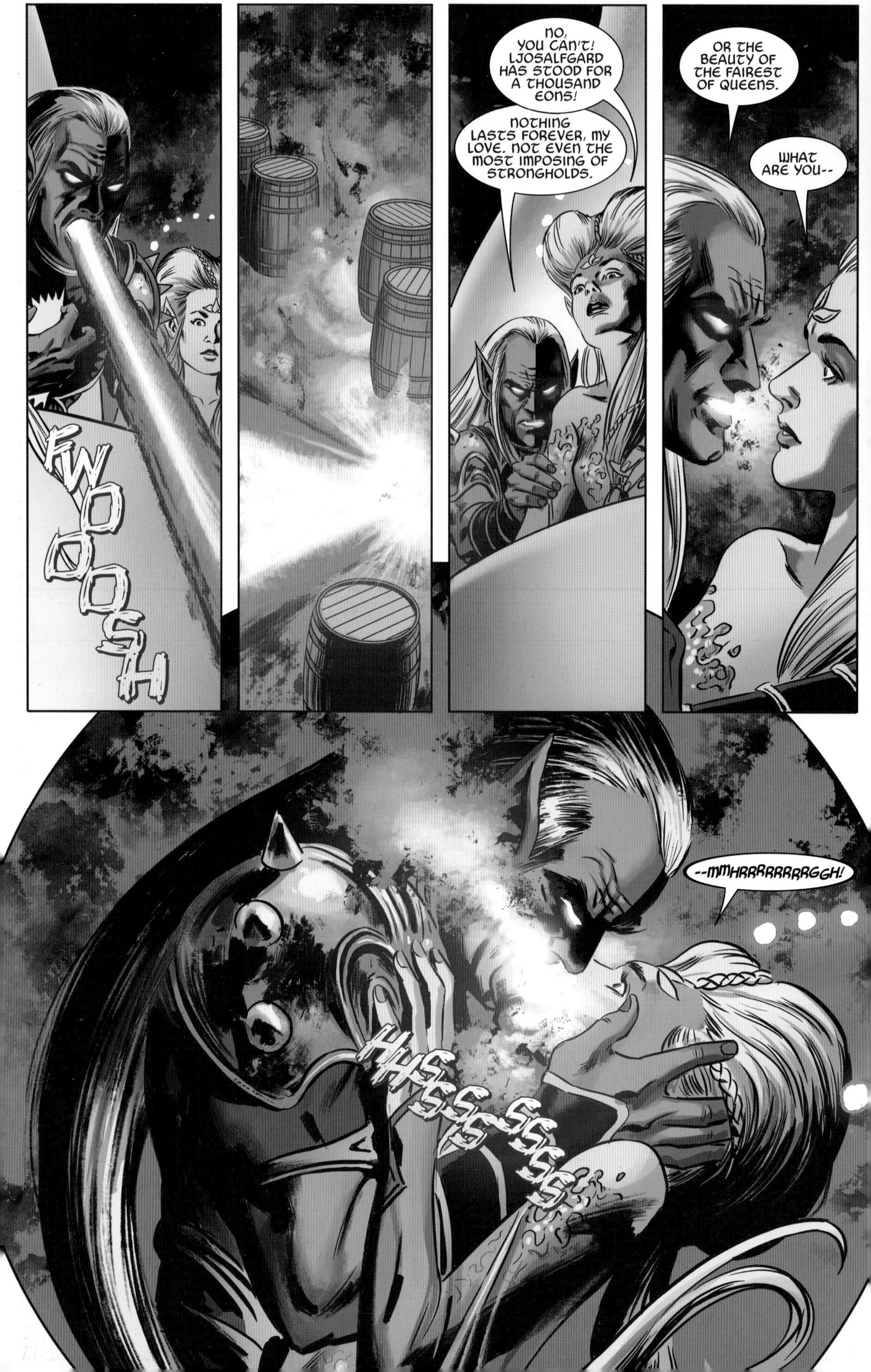
FWOOOSH
NO, YOU CAN'T! LJOSALFGARD HAS STOOD FOR A THOUSAND EONS!
NOTHING LASTS FOREVER, MY LOVE. NOT EVEN THE MOST IMPOSING OF STRONGHOLDS.
OR THE BEAUTY OF THE FAIREST OF QUEENS.
WHAT ARE YOU--
--MMHRRRRRRRRGGH!
HHSSSSSSSSSS

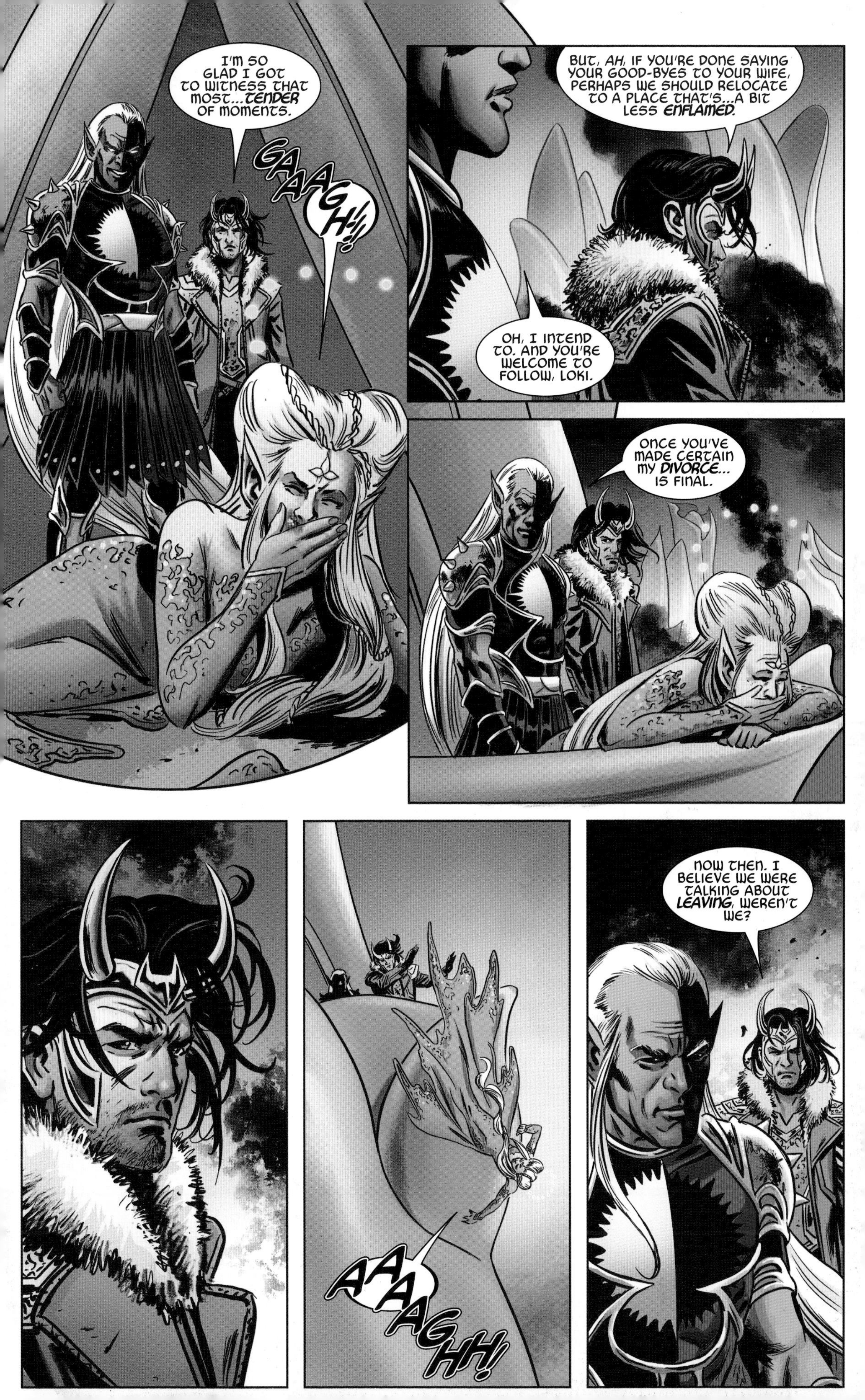
I'M SO GLAD I GOT TO WITNESS THAT MOST...TENDER OF MOMENTS.
GAAAGH!!
BUT, AH, IF YOU'RE DONE SAYING YOUR GOOD-BYES TO YOUR WIFE, PERHAPS WE SHOULD RELOCATE TO A PLACE THAT'S...A BIT LESS ENFLAMED.
OH, I INTEND TO. AND YOU'RE WELCOME TO FOLLOW, LOKI.
ONCE YOU'VE MADE CERTAIN MY DIVORCE... IS FINAL.
AAAAAGHH!
NOW THEN. I BELIEVE WE WERE TALKING ABOUT LEAVING, WEREN'T WE?

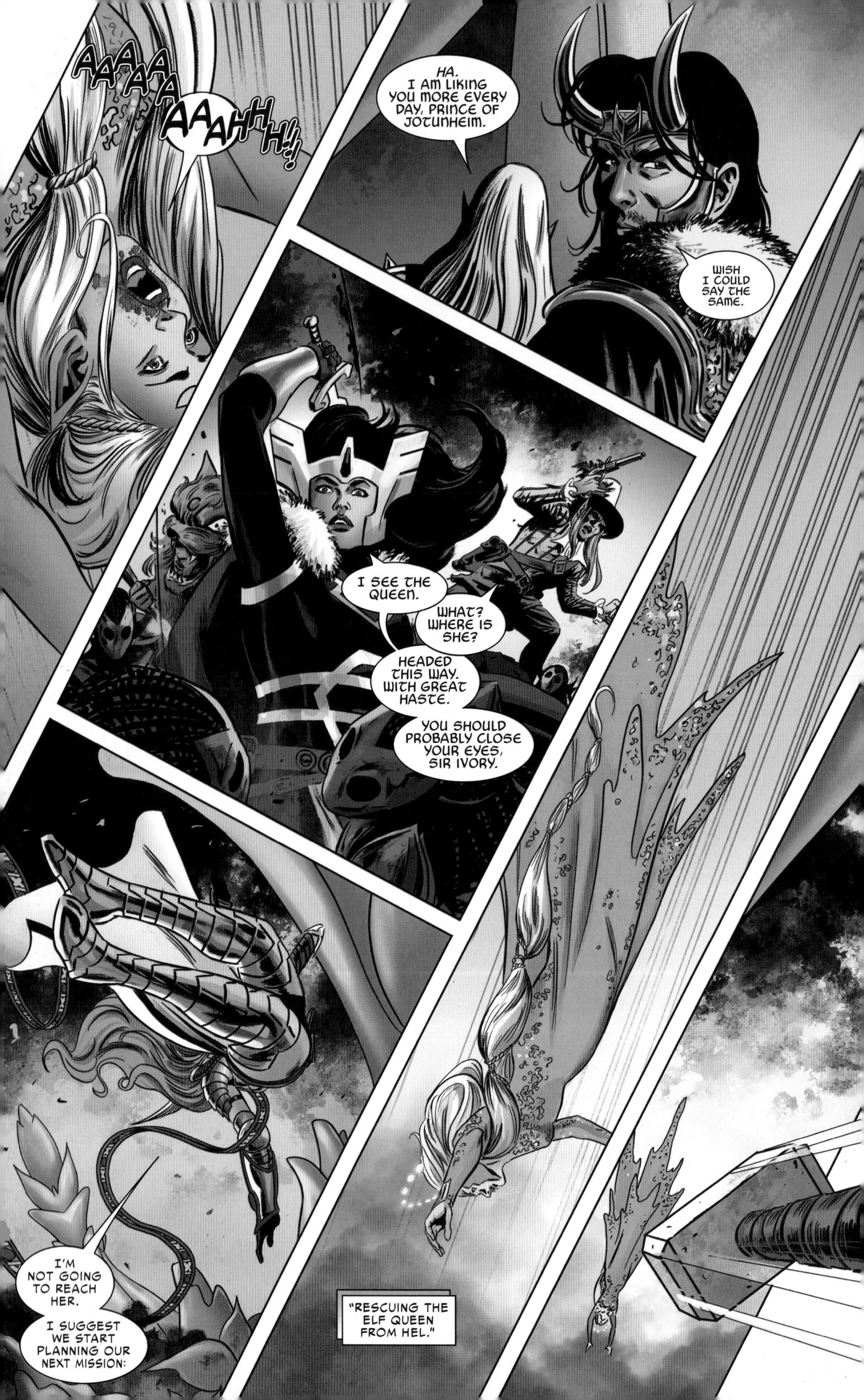
AAAAAAAAAAHHH!!
HA. I AM LIKING YOU MORE EVERY DAY, PRINCE OF JOTUNHEIM.
WISH I COULD SAY THE SAME.
I SEE THE QUEEN.
WHAT? WHERE IS SHE?
HEADED THIS WAY. WITH GREAT HASTE.
YOU SHOULD PROBABLY CLOSE YOUR EYES, SIR IVORY.
I'M NOT GOING TO REACH HER.
I SUGGEST WE START PLANNING OUR NEXT MISSION:
"RESCUING THE ELF QUEEN FROM HEL."

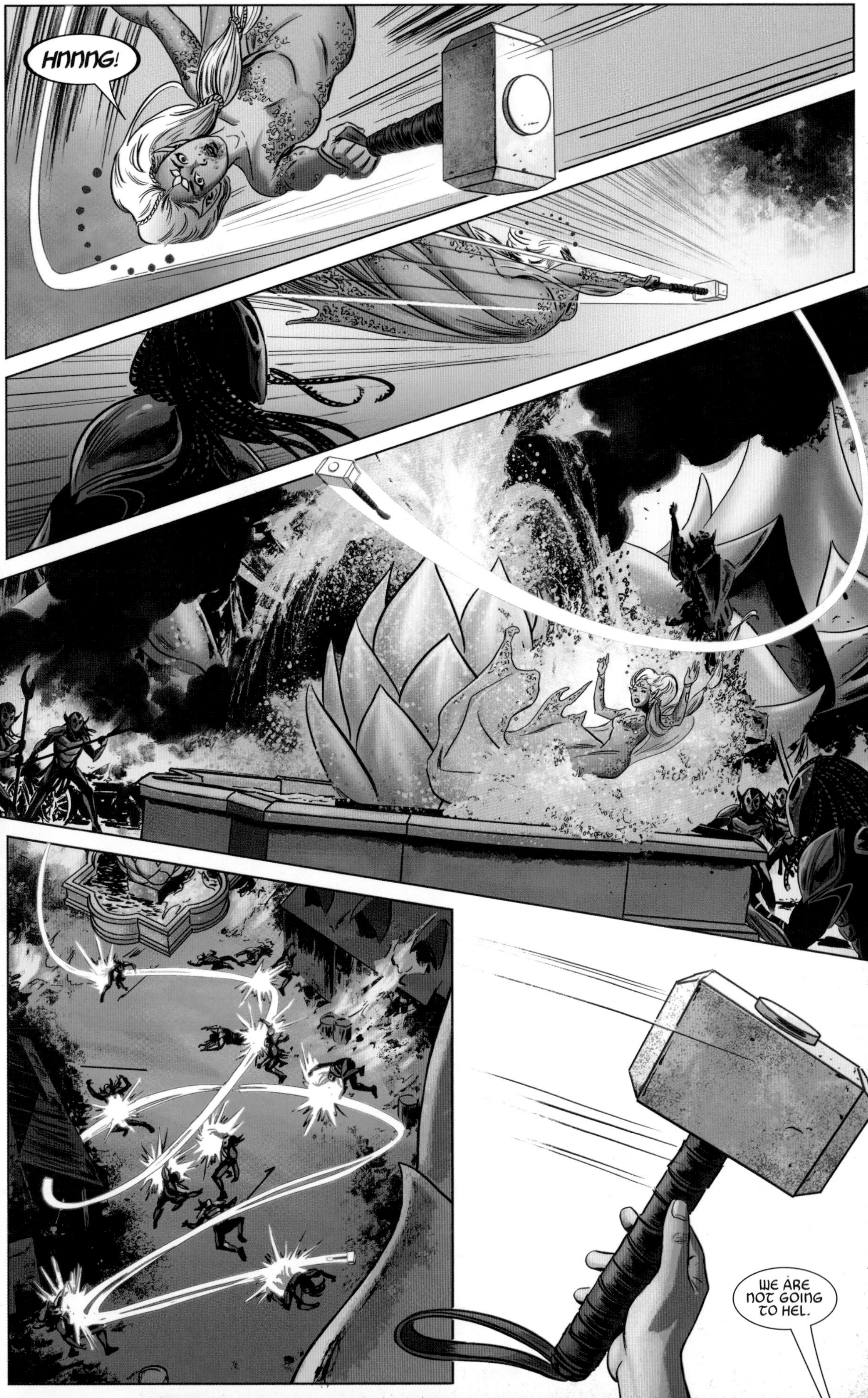
HNNNG!
WE ARE NOT GOING TO HEL.

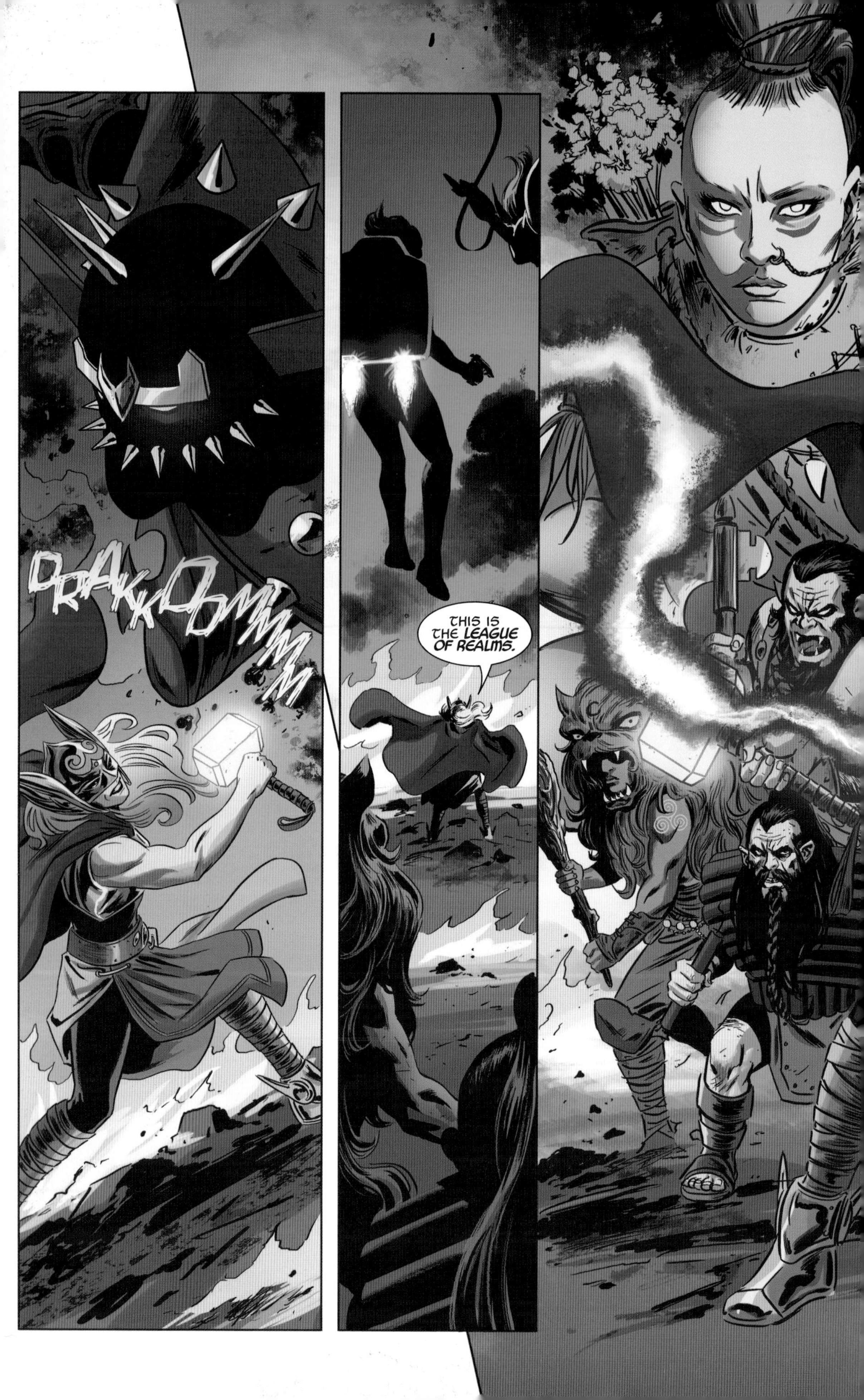
DRAKOOMMM
THIS IS THE LEAGUE OF REALMS.

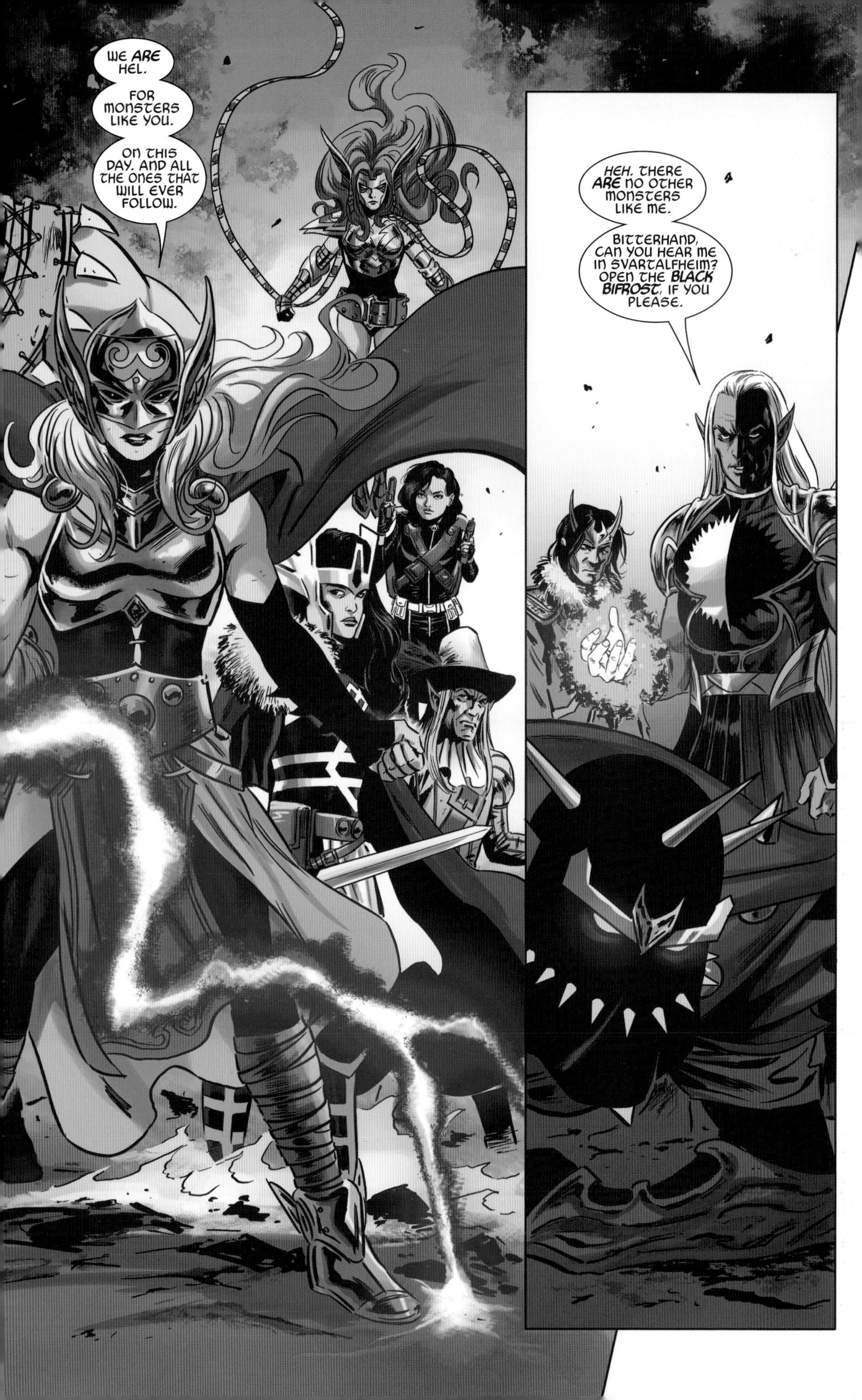
WE **ARE** HEL.
FOR MONSTERS LIKE YOU.
ON THIS DAY. AND ALL THE ONES THAT WILL EVER FOLLOW.
HEH. THERE **ARE** NO OTHER MONSTERS LIKE ME.
BITTERHAND, CAN YOU HEAR ME IN SVARTALFHEIM? OPEN THE **BLACK BIFROST**, IF YOU PLEASE.

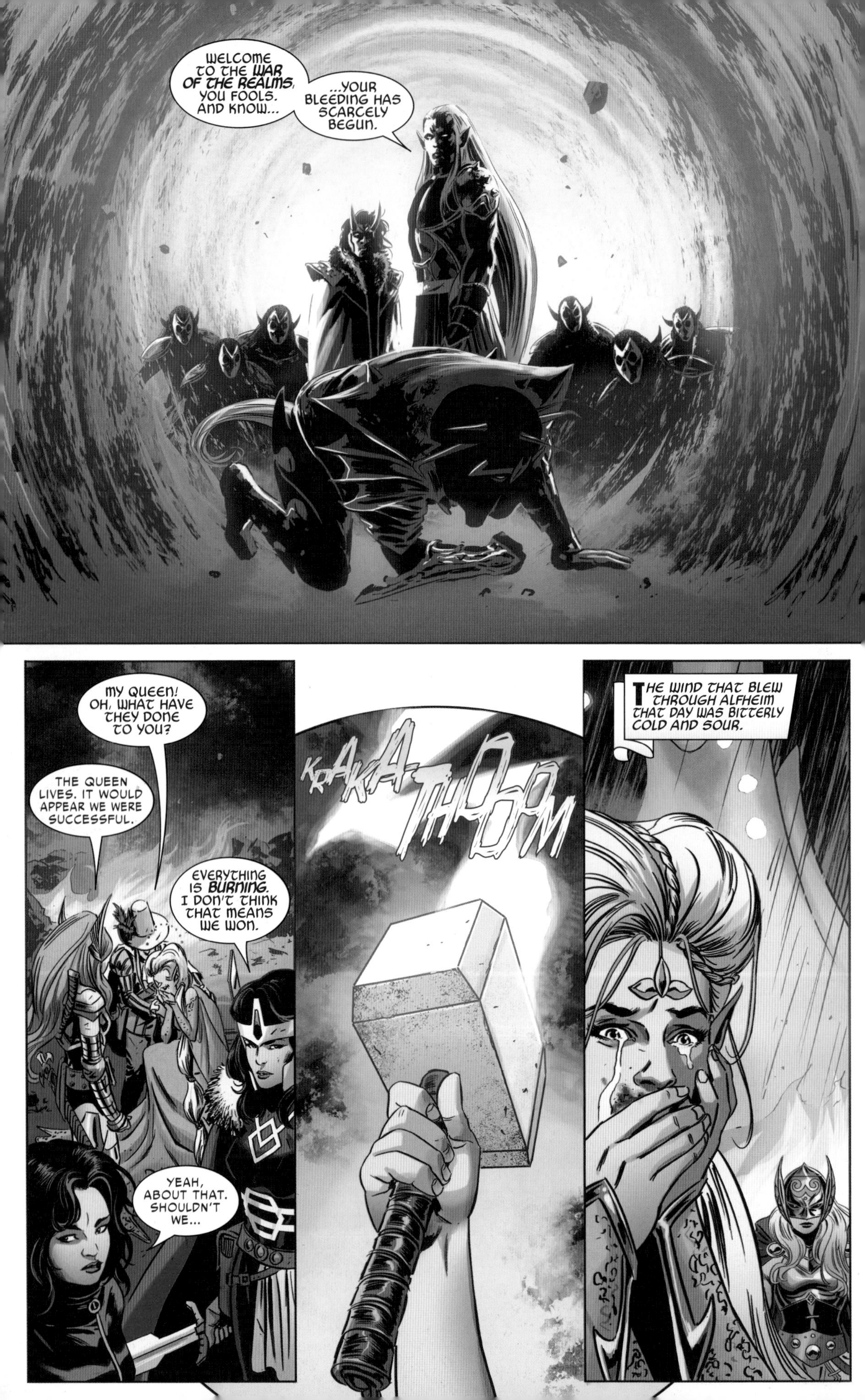

WELCOME TO THE WAR OF THE REALMS, YOU FOOLS. AND KNOW...
...YOUR BLEEDING HAS SCARCELY BEGUN.
MY QUEEN! OH, WHAT HAVE THEY DONE TO YOU?
THE QUEEN LIVES. IT WOULD APPEAR WE WERE SUCCESSFUL.
EVERYTHING IS BURNING. I DON'T THINK THAT MEANS WE WON.
YEAH, ABOUT THAT. SHOULDN'T WE...
KRAKATHOOM
THE WIND THAT BLEW THROUGH ALFHEIM THAT DAY WAS BITTERLY COLD AND SOUR.

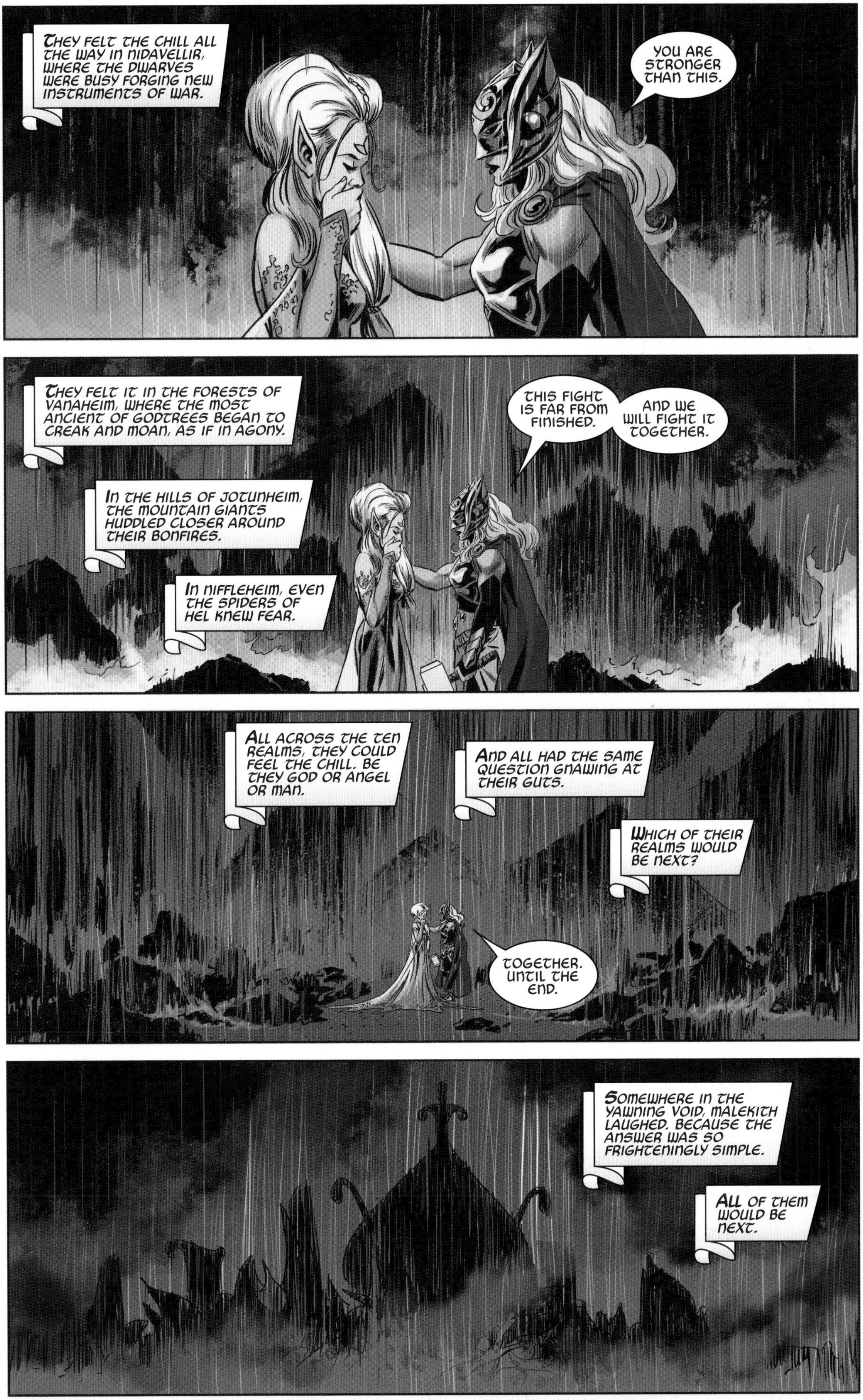
THEY FELT THE CHILL ALL THE WAY IN NIDAVELLIR, WHERE THE DWARVES WERE BUSY FORGING NEW INSTRUMENTS OF WAR.
YOU ARE STRONGER THAN THIS.
THEY FELT IT IN THE FORESTS OF VANAHEIM, WHERE THE MOST ANCIENT OF GODTREES BEGAN TO CREAK AND MOAN, AS IF IN AGONY.
THIS FIGHT IS FAR FROM FINISHED.
AND WE WILL FIGHT IT TOGETHER.
IN THE HILLS OF JOTUNHEIM, THE MOUNTAIN GIANTS HUDDLED CLOSER AROUND THEIR BONFIRES.
IN NIFFLEHEIM, EVEN THE SPIDERS OF HEL KNEW FEAR.
ALL ACROSS THE TEN REALMS, THEY COULD FEEL THE CHILL. BE THEY GOD OR ANGEL OR MAN.
AND ALL HAD THE SAME QUESTION GNAWING AT THEIR GUTS.
WHICH OF THEIR REALMS WOULD BE NEXT?
TOGETHER. UNTIL THE END.
SOMEWHERE IN THE YAWNING VOID, MALEKITH LAUGHED. BECAUSE THE ANSWER WAS SO FRIGHTENINGLY SIMPLE.
ALL OF THEM WOULD BE NEXT.

THE MIGHTY THOR Variant Cover Gallery

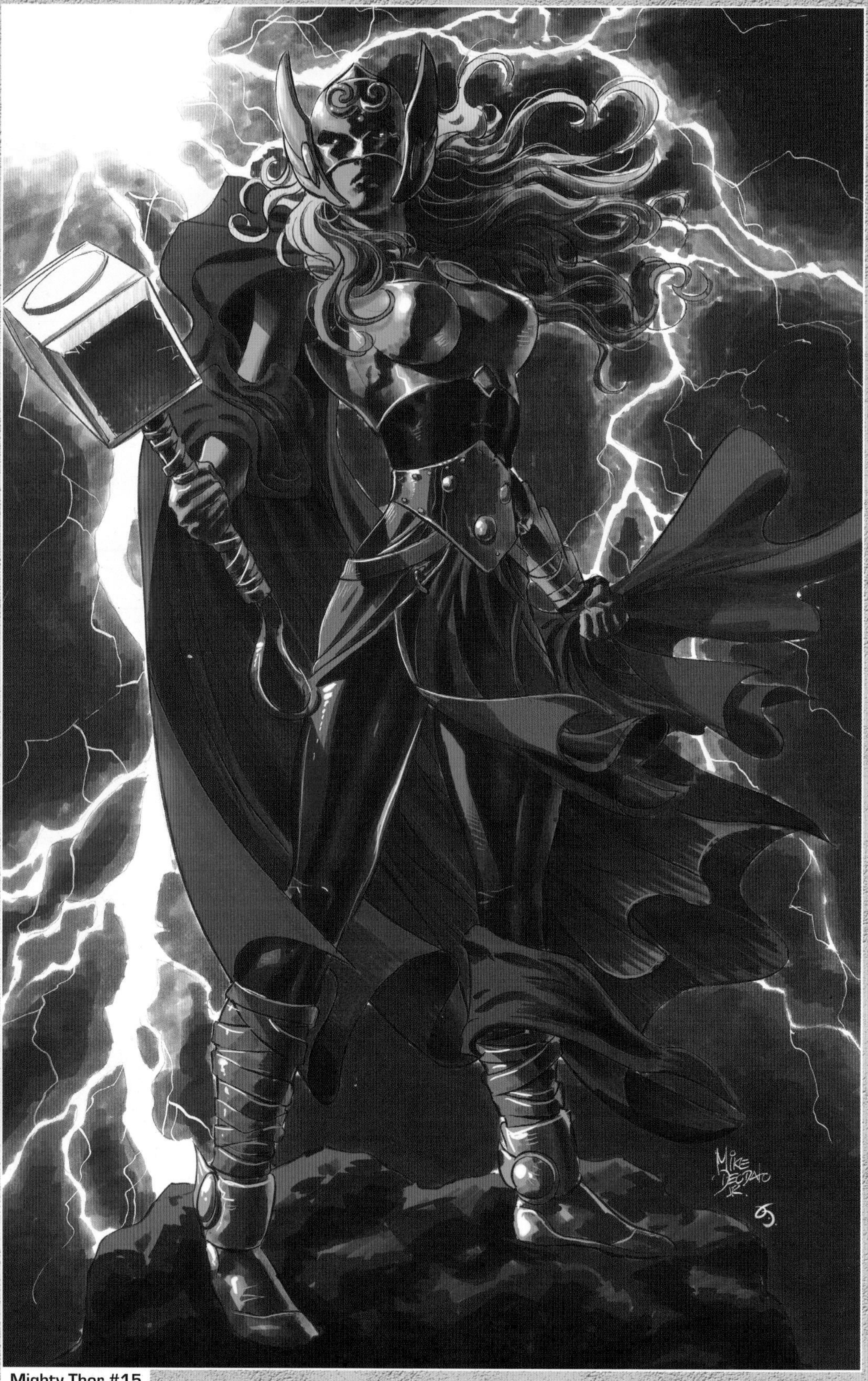
MIKE DEODATO JR.

Mighty Thor #15
By Mike Deodato

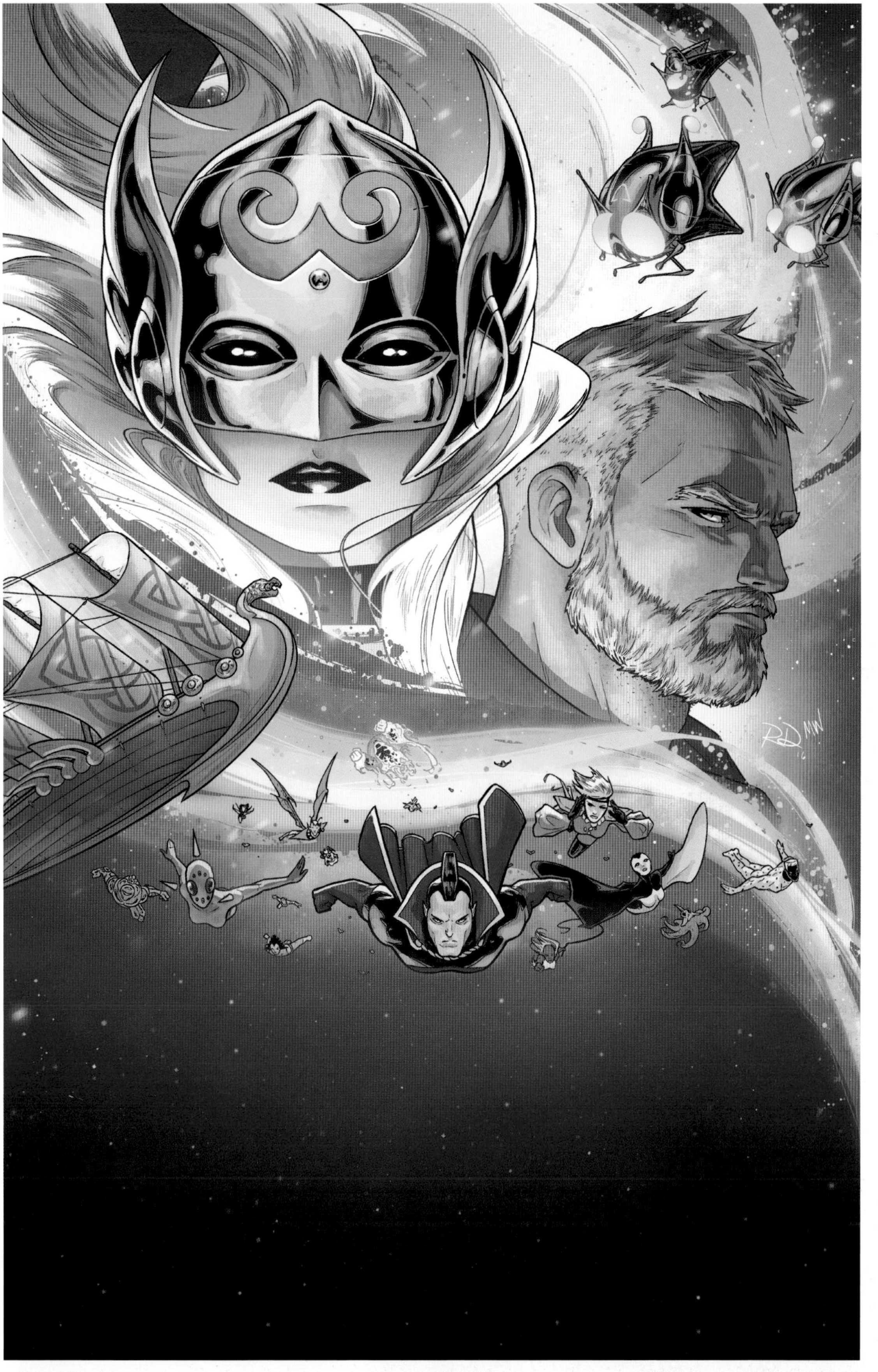

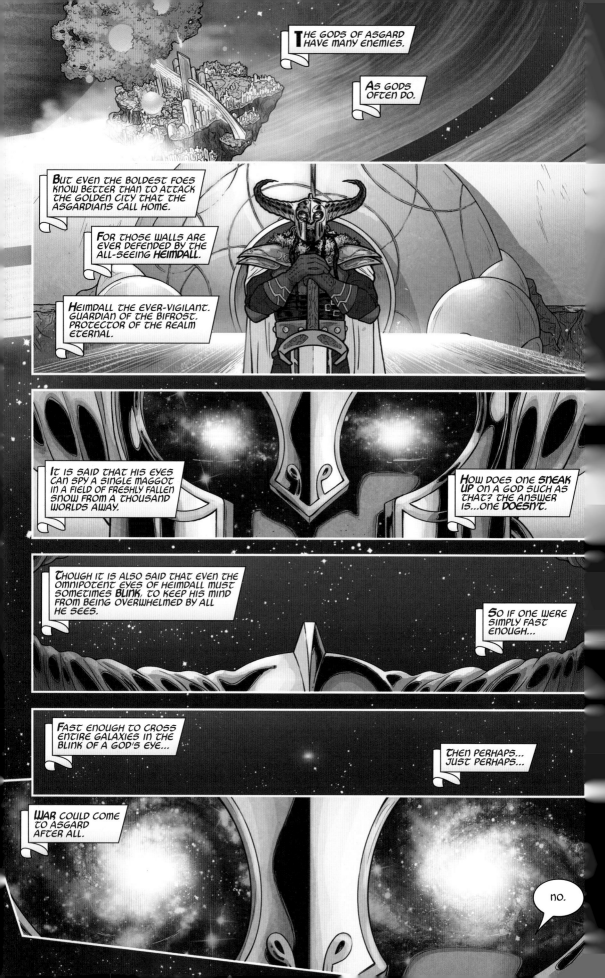

THE GODS OF ASGARD HAVE MANY ENEMIES.

AS GODS OFTEN DO.

BUT EVEN THE BOLDEST FOES KNOW BETTER THAN TO ATTACK THE GOLDEN CITY THAT THE ASGARDIANS CALL HOME.

FOR THOSE WALLS ARE EVER DEFENDED BY THE ALL-SEEING HEIMDALL.

HEIMDALL THE EVER-VIGILANT. GUARDIAN OF THE BIFROST. PROTECTOR OF THE REALM ETERNAL.

IT IS SAID THAT HIS EYES CAN SPY A SINGLE MAGGOT IN A FIELD OF FRESHLY FALLEN SNOW FROM A THOUSAND WORLDS AWAY.

HOW DOES ONE SNEAK UP ON A GOD SUCH AS THAT? THE ANSWER IS...ONE DOESN'T.

THOUGH IT IS ALSO SAID THAT EVEN THE OMNIPOTENT EYES OF HEIMDALL MUST SOMETIMES BLINK, TO KEEP HIS MIND FROM BEING OVERWHELMED BY ALL HE SEES.

SO IF ONE WERE SIMPLY FAST ENOUGH...

FAST ENOUGH TO CROSS ENTIRE GALAXIES IN THE BLINK OF A GOD'S EYE...

THEN PERHAPS... JUST PERHAPS...

WAR COULD COME TO ASGARD AFTER ALL.

no.

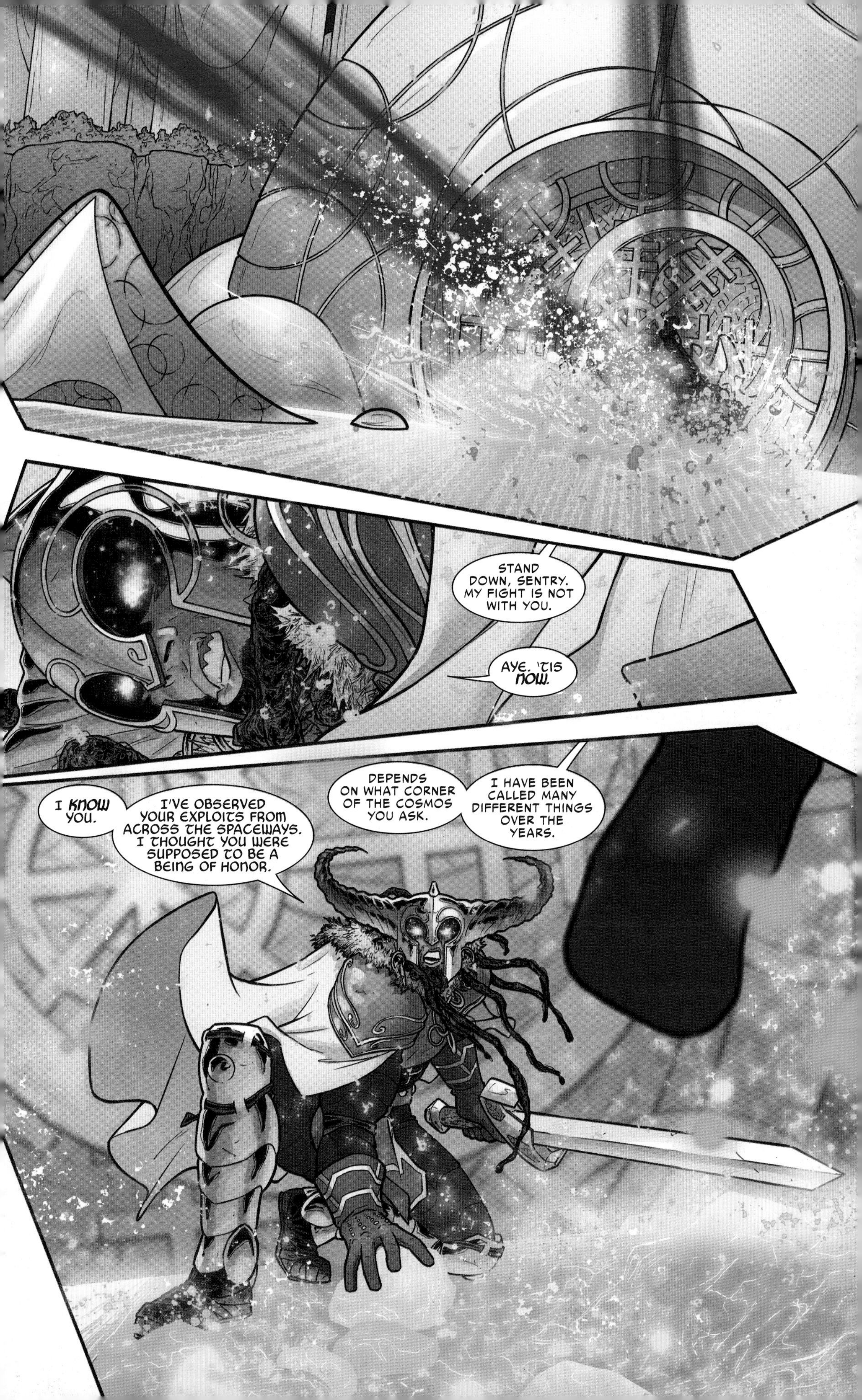

STAND DOWN, SENTRY. MY FIGHT IS NOT WITH YOU.
AYE. 'TIS NOW.
I KNOW YOU.
I'VE OBSERVED YOUR EXPLOITS FROM ACROSS THE SPACEWAYS. I THOUGHT YOU WERE SUPPOSED TO BE A BEING OF HONOR.
DEPENDS ON WHAT CORNER OF THE COSMOS YOU ASK.
I HAVE BEEN CALLED MANY DIFFERENT THINGS OVER THE YEARS.

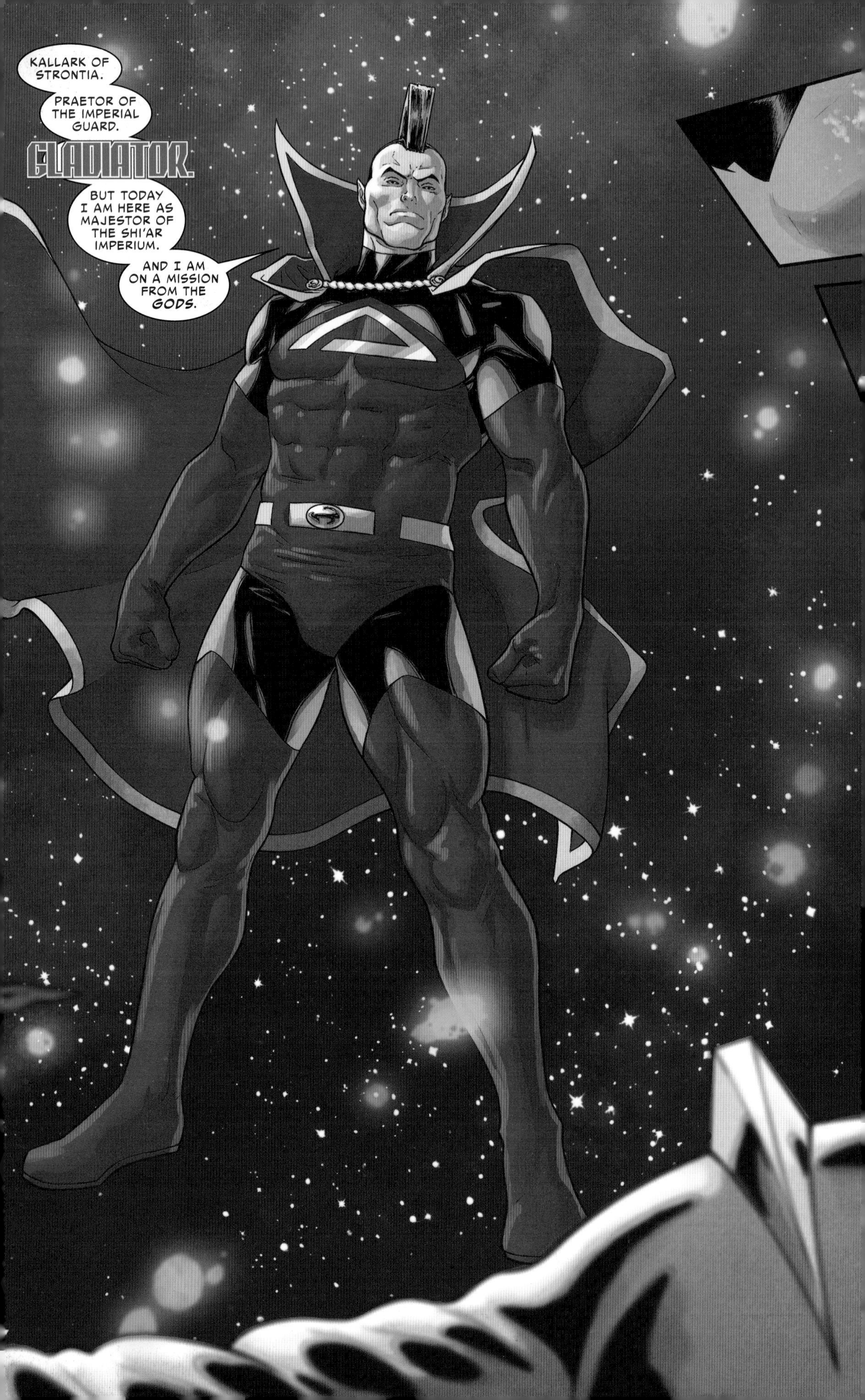
KALLARK OF STRONTIA.
PRAETOR OF THE IMPERIAL GUARD.
GLADIATOR.
BUT TODAY I AM HERE AS MAJESTOR OF THE SHI'AR IMPERIUM.
AND I AM ON A MISSION FROM THE *GODS*.

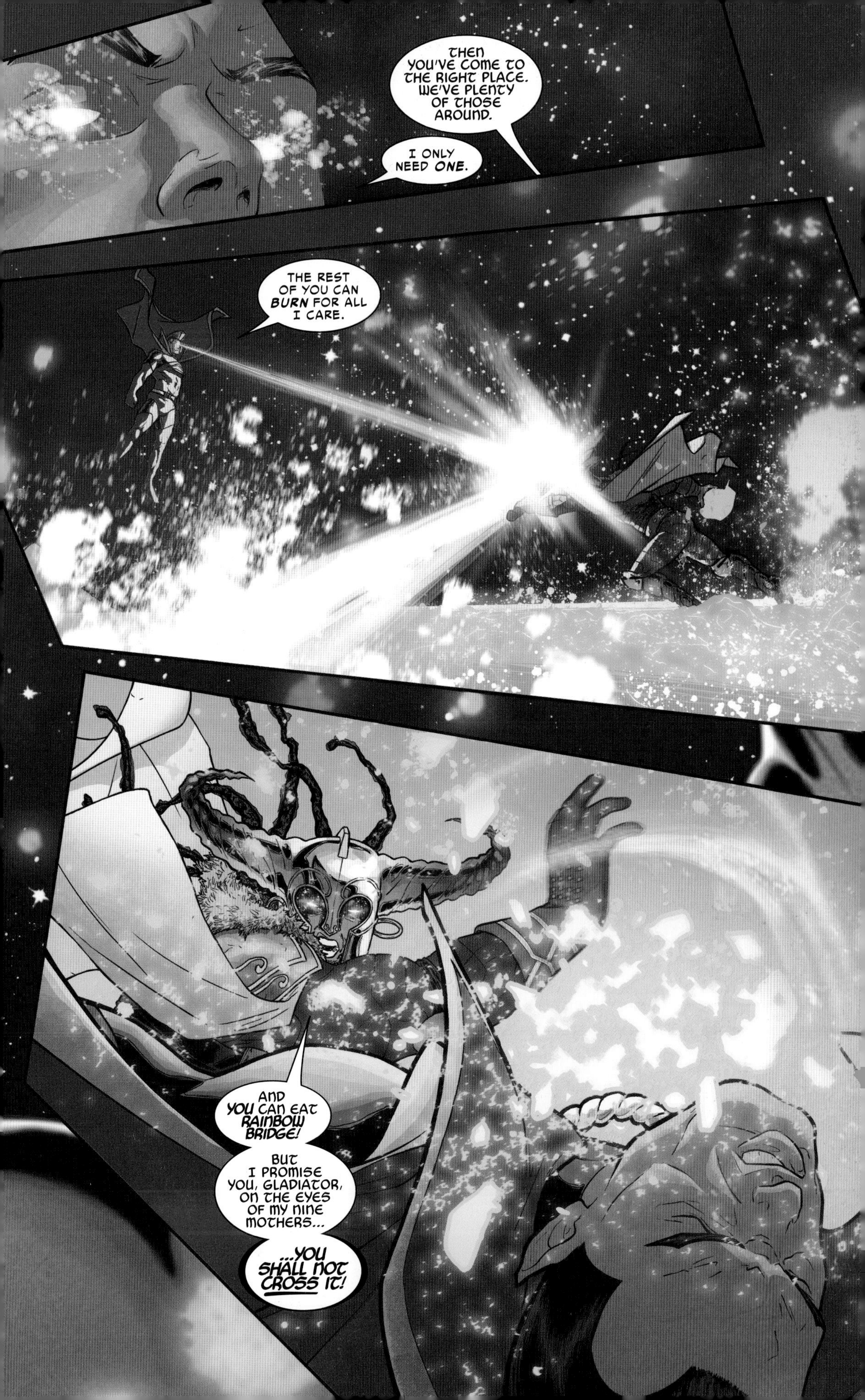
THEN YOU'VE COME TO THE RIGHT PLACE. WE'VE PLENTY OF THOSE AROUND.
I ONLY NEED *ONE*.
THE REST OF YOU CAN *BURN* FOR ALL I CARE.
AND *YOU* CAN EAT *RAINBOW BRIDGE*!
BUT I PROMISE YOU, GLADIATOR, ON THE EYES OF MY NINE MOTHERS...
...YOU SHALL NOT CROSS IT!

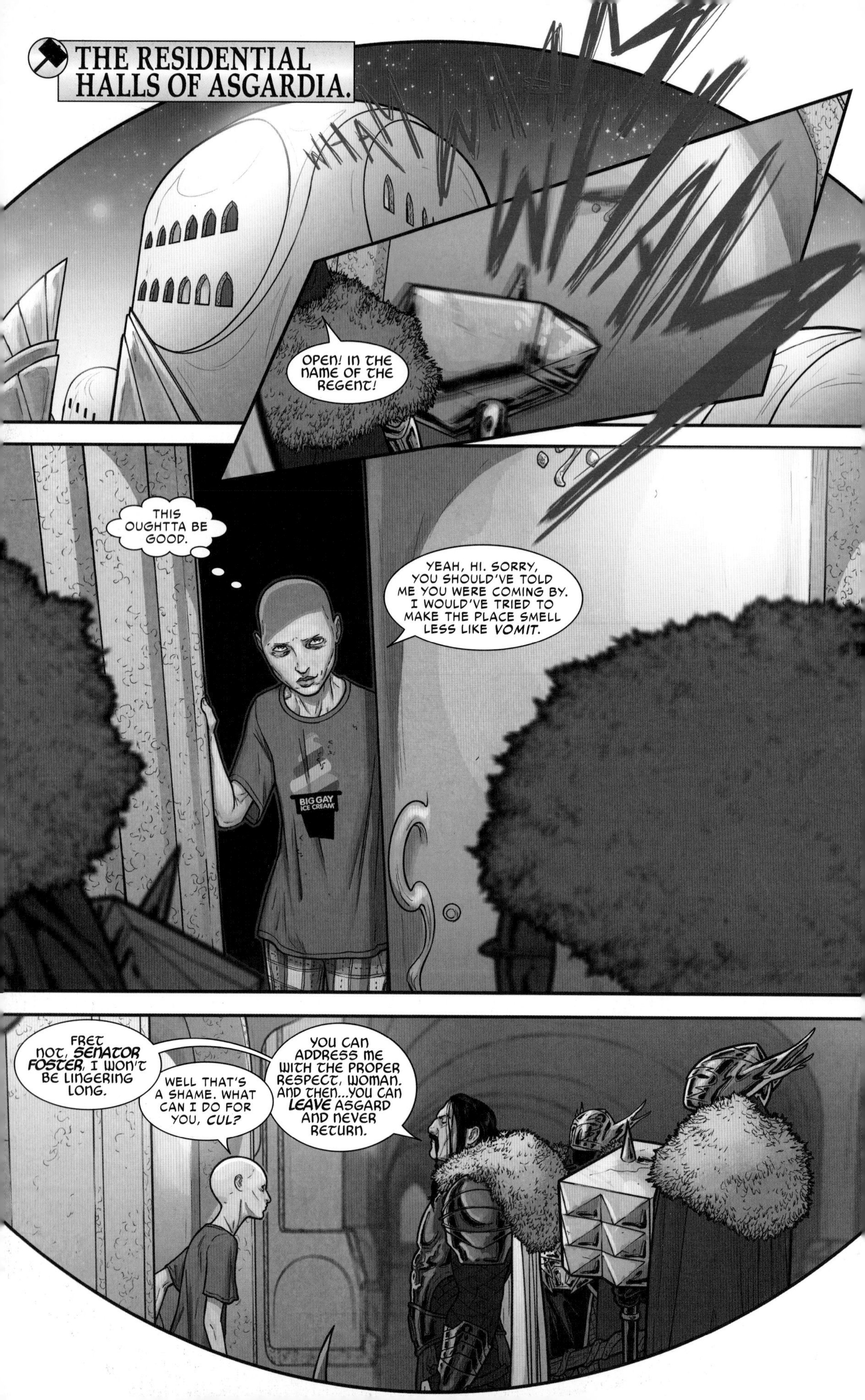
THE RESIDENTIAL HALLS OF ASGARDIA.
WHAM WHAM WHAM
OPEN! IN THE NAME OF THE REGENT!
THIS OUGHTTA BE GOOD.
YEAH, HI. SORRY, YOU SHOULD'VE TOLD ME YOU WERE COMING BY. I WOULD'VE TRIED TO MAKE THE PLACE SMELL LESS LIKE VOMIT.
BIG GAY ICE CREAM
FRET NOT, SENATOR FOSTER, I WON'T BE LINGERING LONG.
WELL THAT'S A SHAME. WHAT CAN I DO FOR YOU, CUL?
YOU CAN ADDRESS ME WITH THE PROPER RESPECT, WOMAN. AND THEN...YOU CAN LEAVE ASGARD AND NEVER RETURN.

AFRAID I CAN'T DO THAT. I REPRESENT *MIDGARD* IN THE *CONGRESS OF WORLDS.*

LIKE IT OR NOT, CULLY, I'M AS MUCH A PART OF THE COURT OF *ASGARDIA* AS YOU ARE.

YES, BUT EXACTLY HOW ARE YOU SUPPOSED TO EFFECTIVELY REPRESENT YOUR BELOVED LITTLE MUDBALL...

...WHEN YOU ARE HOLED UP INSIDE YOUR QUARTERS FOR DAYS ON END, *VOMITING* LIKE A DRUNKEN DWARF?

IT'S BEEN A ROUGH WEEK. BUT YOU'LL FORGIVE ME IF I DON'T FEEL LIKE TALKING CHEMOTHERAPY WITH THE GOD OF FEAR. NOW IF YOU'LL EXCUSE--

NINE DAYS.

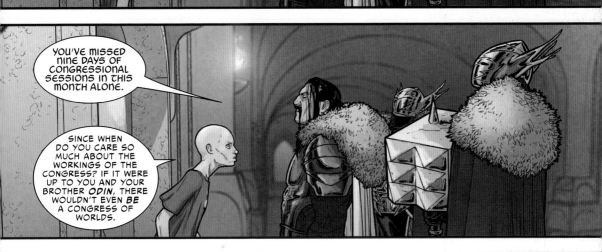

YOU'VE MISSED NINE DAYS OF CONGRESSIONAL SESSIONS IN THIS MONTH ALONE.

SINCE WHEN DO YOU CARE SO MUCH ABOUT THE WORKINGS OF THE CONGRESS? IF IT WERE UP TO YOU AND YOUR BROTHER *ODIN*, THERE WOULDN'T EVEN *BE* A CONGRESS OF WORLDS.

YOU ARE RIGHT.

IF IT WERE UP TO CUL BORSON, MIDGARD WOULD STILL BE BURNING IN A BONFIRE OF FEAR.

AND ALL THE OTHER REALMS WOULD BE GROVELING IN THEIR OWN BLOOD BEFORE THE FEARSOME, UNRELENTING MAJESTY OF ASGARD.

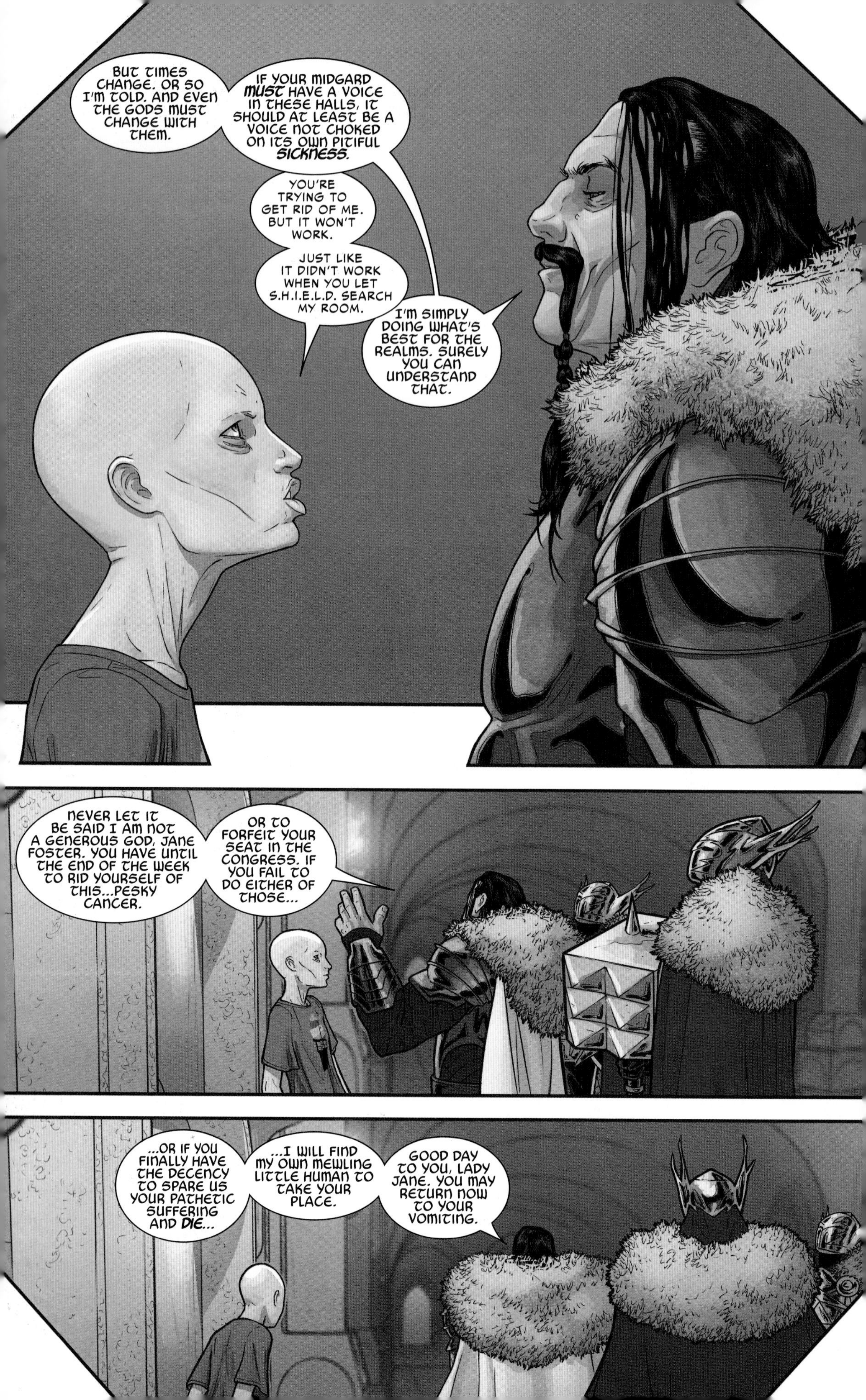

BUT TIMES CHANGE. OR SO I'M TOLD. AND EVEN THE GODS MUST CHANGE WITH THEM.
IF YOUR MIDGARD MUST HAVE A VOICE IN THESE HALLS, IT SHOULD AT LEAST BE A VOICE NOT CHOKED ON ITS OWN PITIFUL SICKNESS.
YOU'RE TRYING TO GET RID OF ME. BUT IT WON'T WORK.
JUST LIKE IT DIDN'T WORK WHEN YOU LET S.H.I.E.L.D. SEARCH MY ROOM.
I'M SIMPLY DOING WHAT'S BEST FOR THE REALMS. SURELY YOU CAN UNDERSTAND THAT.
NEVER LET IT BE SAID I AM NOT A GENEROUS GOD, JANE FOSTER. YOU HAVE UNTIL THE END OF THE WEEK TO RID YOURSELF OF THIS...PESKY CANCER.
OR TO FORFEIT YOUR SEAT IN THE CONGRESS. IF YOU FAIL TO DO EITHER OF THOSE...
...OR IF YOU FINALLY HAVE THE DECENCY TO SPARE US YOUR PATHETIC SUFFERING AND DIE...
...I WILL FIND MY OWN MEWLING LITTLE HUMAN TO TAKE YOUR PLACE.
GOOD DAY TO YOU, LADY JANE. YOU MAY RETURN NOW TO YOUR VOMITING.

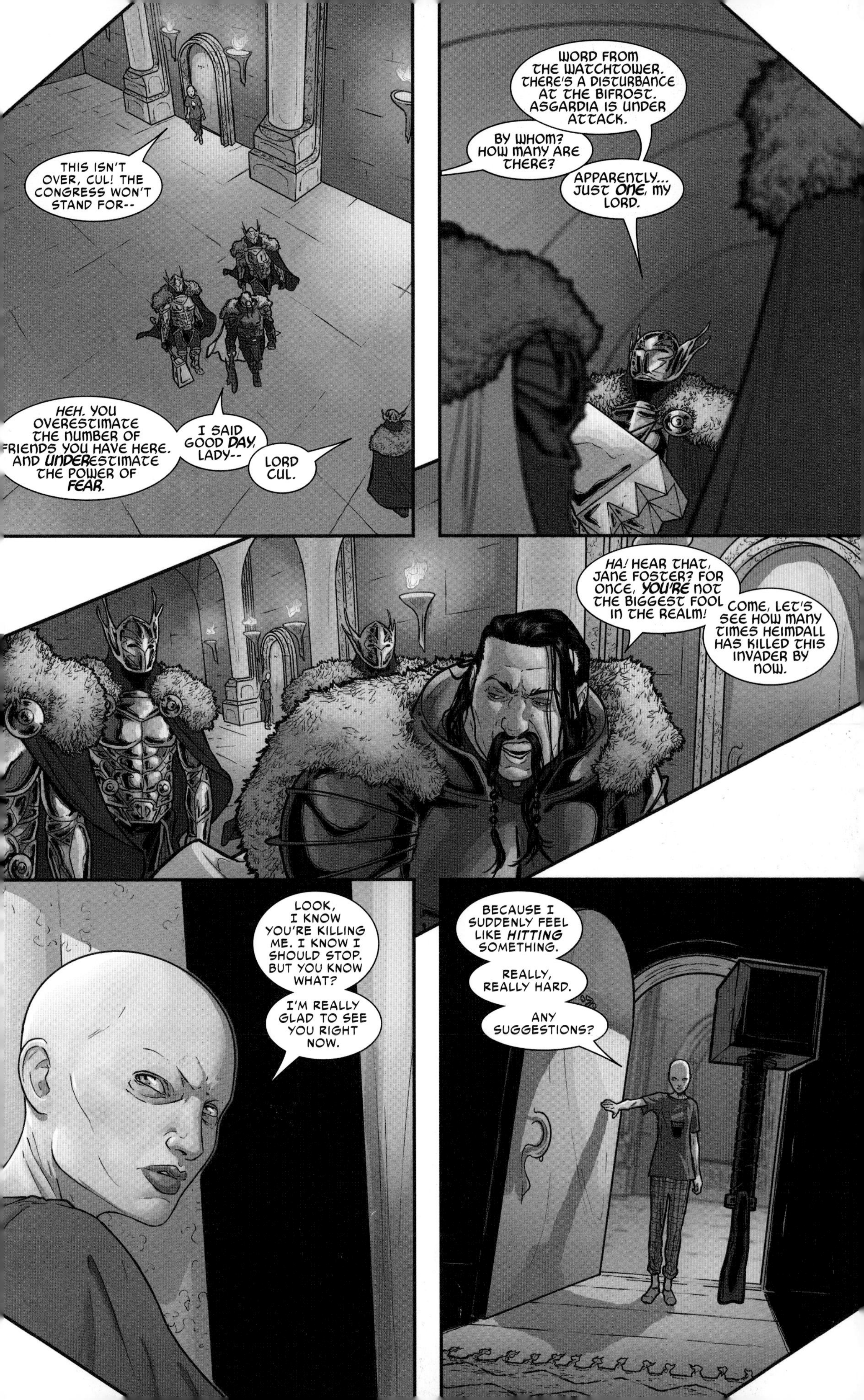

THIS ISN'T OVER, CUL! THE CONGRESS WON'T STAND FOR--
HEH. YOU OVERESTIMATE THE NUMBER OF FRIENDS YOU HAVE HERE. AND UNDERESTIMATE THE POWER OF FEAR.
I SAID GOOD DAY, LADY--
LORD CUL.
WORD FROM THE WATCHTOWER. THERE'S A DISTURBANCE AT THE BIFROST. ASGARDIA IS UNDER ATTACK.
BY WHOM? HOW MANY ARE THERE?
APPARENTLY... JUST ONE, MY LORD.
HA! HEAR THAT, JANE FOSTER? FOR ONCE, YOU'RE NOT THE BIGGEST FOOL IN THE REALM!
COME, LET'S SEE HOW MANY TIMES HEIMDALL HAS KILLED THIS INVADER BY NOW.
LOOK, I KNOW YOU'RE KILLING ME. I KNOW I SHOULD STOP. BUT YOU KNOW WHAT?
I'M REALLY GLAD TO SEE YOU RIGHT NOW.
BECAUSE I SUDDENLY FEEL LIKE HITTING SOMETHING.
REALLY, REALLY HARD.
ANY SUGGESTIONS?

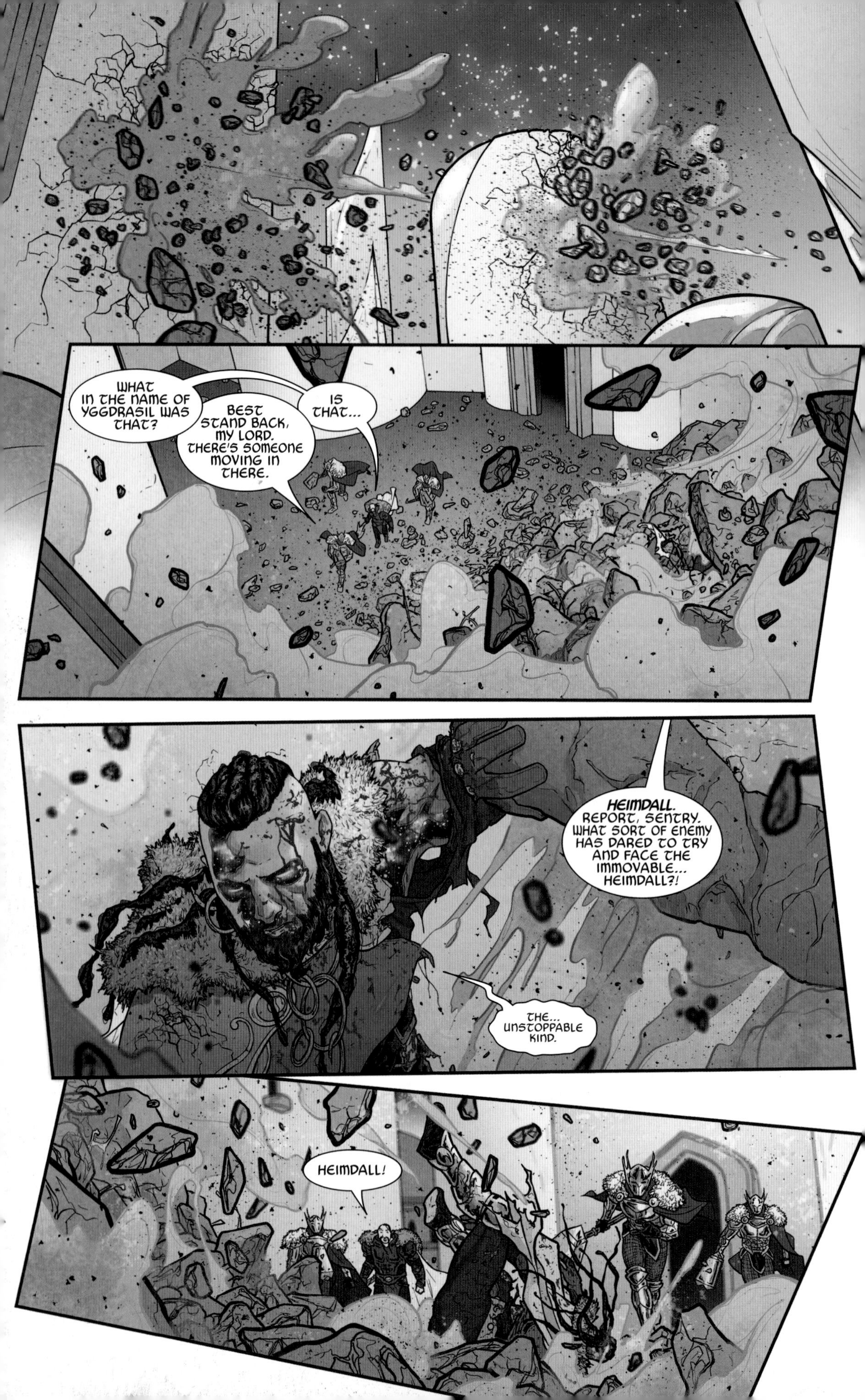
WHAT IN THE NAME OF YGGDRASIL WAS THAT?
IS THAT...
BEST STAND BACK, MY LORD. THERE'S SOMEONE MOVING IN THERE.
HEIMDALL. REPORT, SENTRY. WHAT SORT OF ENEMY HAS DARED TO TRY AND FACE THE IMMOVABLE... HEIMDALL?!
THE... UNSTOPPABLE KIND.
HEIMDALL!

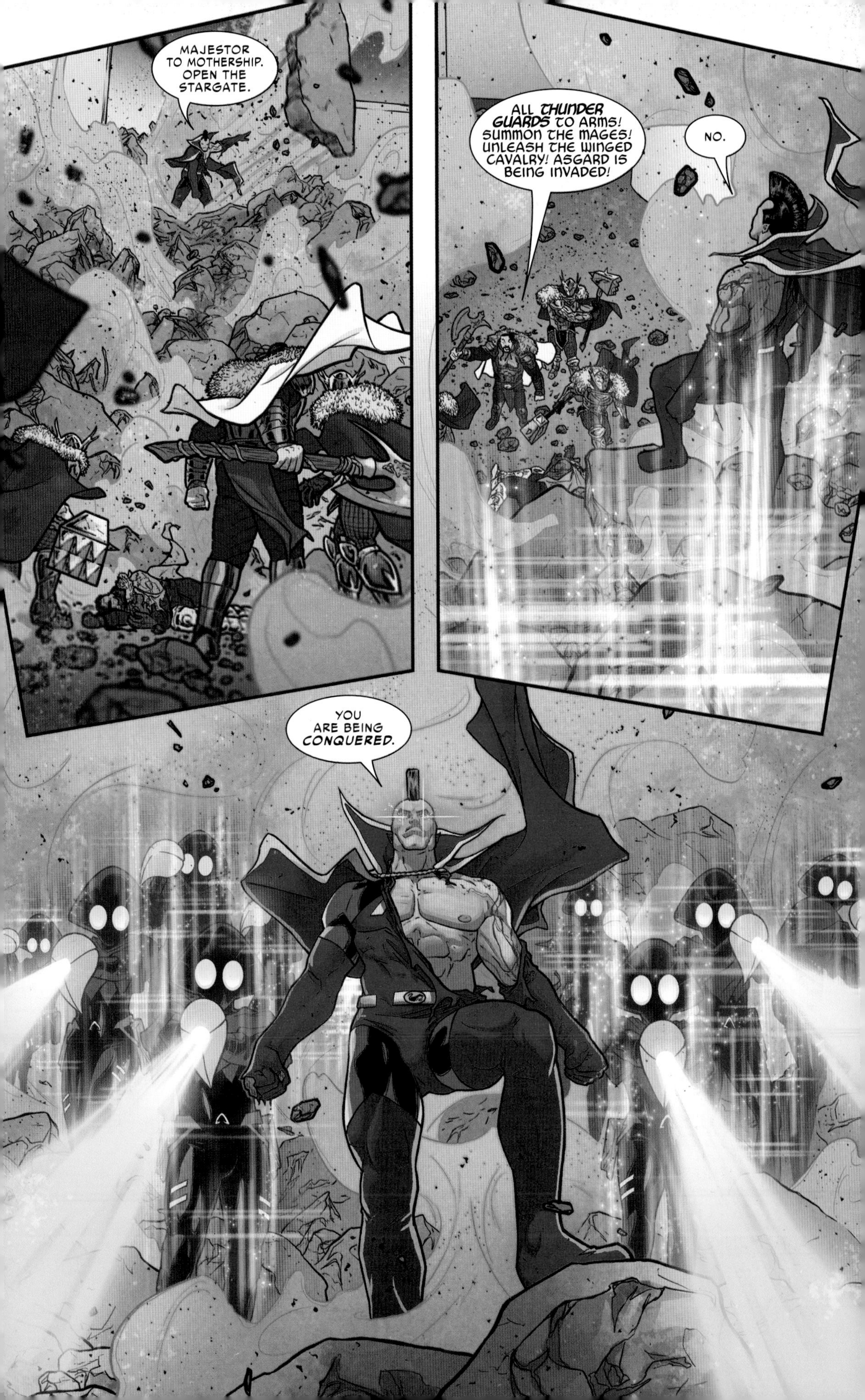
MAJESTOR TO MOTHERSHIP. OPEN THE STARGATE.
ALL THUNDER GUARDS TO ARMS! SUMMON THE MAGES! UNLEASH THE WINGED CAVALRY! ASGARD IS BEING INVADED!
NO.
YOU ARE BEING CONQUERED.

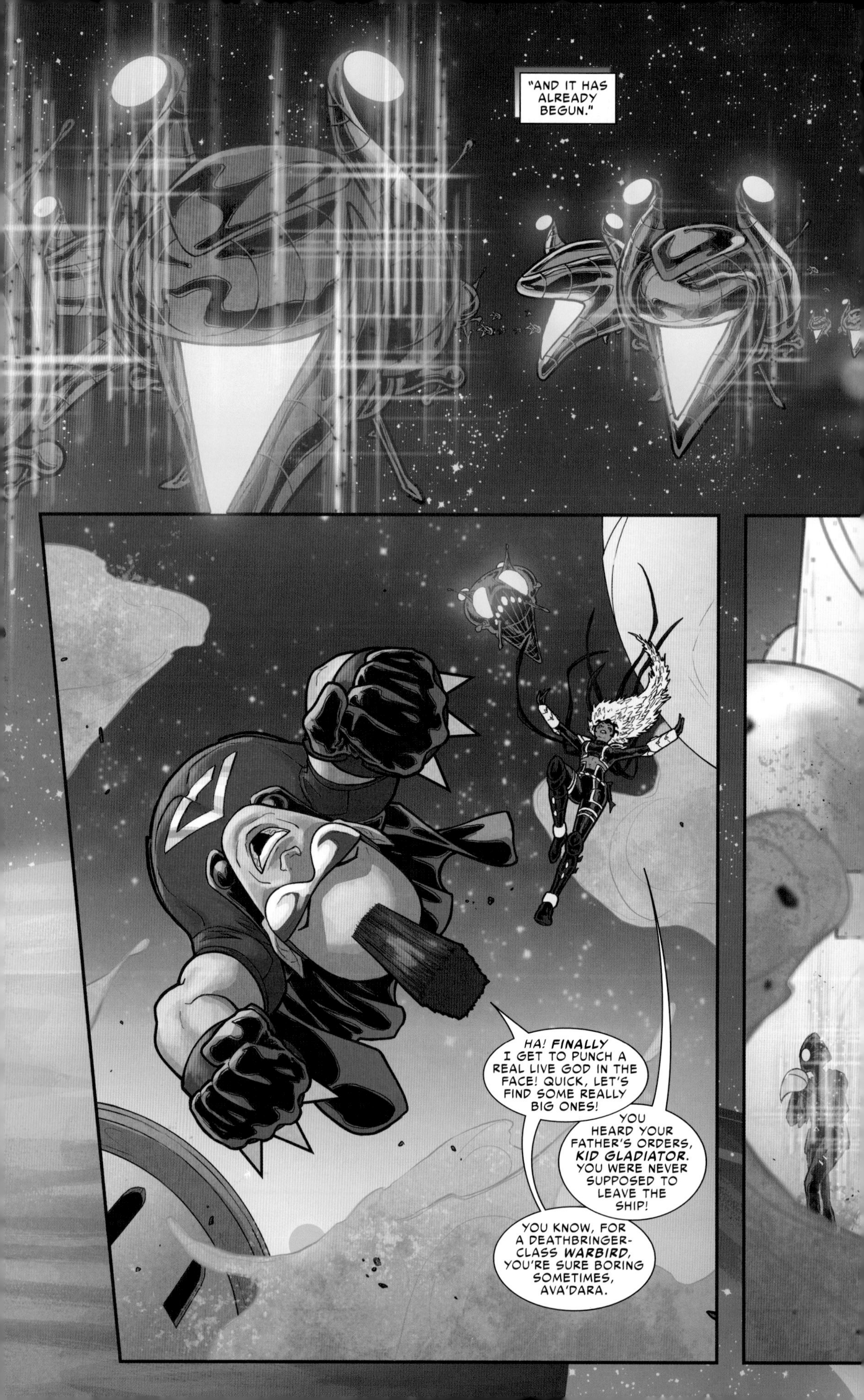
"AND IT HAS ALREADY BEGUN."
HA! FINALLY I GET TO PUNCH A REAL LIVE GOD IN THE FACE! QUICK, LET'S FIND SOME REALLY BIG ONES!
YOU HEARD YOUR FATHER'S ORDERS, KID GLADIATOR. YOU WERE NEVER SUPPOSED TO LEAVE THE SHIP!
YOU KNOW, FOR A DEATHBRINGER-CLASS WARBIRD, YOU'RE SURE BORING SOMETIMES, AVA'DARA.

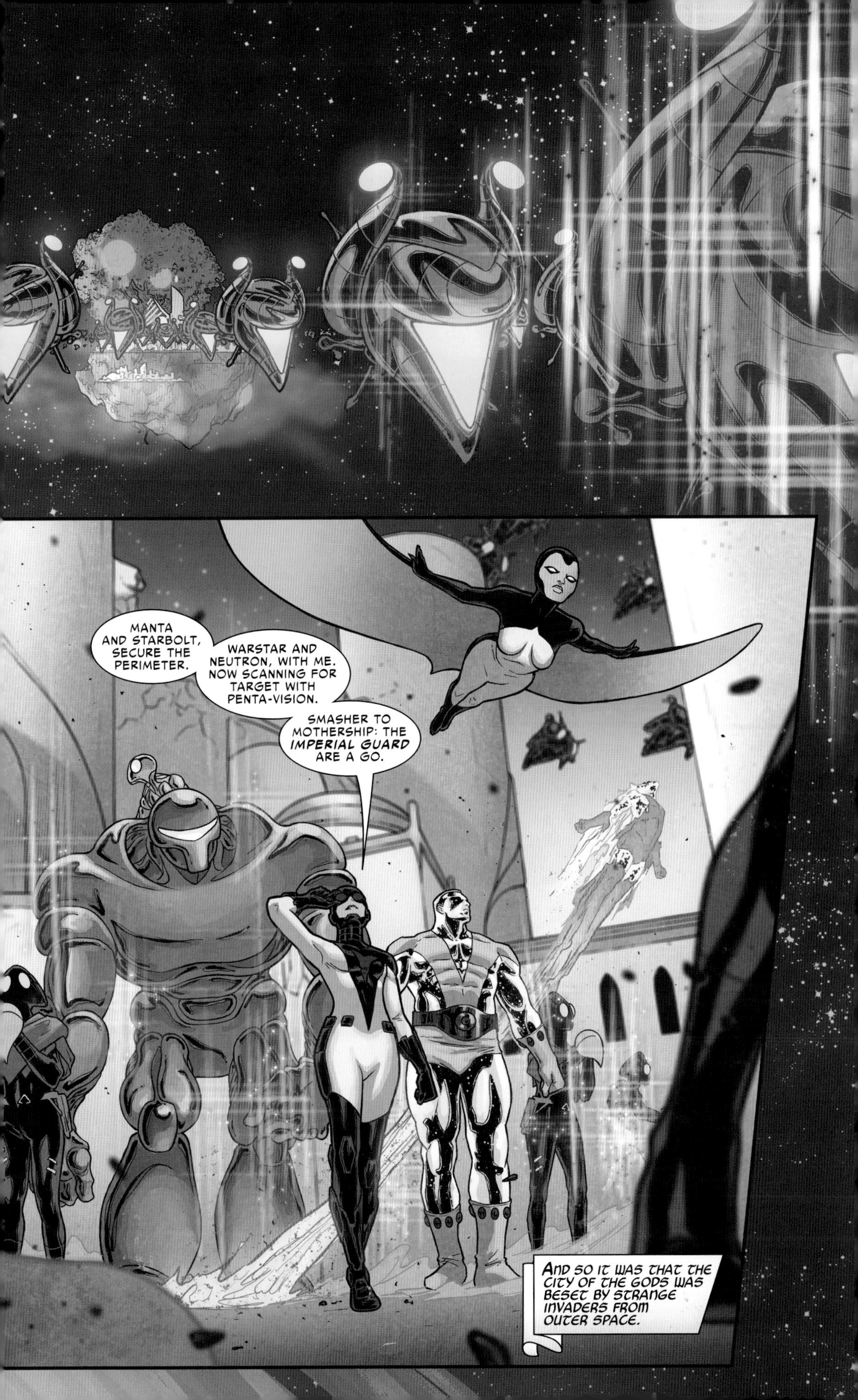
MANTA AND STARBOLT, SECURE THE PERIMETER.
WARSTAR AND NEUTRON, WITH ME. NOW SCANNING FOR TARGET WITH PENTA-VISION.
SMASHER TO MOTHERSHIP: THE *IMPERIAL GUARD* ARE A GO.
AND SO IT WAS THAT THE CITY OF THE GODS WAS BESET BY STRANGE INVADERS FROM OUTER SPACE.

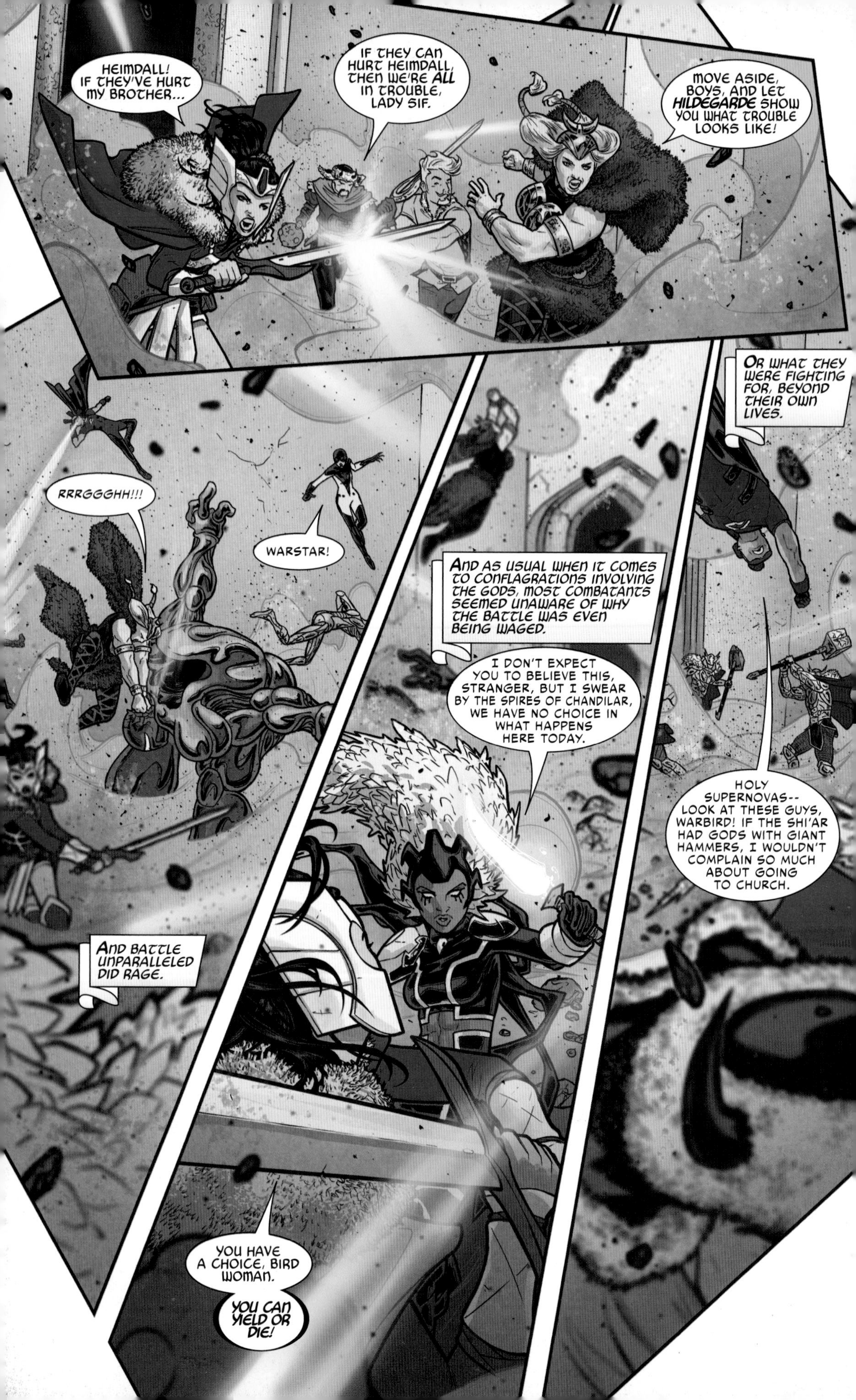
HEIMDALL! IF THEY'VE HURT MY BROTHER...
IF THEY CAN HURT HEIMDALL, THEN WE'RE ALL IN TROUBLE, LADY SIF.
MOVE ASIDE, BOYS, AND LET HILDEGARDE SHOW YOU WHAT TROUBLE LOOKS LIKE!
RRRGGGHH!!!
WARSTAR!
AND BATTLE UNPARALLELED DID RAGE.
AND AS USUAL WHEN IT COMES TO CONFLAGRATIONS INVOLVING THE GODS, MOST COMBATANTS SEEMED UNAWARE OF WHY THE BATTLE WAS EVEN BEING WAGED.
I DON'T EXPECT YOU TO BELIEVE THIS, STRANGER, BUT I SWEAR BY THE SPIRES OF CHANDILAR, WE HAVE NO CHOICE IN WHAT HAPPENS HERE TODAY.
YOU HAVE A CHOICE, BIRD WOMAN.
YOU CAN YIELD OR DIE!
OR WHAT THEY WERE FIGHTING FOR, BEYOND THEIR OWN LIVES.
HOLY SUPERNOVAS-- LOOK AT THESE GUYS, WARBIRD! IF THE SHI'AR HAD GODS WITH GIANT HAMMERS, I WOULDN'T COMPLAIN SO MUCH ABOUT GOING TO CHURCH.

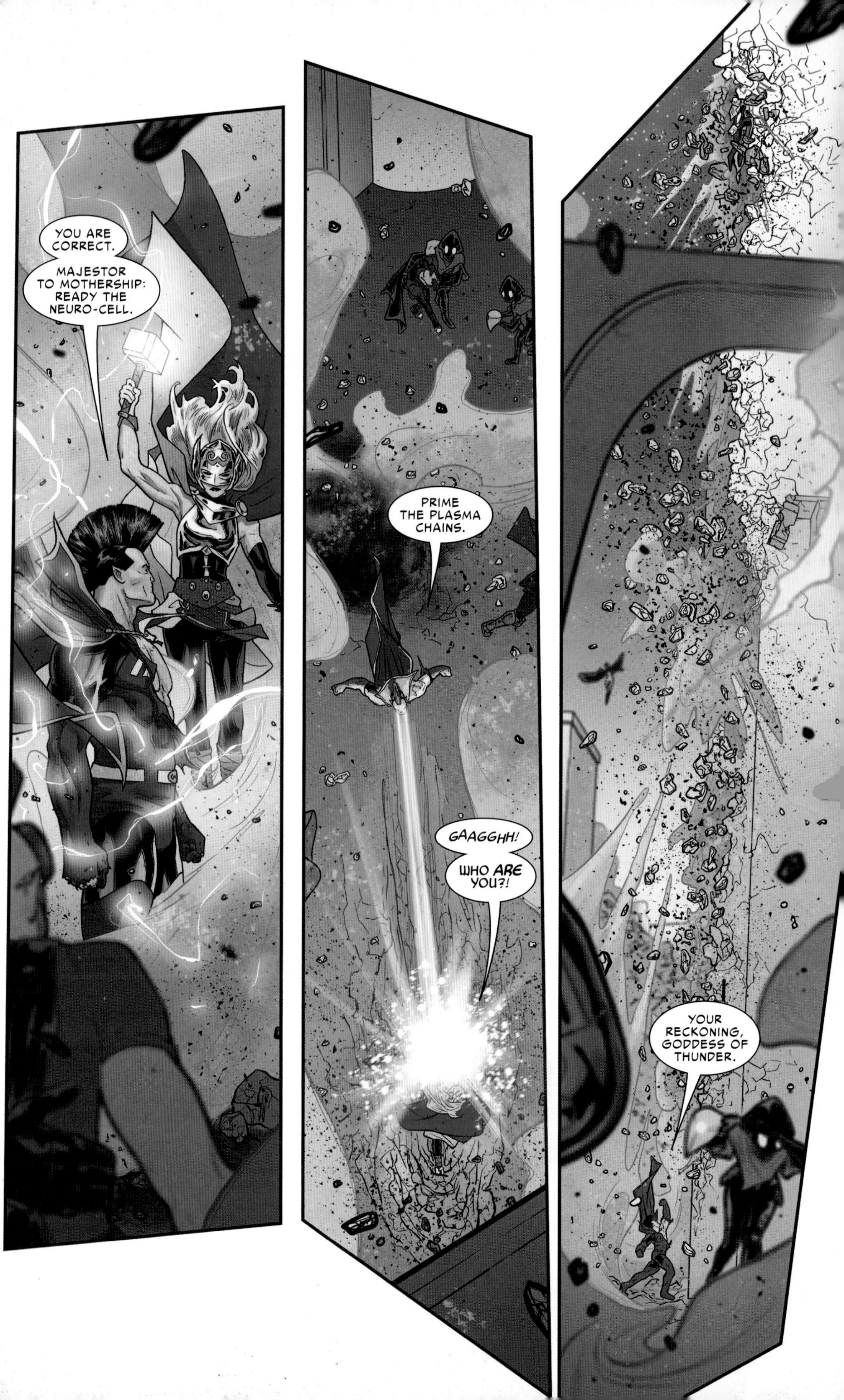
YOU ARE CORRECT.
MAJESTOR TO MOTHERSHIP: READY THE NEURO-CELL.
PRIME THE PLASMA CHAINS.
GAAGGHH!
WHO ARE YOU?!
YOUR RECKONING, GODDESS OF THUNDER.

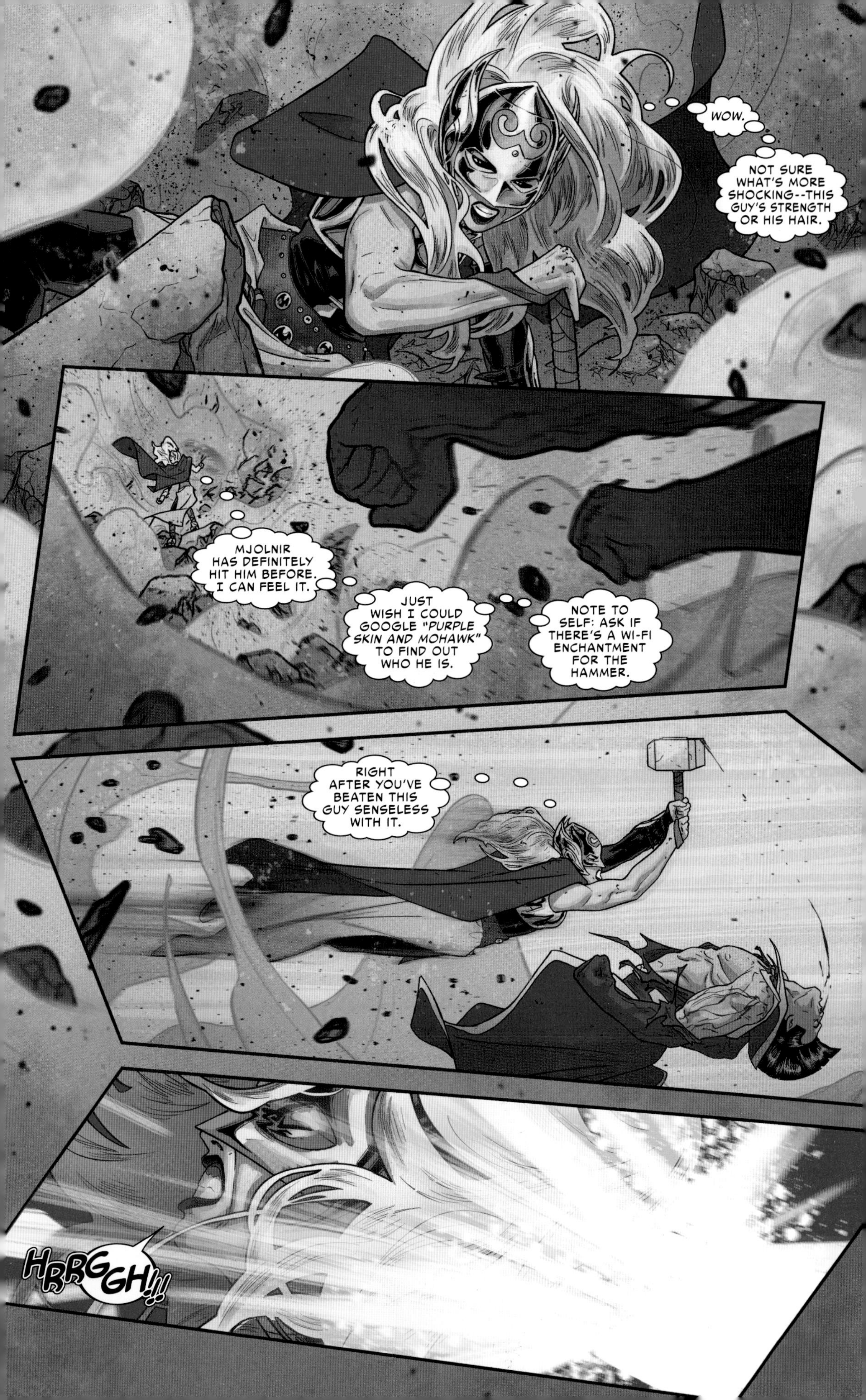
WOW.
NOT SURE WHAT'S MORE SHOCKING--THIS GUY'S STRENGTH OR HIS HAIR.
MJOLNIR HAS DEFINITELY HIT HIM BEFORE. I CAN FEEL IT.
JUST WISH I COULD GOOGLE "PURPLE SKIN AND MOHAWK" TO FIND OUT WHO HE IS.
NOTE TO SELF: ASK IF THERE'S A WI-FI ENCHANTMENT FOR THE HAMMER.
RIGHT AFTER YOU'VE BEATEN THIS GUY SENSELESS WITH IT.
HRRRGGH!!!

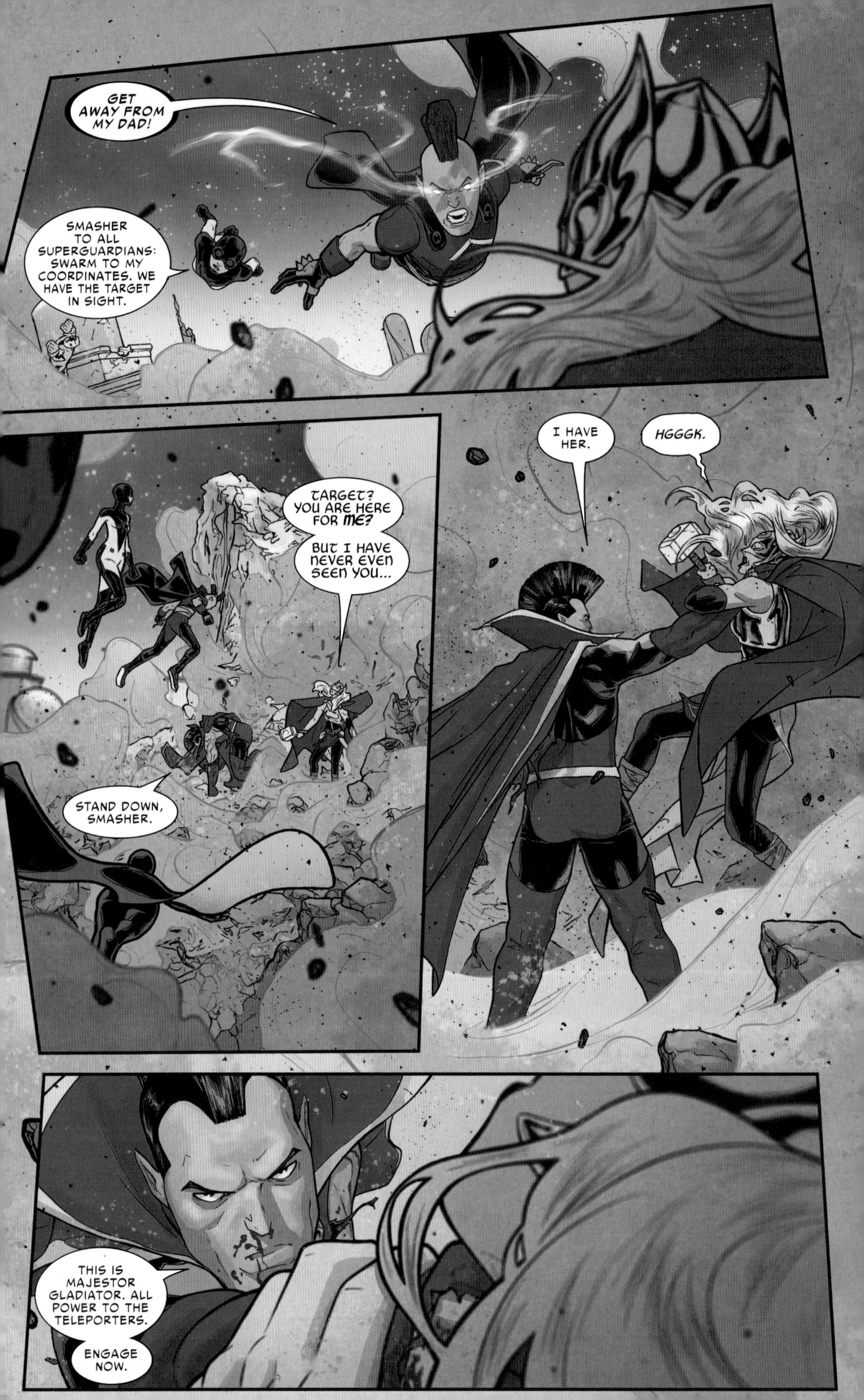
GET AWAY FROM MY DAD!
SMASHER TO ALL SUPERGUARDIANS: SWARM TO MY COORDINATES. WE HAVE THE TARGET IN SIGHT.
TARGET? YOU ARE HERE FOR ME?
BUT I HAVE NEVER EVEN SEEN YOU...
STAND DOWN, SMASHER.
I HAVE HER.
HGGGK.
THIS IS MAJESTOR GLADIATOR. ALL POWER TO THE TELEPORTERS.
ENGAGE NOW.

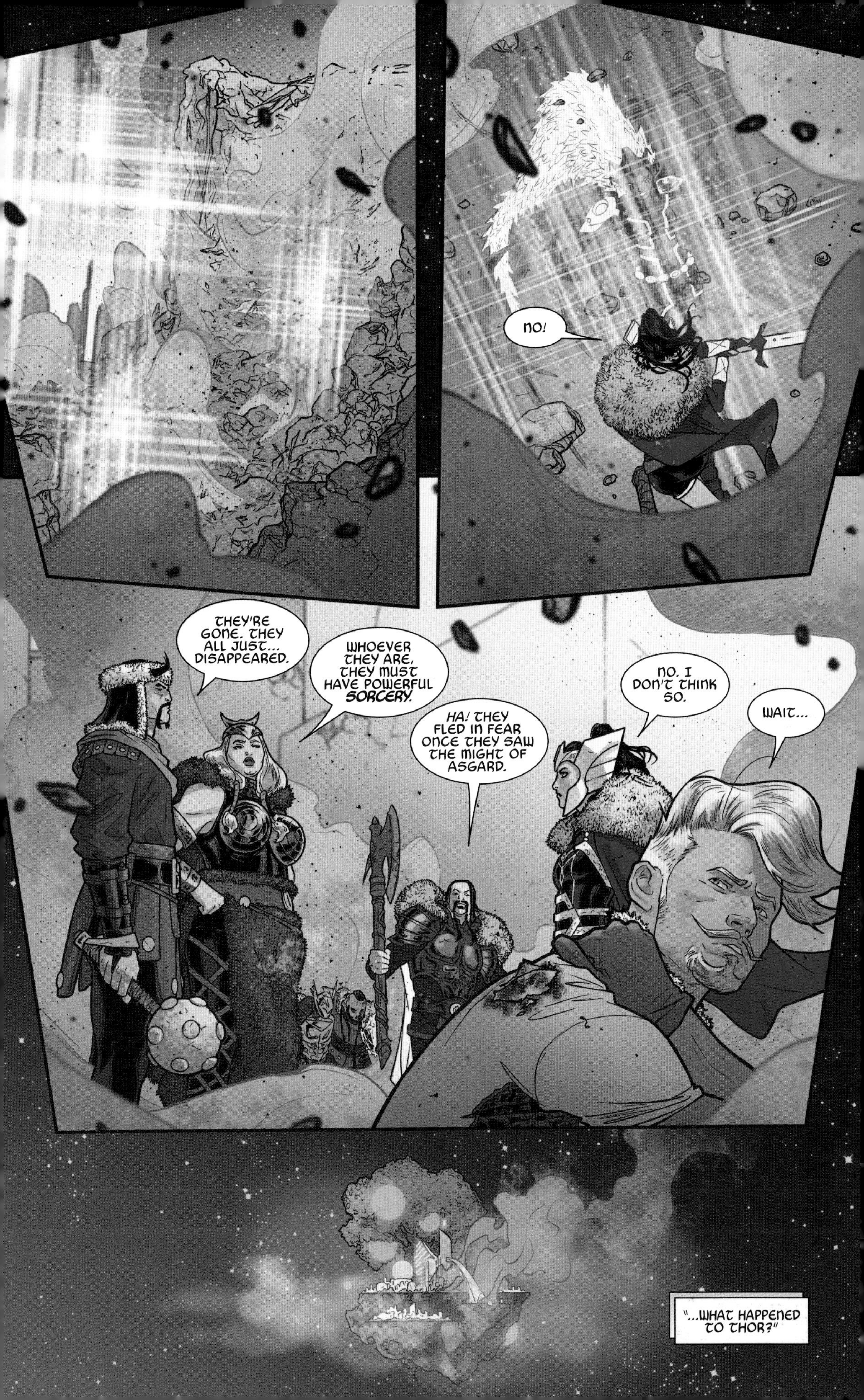
NO!
THEY'RE GONE. THEY ALL JUST... DISAPPEARED.
WHOEVER THEY ARE, THEY MUST HAVE POWERFUL SORCERY.
HA! THEY FLED IN FEAR ONCE THEY SAW THE MIGHT OF ASGARD.
NO. I DON'T THINK SO.
WAIT...
"...WHAT HAPPENED TO THOR?"

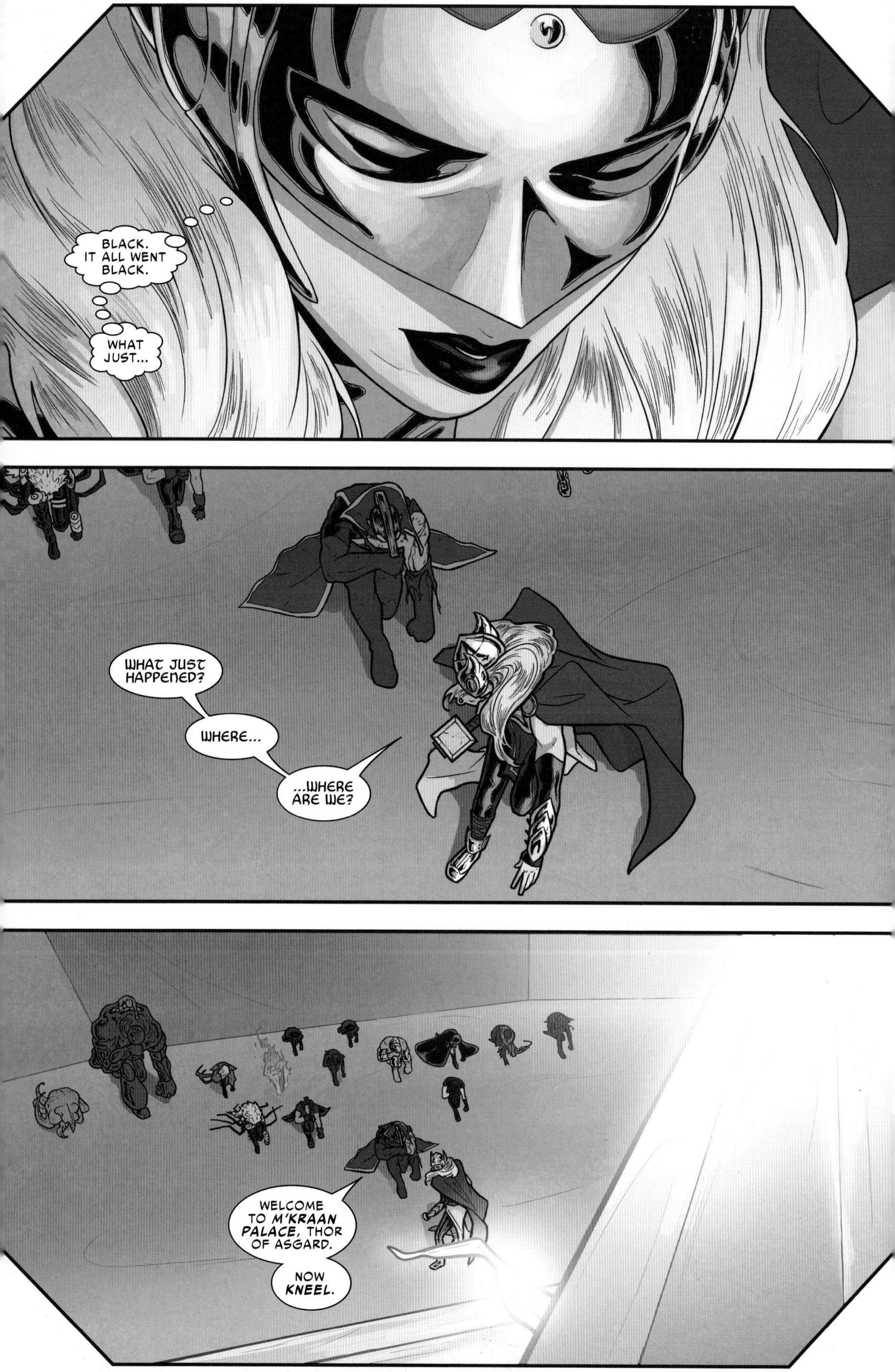
BLACK. IT ALL WENT BLACK.
WHAT JUST...
WHAT JUST HAPPENED?
WHERE...
...WHERE ARE WE?
WELCOME TO M'KRAAN PALACE, THOR OF ASGARD.
NOW KNEEL.

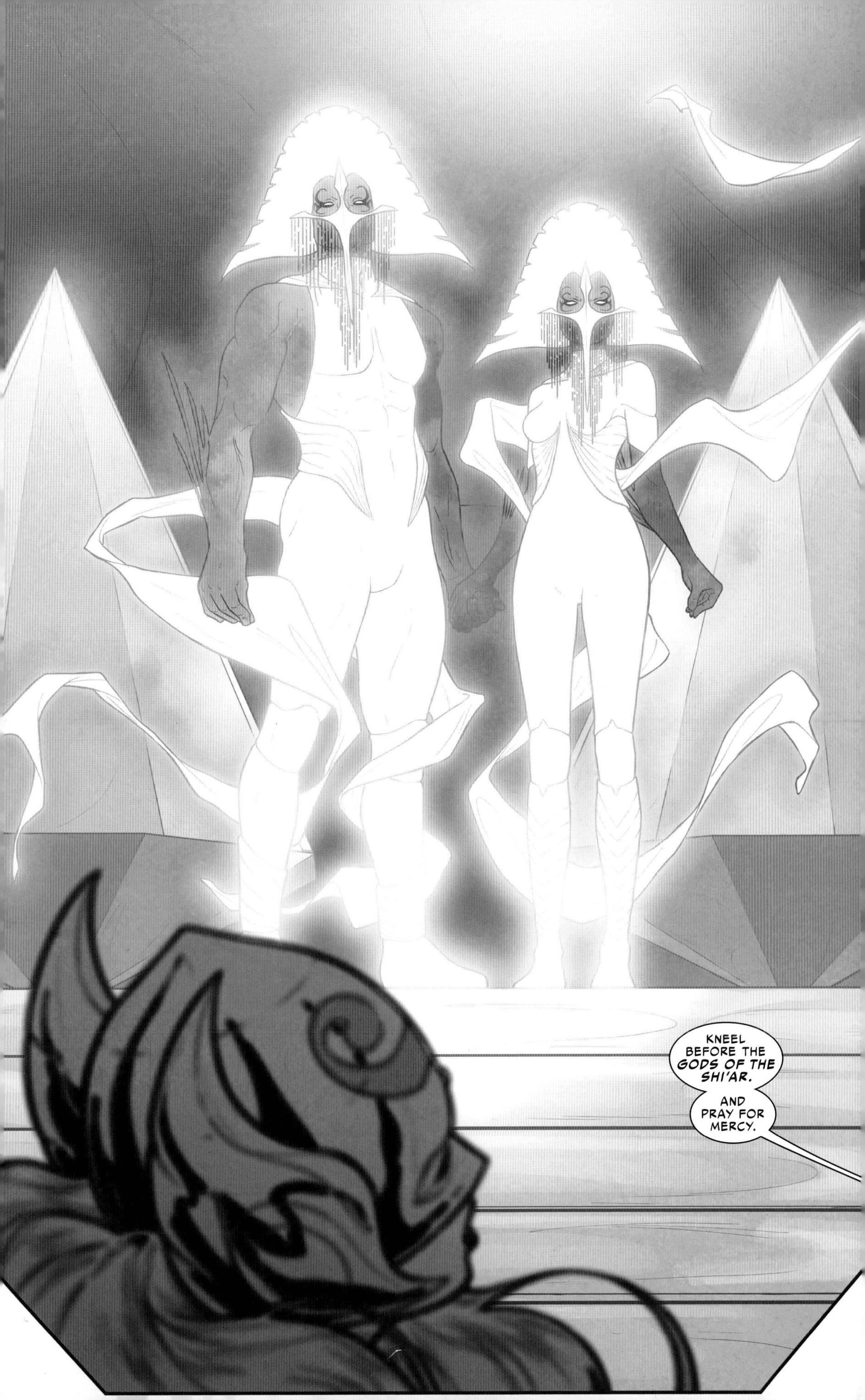

KNEEL BEFORE THE GODS OF THE SHI'AR.
AND PRAY FOR MERCY.

THE MIGHTY THOR Variant Cover Gallery

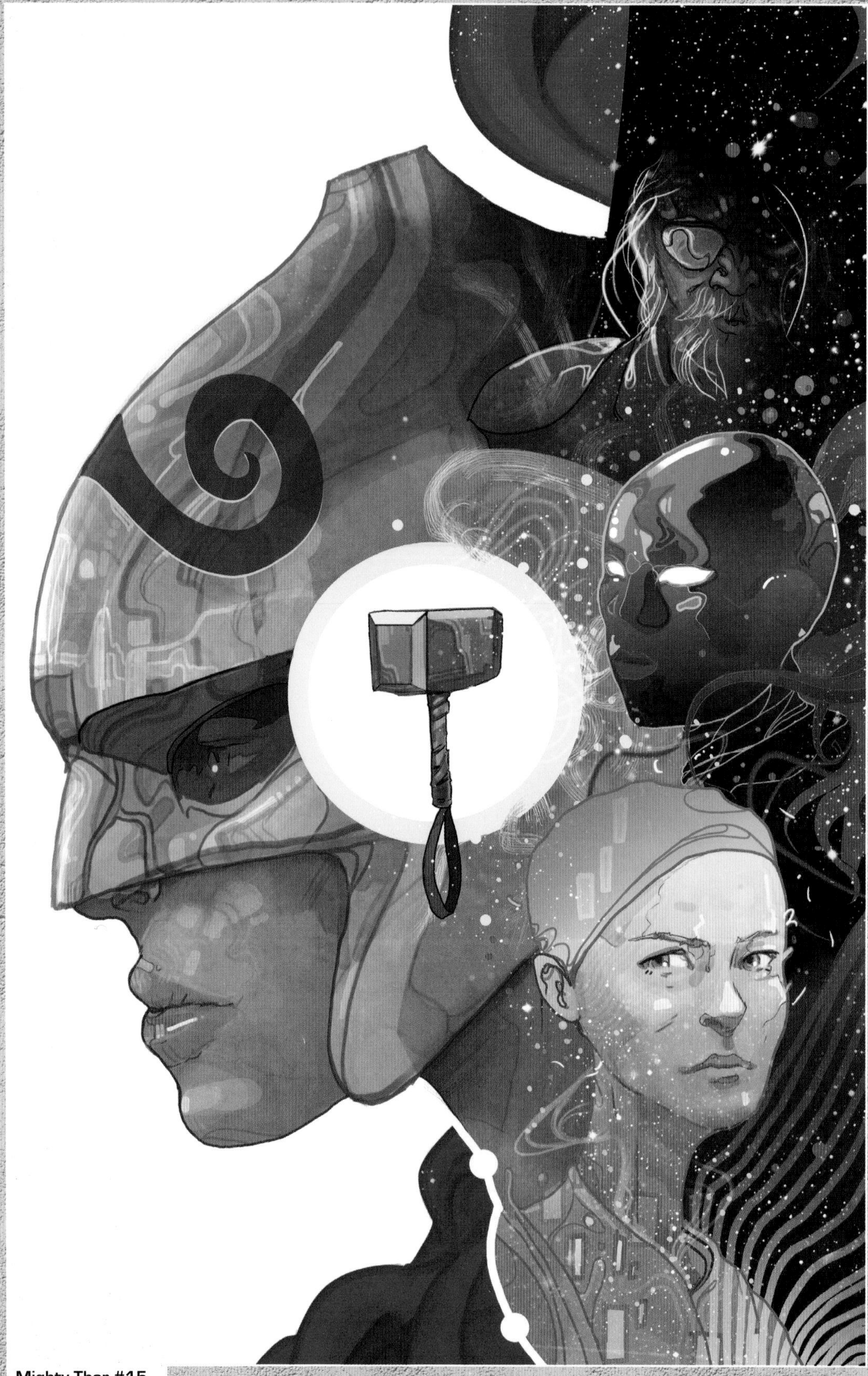

Mighty Thor #15
By Christian Ward

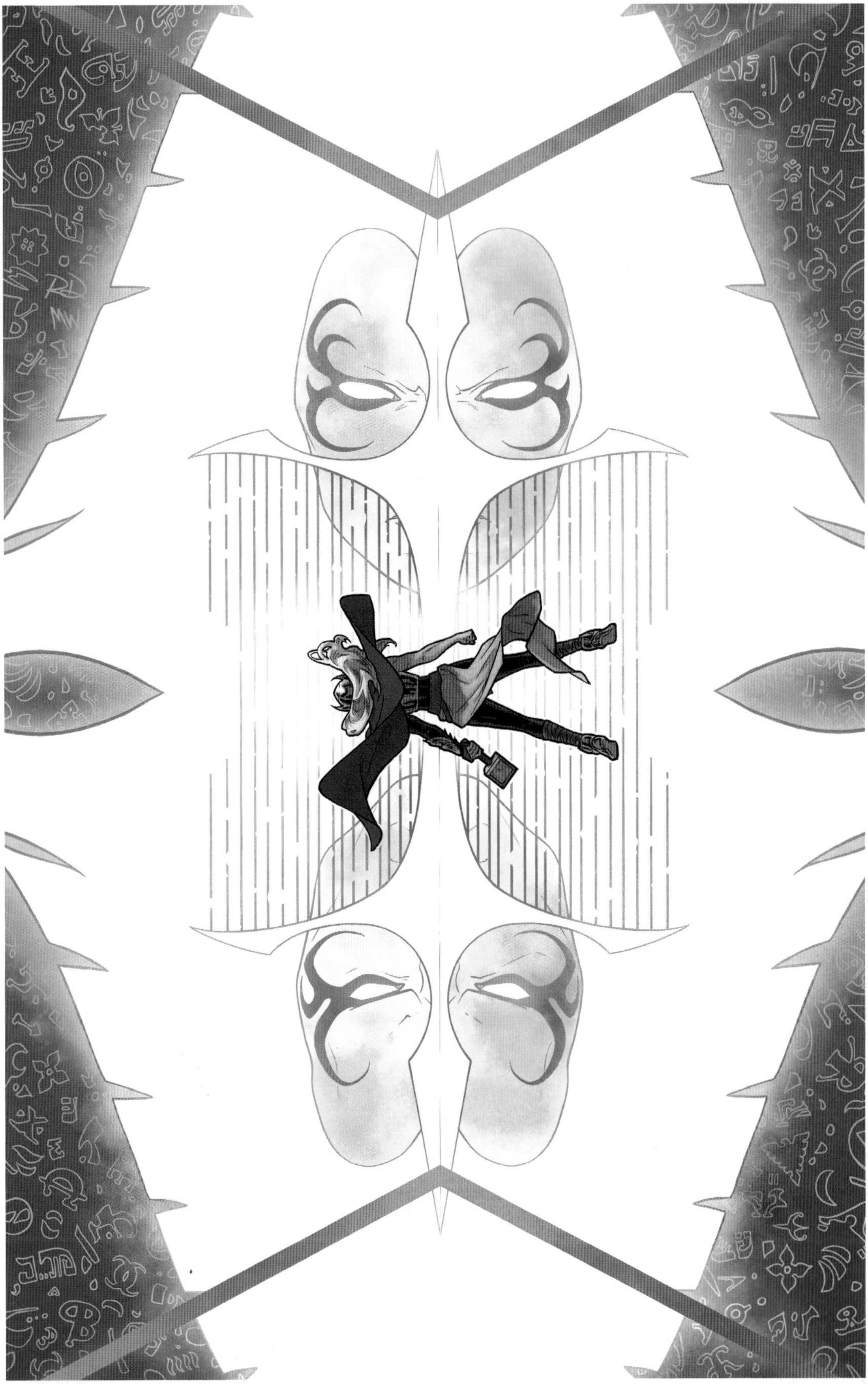

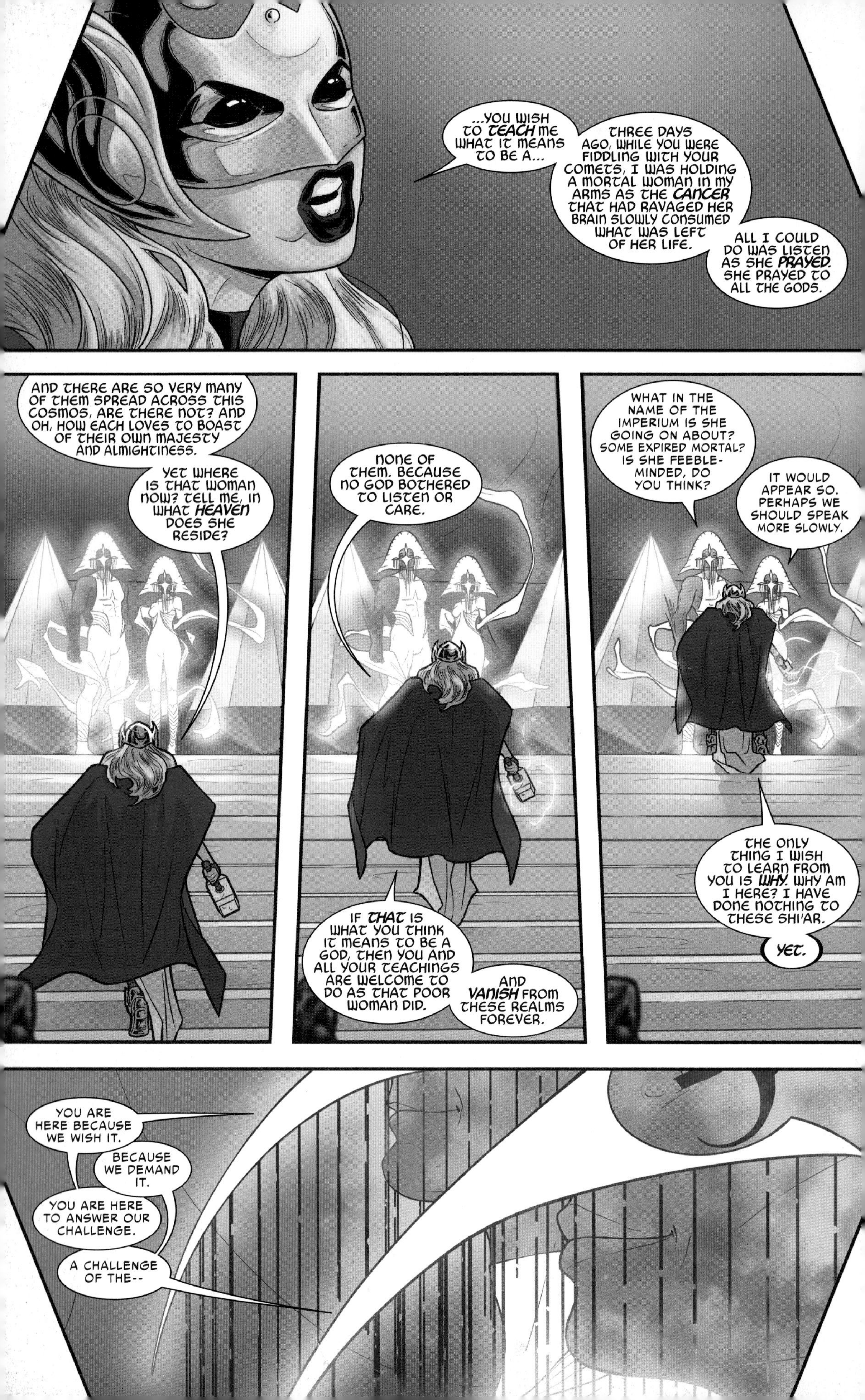
...YOU WISH TO TEACH ME WHAT IT MEANS TO BE A...
THREE DAYS AGO, WHILE YOU WERE FIDDLING WITH YOUR COMETS, I WAS HOLDING A MORTAL WOMAN IN MY ARMS AS THE CANCER THAT HAD RAVAGED HER BRAIN SLOWLY CONSUMED WHAT WAS LEFT OF HER LIFE.
ALL I COULD DO WAS LISTEN AS SHE PRAYED. SHE PRAYED TO ALL THE GODS.
AND THERE ARE SO VERY MANY OF THEM SPREAD ACROSS THIS COSMOS, ARE THERE NOT? AND OH, HOW EACH LOVES TO BOAST OF THEIR OWN MAJESTY AND ALMIGHTINESS.
YET WHERE IS THAT WOMAN NOW? TELL ME, IN WHAT HEAVEN DOES SHE RESIDE?
NONE OF THEM. BECAUSE NO GOD BOTHERED TO LISTEN OR CARE.
IF THAT IS WHAT YOU THINK IT MEANS TO BE A GOD, THEN YOU AND ALL YOUR TEACHINGS ARE WELCOME TO DO AS THAT POOR WOMAN DID.
AND VANISH FROM THESE REALMS FOREVER.
WHAT IN THE NAME OF THE IMPERIUM IS SHE GOING ON ABOUT? SOME EXPIRED MORTAL? IS SHE FEEBLE-MINDED, DO YOU THINK?
IT WOULD APPEAR SO. PERHAPS WE SHOULD SPEAK MORE SLOWLY.
THE ONLY THING I WISH TO LEARN FROM YOU IS WHY. WHY AM I HERE? I HAVE DONE NOTHING TO THESE SHI'AR.
YET.
YOU ARE HERE BECAUSE WE WISH IT.
BECAUSE WE DEMAND IT.
YOU ARE HERE TO ANSWER OUR CHALLENGE.
A CHALLENGE OF THE--

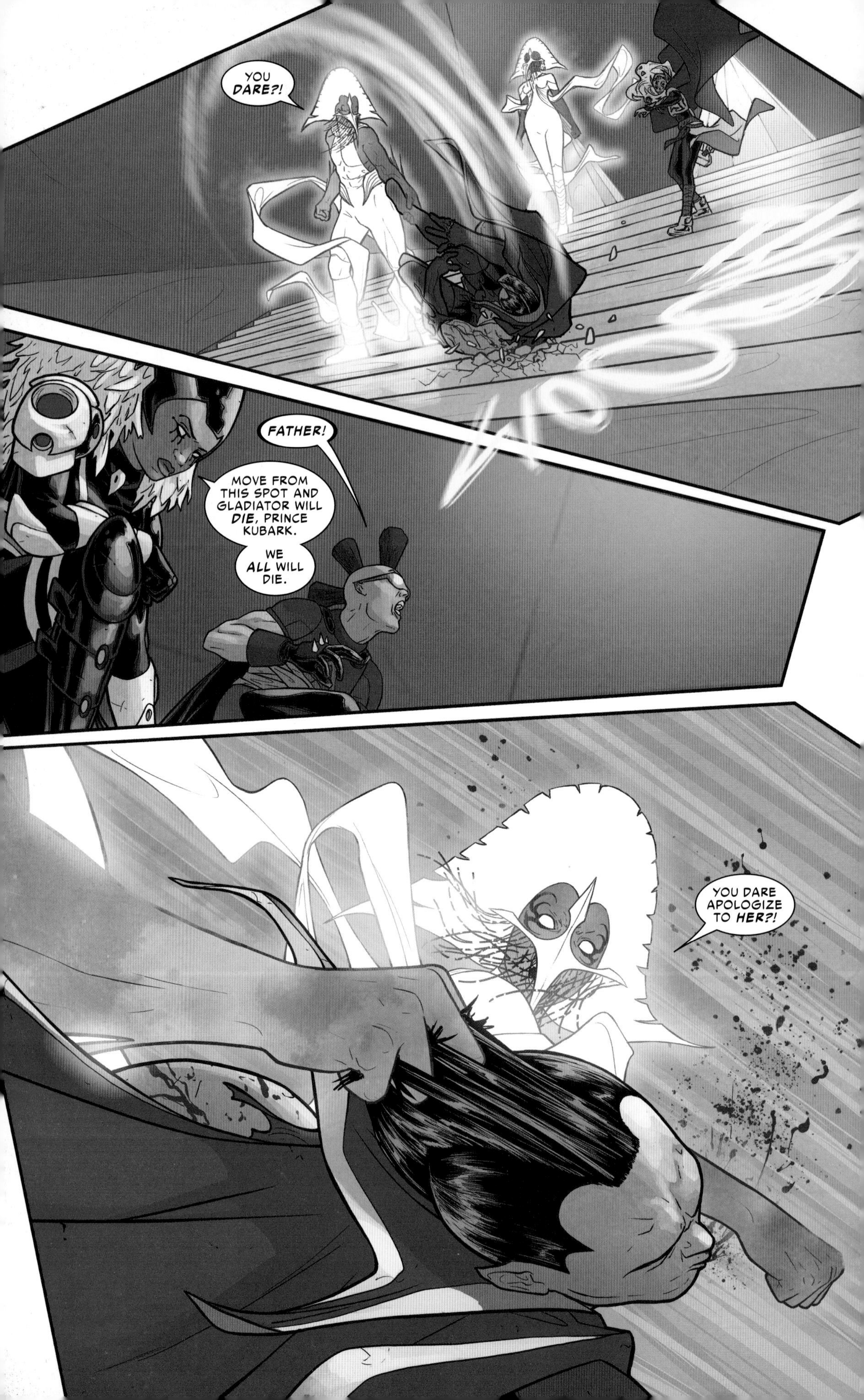
YOU DARE?!
FATHER!
MOVE FROM THIS SPOT AND GLADIATOR WILL DIE, PRINCE KUBARK.
WE ALL WILL DIE.
YOU DARE APOLOGIZE TO HER?!

ASGARDIA.

AND THEN THERE WAS THE TIME I DONNED THE ARMOR OF THE DESTROYER AND WENT OFF, SWORD IN HAND, TO BATTLE THE CELESTIALS!

THE CONGRESS OF WORLDS.

‡SIGH‡

OR WAIT, WAS IT ODIN WHO DID THAT?

NO, NO, IT WAS DEFINITELY ME. I REMEMBER IT LIKE IT WAS YESTERDAY!

THE DAY BEGAN WITH A QUICK BREAKFAST OF BILGESNIPE BACON, POACHED LEVIATHAN EGGS, SAUTÉED SPACE MUSHROOMS, BAKED ASGARDIAN BEANS, BLACK DRAGON PUDDING, CROW BLOOD SAUSAGE, HORSE STEW, DWARVEN MOUNTAIN OYSTERS, VANIR FLATBREAD WITH RAW HONEY, MIDGARDIAN BAGELS, ELVEN ELDERBERRY PIE WITH A DOLLOP OF CREAM, A TALL GLASS OF WARM BUTTERMILK, A TANKARD OF HOME-BREWED ALE, A BOTTLE OF--

SENATOR VOLSTAGG, THIS IS MADNESS.

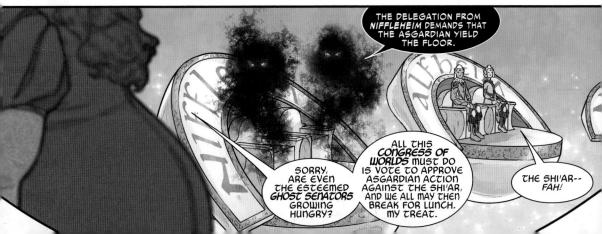

THE DELEGATION FROM NIFFLEHEIM DEMANDS THAT THE ASGARDIAN YIELD THE FLOOR.

SORRY, ARE EVEN THE ESTEEMED GHOST SENATORS GROWING HUNGRY?

ALL THIS CONGRESS OF WORLDS MUST DO IS VOTE TO APPROVE ASGARDIAN ACTION AGAINST THE SHI'AR, AND WE ALL MAY THEN BREAK FOR LUNCH. MY TREAT.

THE SHI'AR-- FAH!

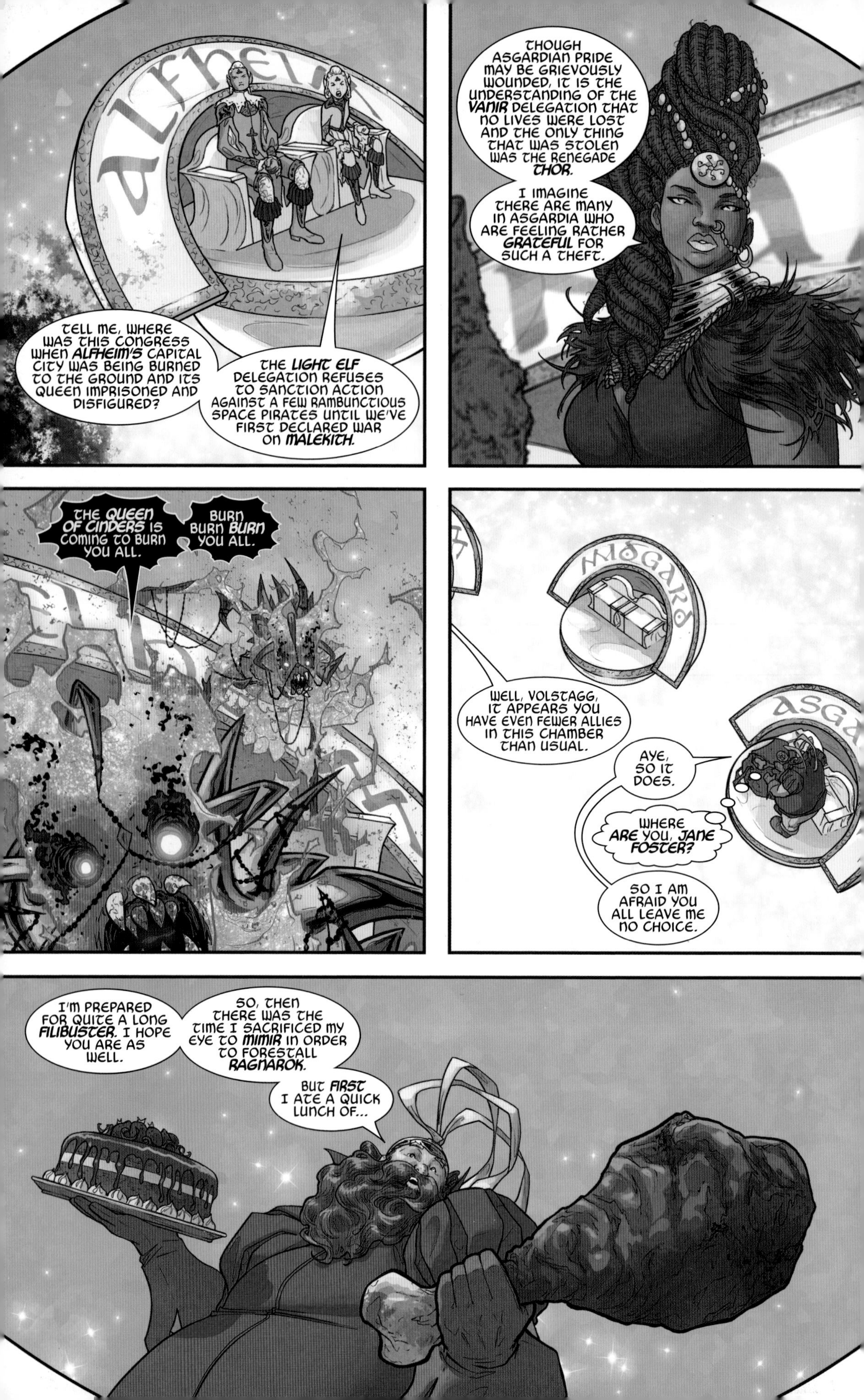
TELL ME, WHERE WAS THIS CONGRESS WHEN ALFHEIM'S CAPITAL CITY WAS BEING BURNED TO THE GROUND AND ITS QUEEN IMPRISONED AND DISFIGURED?
THE LIGHT ELF DELEGATION REFUSES TO SANCTION ACTION AGAINST A FEW RAMBUNCTIOUS SPACE PIRATES UNTIL WE'VE FIRST DECLARED WAR ON MALEKITH.
THOUGH ASGARDIAN PRIDE MAY BE GRIEVOUSLY WOUNDED, IT IS THE UNDERSTANDING OF THE VANIR DELEGATION THAT NO LIVES WERE LOST AND THE ONLY THING THAT WAS STOLEN WAS THE RENEGADE THOR.
I IMAGINE THERE ARE MANY IN ASGARDIA WHO ARE FEELING RATHER GRATEFUL FOR SUCH A THEFT.
THE QUEEN OF CINDERS IS COMING TO BURN YOU ALL.
BURN BURN BURN YOU ALL.
WELL, VOLSTAGG, IT APPEARS YOU HAVE EVEN FEWER ALLIES IN THIS CHAMBER THAN USUAL.
AYE, SO IT DOES.
WHERE ARE YOU, JANE FOSTER?
SO I AM AFRAID YOU ALL LEAVE ME NO CHOICE.
I'M PREPARED FOR QUITE A LONG FILIBUSTER. I HOPE YOU ARE AS WELL.
SO, THEN THERE WAS THE TIME I SACRIFICED MY EYE TO MIMIR IN ORDER TO FORESTALL RAGNAROK.
BUT FIRST I ATE A QUICK LUNCH OF...

I NEVER THOUGHT I WOULD LIVE TO SEE THE DAY--

--WHEN THE LORD OF ASGARD WOULD RUN FROM A FIGHT LIKE A WOUNDED PUP.

MIND YOUR TONGUE, *LADY SIF,* OR I'LL HAVE SOMEONE MIND IT FOR YOU.

WITH A PAIR OF *PLIERS.*

I AM *CUL BORSON.* THE DAY I RUN FROM BATTLE IS THE DAY THE STARS TURN TO SNOWSTORMS AND THE SEAS BURN WITH FIRE.

IF THESE *SHI'AR DOGS* EVER DARE SHOW THEIR FACES HERE AGAIN, I WILL HAVE THEIR HEADS MOUNTED ON PIKES FOR ALL THE REALMS TO SEE.

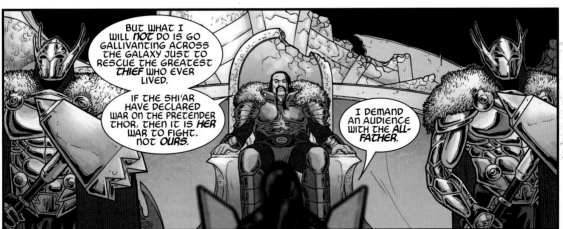

BUT WHAT I WILL *NOT* DO IS GO GALLIVANTING ACROSS THE GALAXY JUST TO RESCUE THE GREATEST *THIEF* WHO EVER LIVED.

IF THE SHI'AR HAVE DECLARED WAR ON THE PRETENDER THOR, THEN IT IS *HER* WAR TO FIGHT. NOT *OURS.*

I DEMAND AN AUDIENCE WITH THE *ALL-FATHER.*

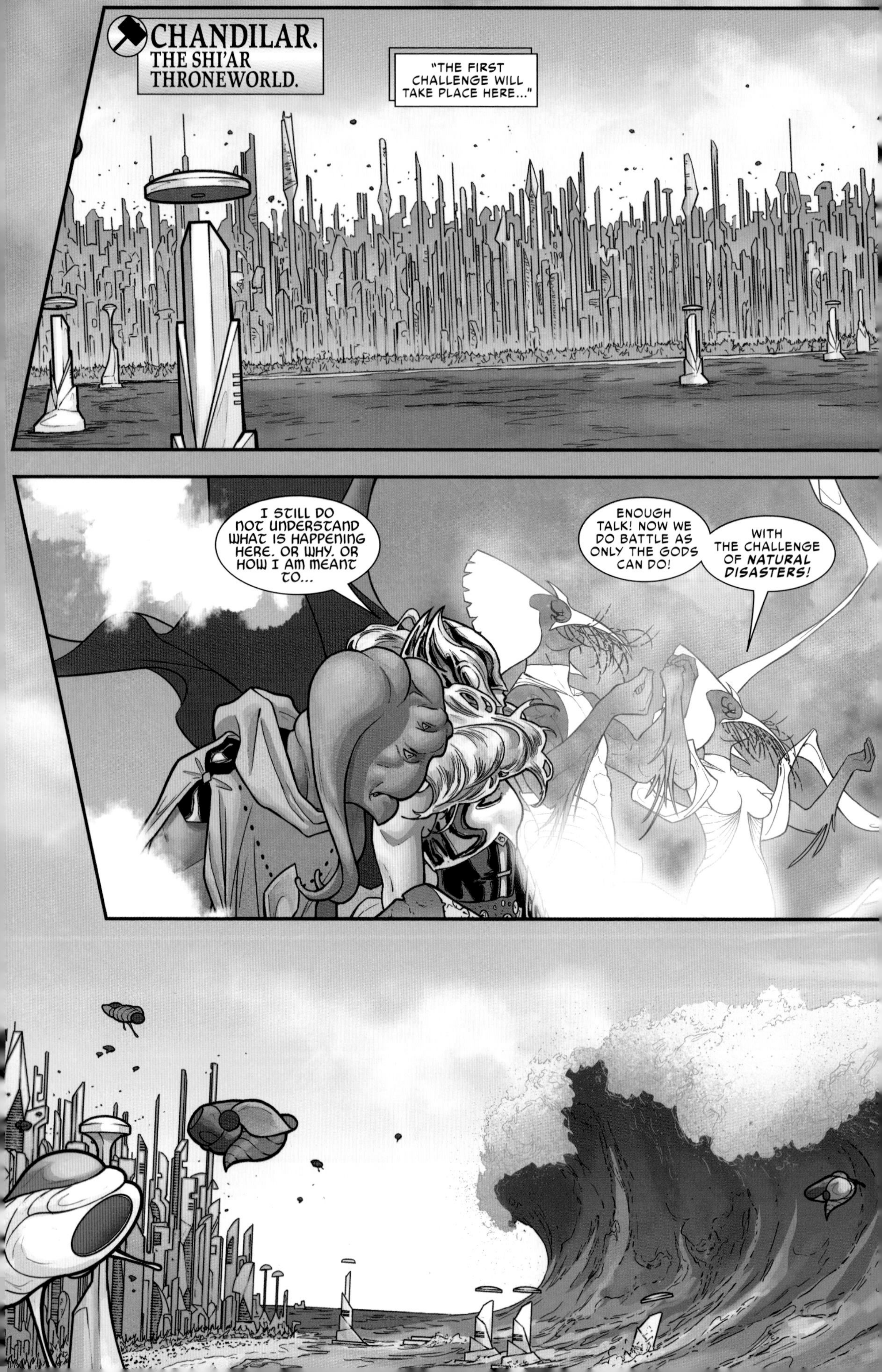
CHANDILAR. THE SHI'AR THRONEWORLD.
"THE FIRST CHALLENGE WILL TAKE PLACE HERE..."
I STILL DO NOT UNDERSTAND WHAT IS HAPPENING HERE. OR WHY. OR HOW I AM MEANT TO...
ENOUGH TALK! NOW WE DO BATTLE AS ONLY THE GODS CAN DO!
WITH THE CHALLENGE OF *NATURAL DISASTERS!*

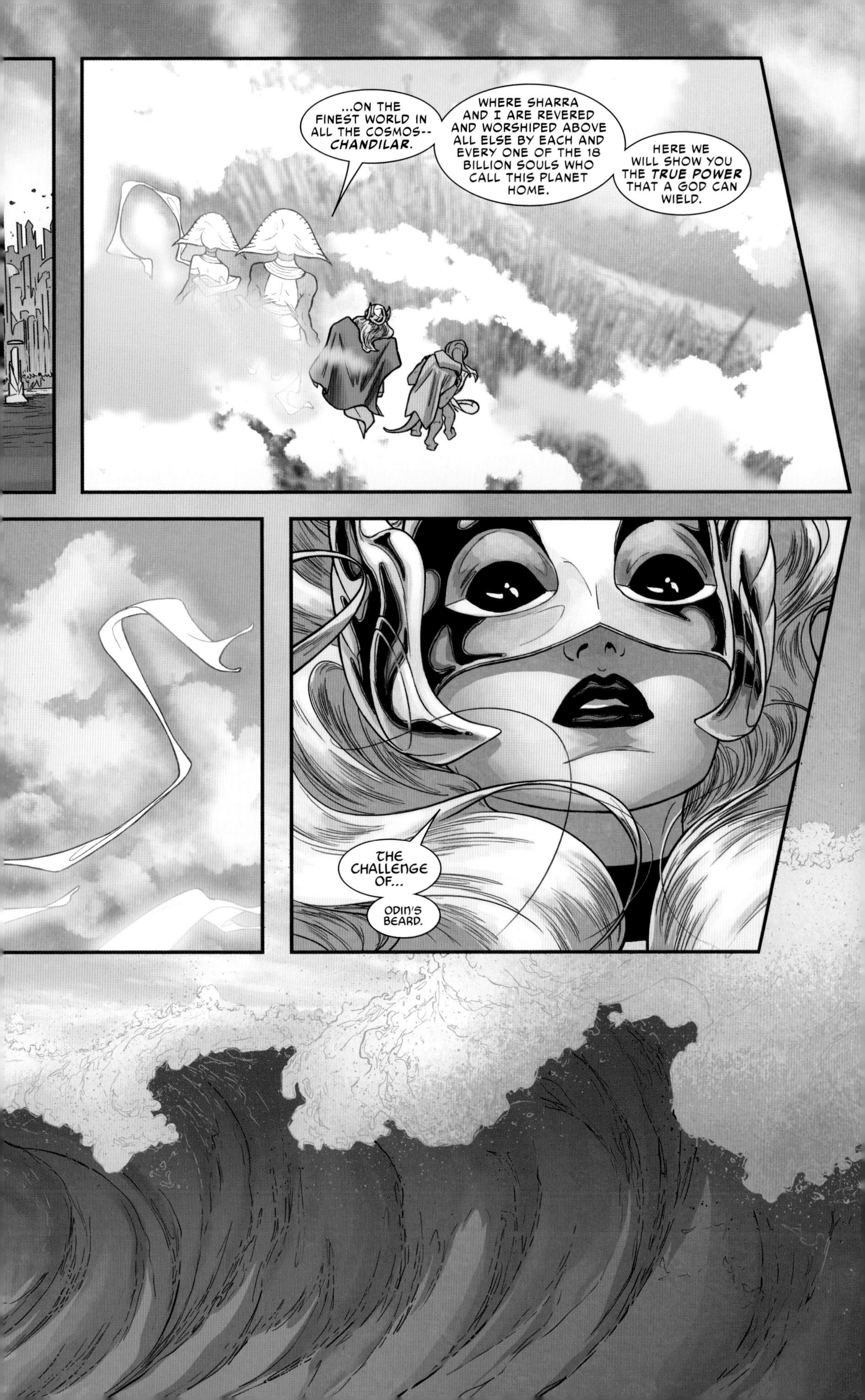
...ON THE FINEST WORLD IN ALL THE COSMOS-- *CHANDILAR*.
WHERE SHARRA AND I ARE REVERED AND WORSHIPED ABOVE ALL ELSE BY EACH AND EVERY ONE OF THE 18 BILLION SOULS WHO CALL THIS PLANET HOME.
HERE WE WILL SHOW YOU THE *TRUE POWER* THAT A GOD CAN WIELD.
THE CHALLENGE OF...
ODIN'S BEARD.

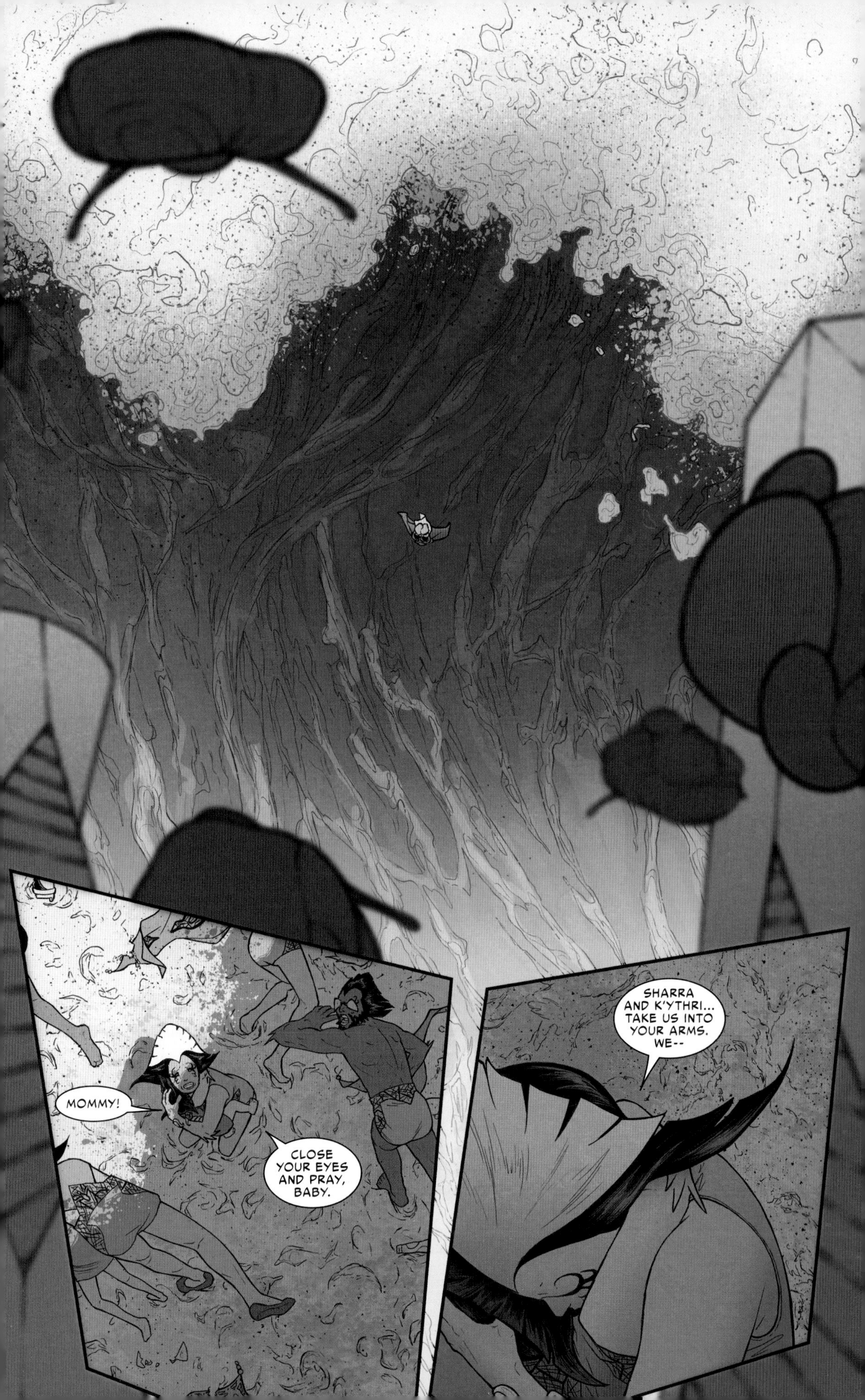
MOMMY!
CLOSE YOUR EYES AND PRAY, BABY.
SHARRA AND K'YTHRI... TAKE US INTO YOUR ARMS. WE--

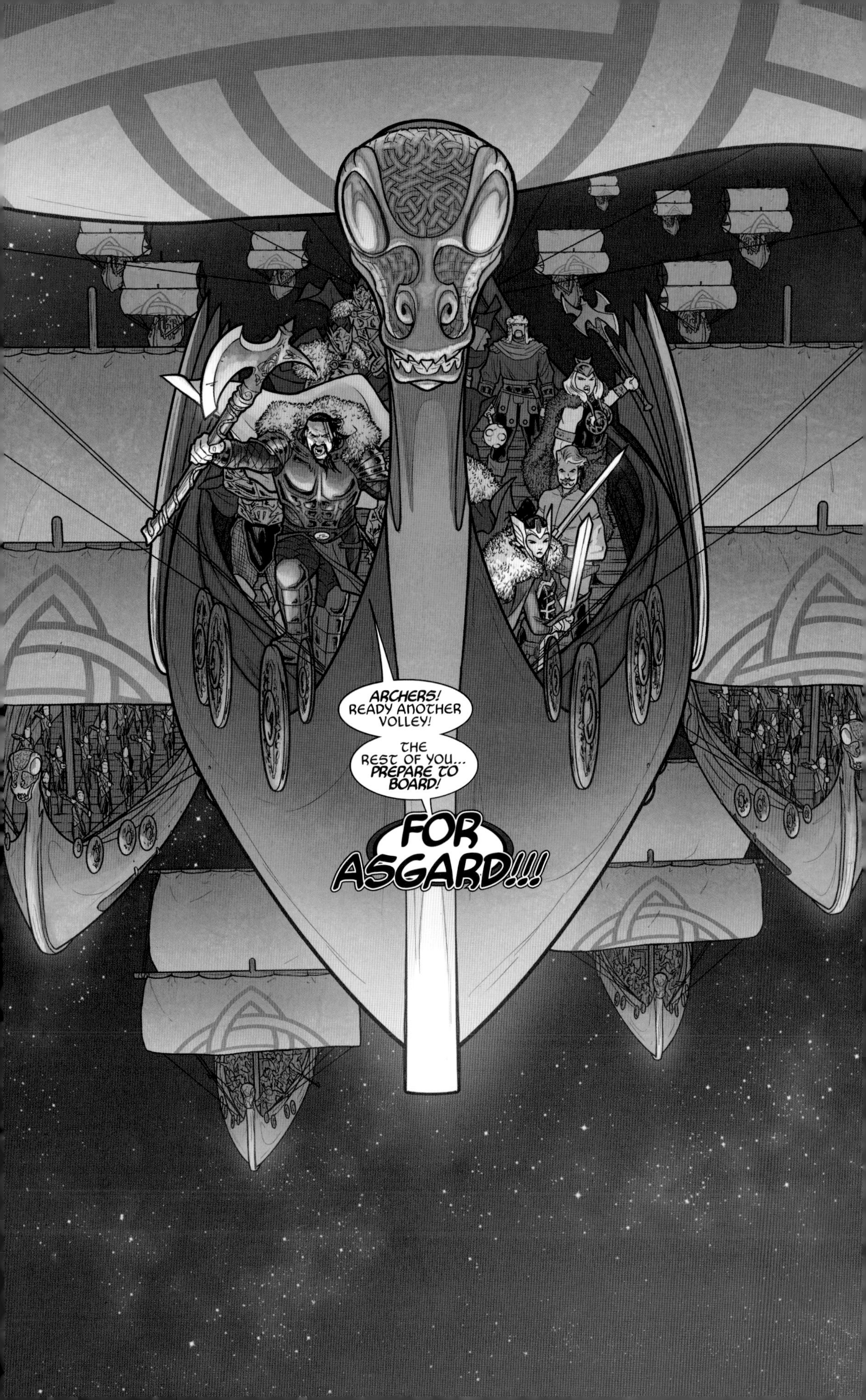
ARCHERS! READY ANOTHER VOLLEY!
THE REST OF YOU... PREPARE TO BOARD!
FOR ASGARD!!!

THE MIGHTY THOR Variant Cover Gallery

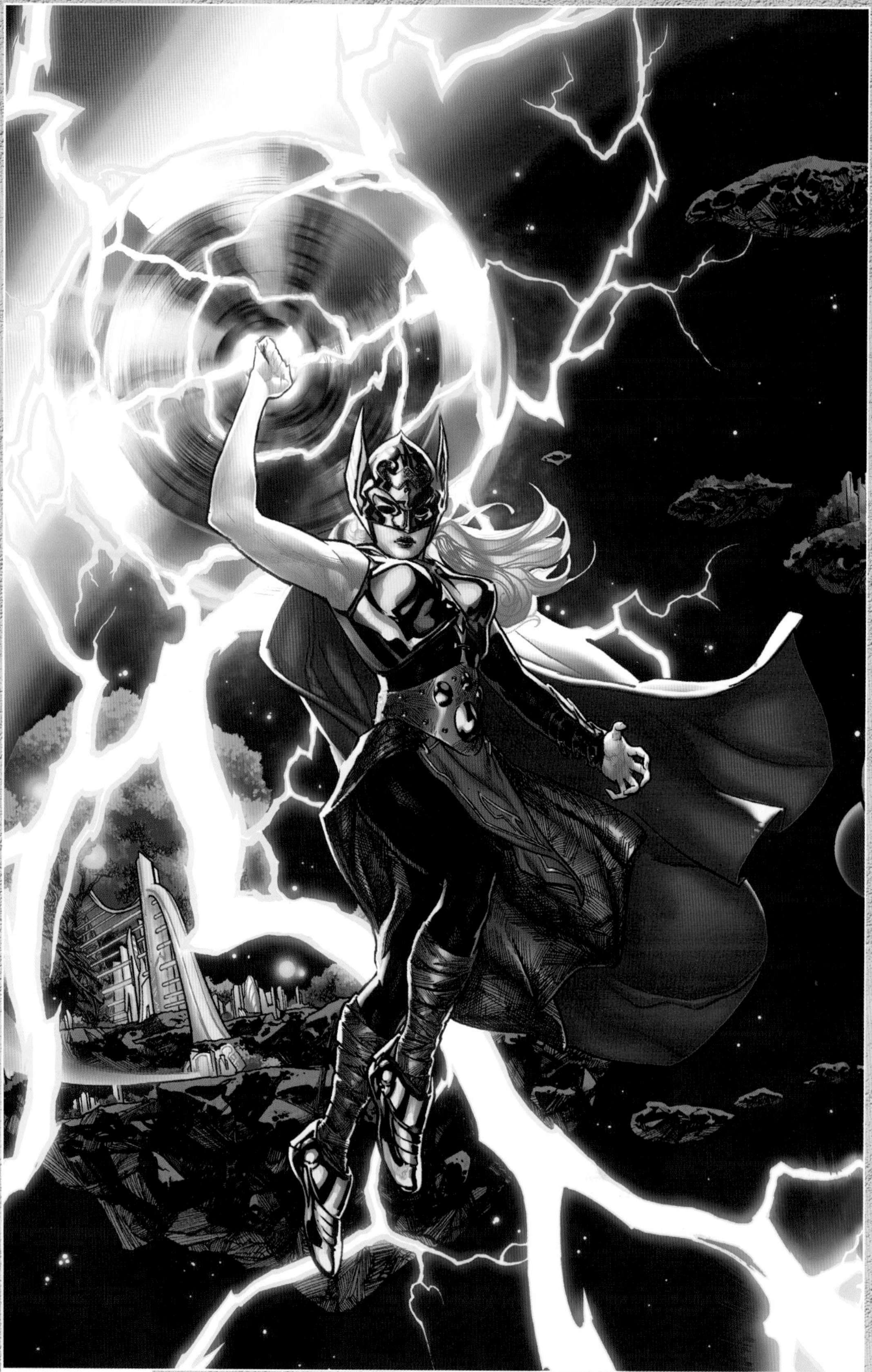

Mighty Thor #15
By Ryan Sook

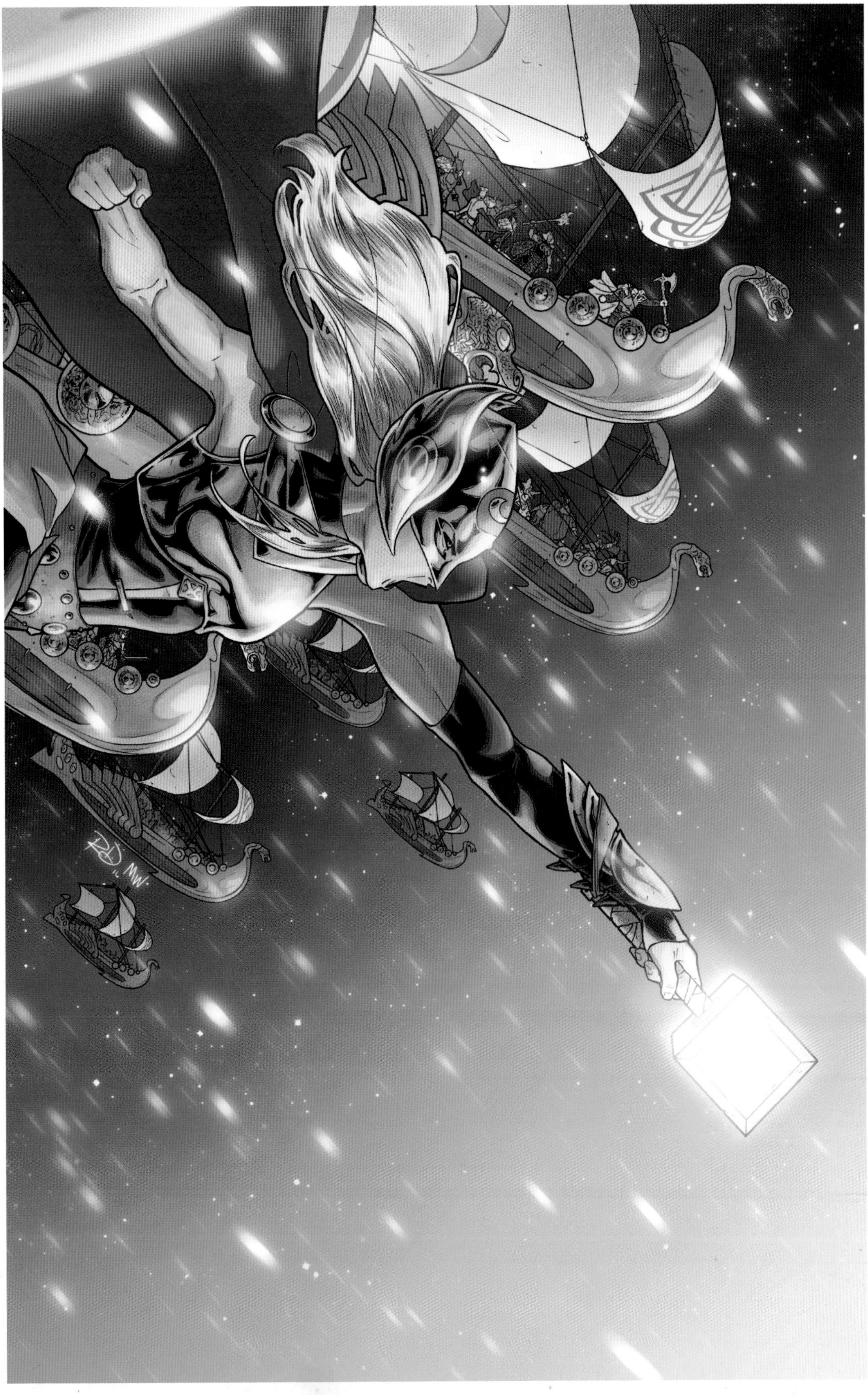

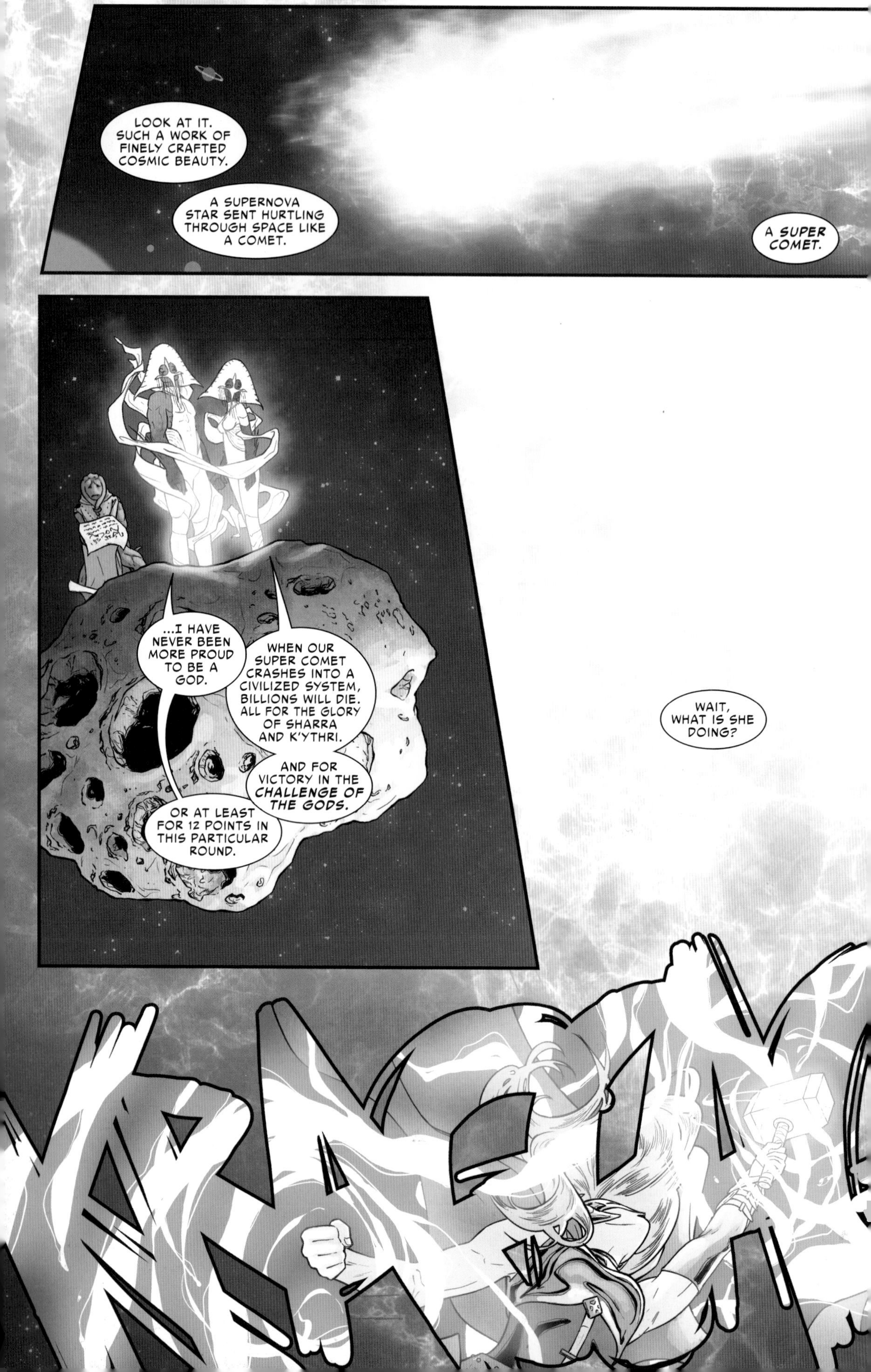

LOOK AT IT. SUCH A WORK OF FINELY CRAFTED COSMIC BEAUTY.
A SUPERNOVA STAR SENT HURTLING THROUGH SPACE LIKE A COMET.
A *SUPER* COMET.
...I HAVE NEVER BEEN MORE PROUD TO BE A GOD.
WHEN OUR SUPER COMET CRASHES INTO A CIVILIZED SYSTEM, BILLIONS WILL DIE. ALL FOR THE GLORY OF SHARRA AND K'YTHRI.
AND FOR VICTORY IN THE *CHALLENGE OF THE GODS.*
OR AT LEAST FOR 12 POINTS IN THIS PARTICULAR ROUND.
WAIT, WHAT IS SHE DOING?

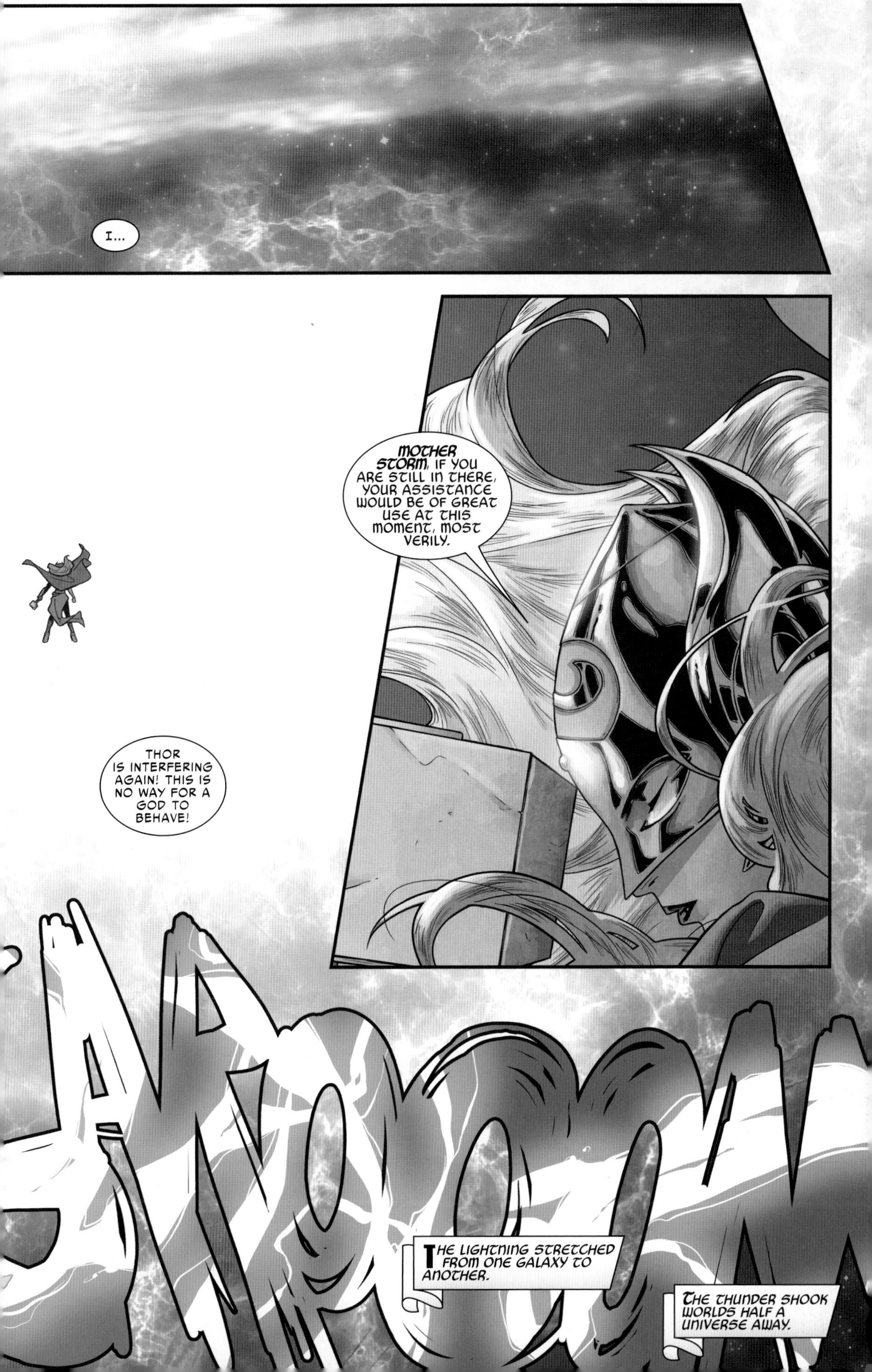
I...
MOTHER STORM, IF YOU ARE STILL IN THERE, YOUR ASSISTANCE WOULD BE OF GREAT USE AT THIS MOMENT, MOST VERILY.
THOR IS INTERFERING AGAIN! THIS IS NO WAY FOR A GOD TO BEHAVE!
THE LIGHTNING STRETCHED FROM ONE GALAXY TO ANOTHER.
THE THUNDER SHOOK WORLDS HALF A UNIVERSE AWAY.

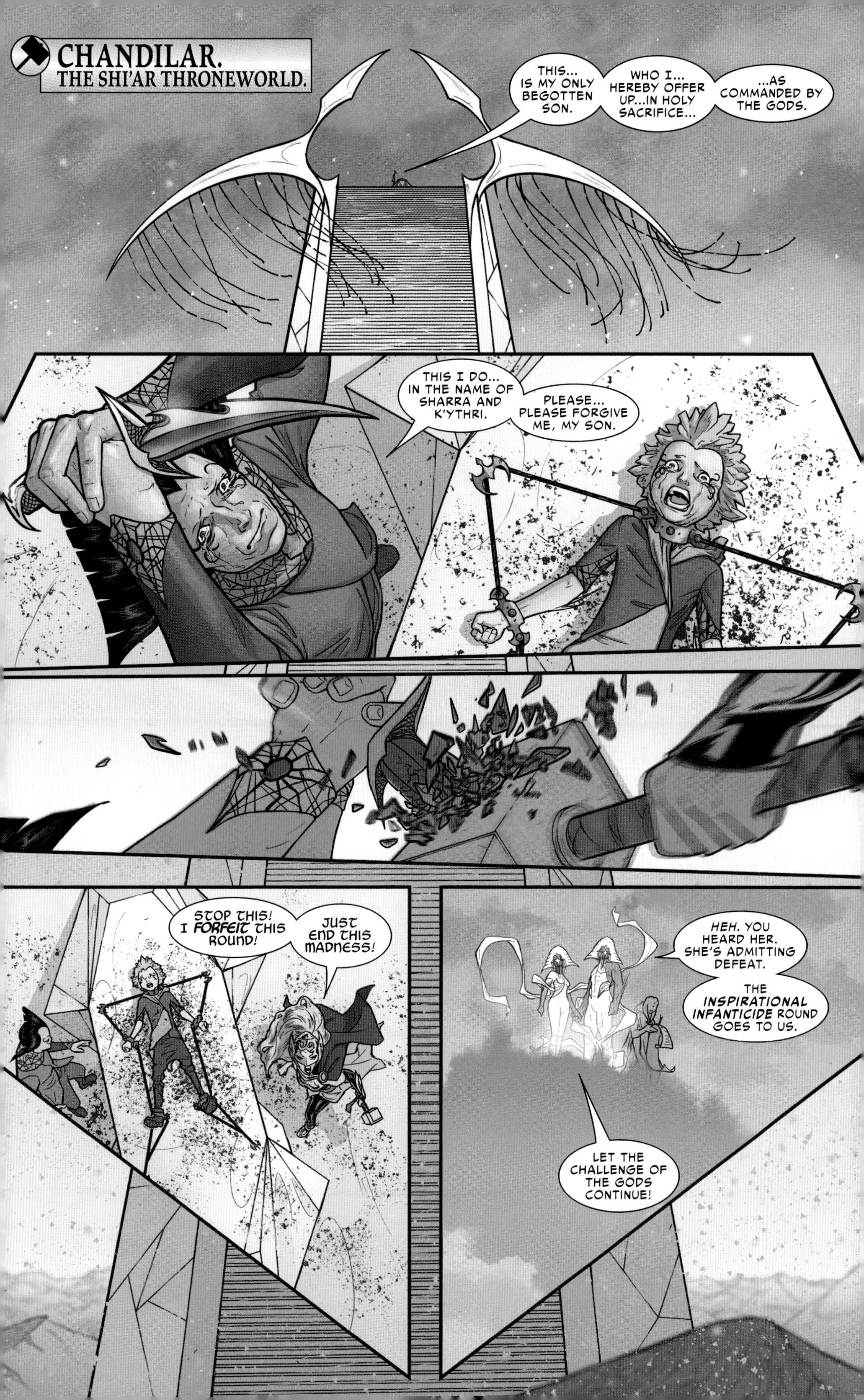
CHANDILAR. THE SHI'AR THRONEWORLD.
THIS... IS MY ONLY BEGOTTEN SON.
WHO I... HEREBY OFFER UP...IN HOLY SACRIFICE...
...AS COMMANDED BY THE GODS.
THIS I DO... IN THE NAME OF SHARRA AND K'YTHRI.
PLEASE... PLEASE FORGIVE ME, MY SON.
STOP THIS! I FORFEIT THIS ROUND!
JUST END THIS MADNESS!
HEH. YOU HEARD HER. SHE'S ADMITTING DEFEAT.
THE INSPIRATIONAL INFANTICIDE ROUND GOES TO US.
LET THE CHALLENGE OF THE GODS CONTINUE!

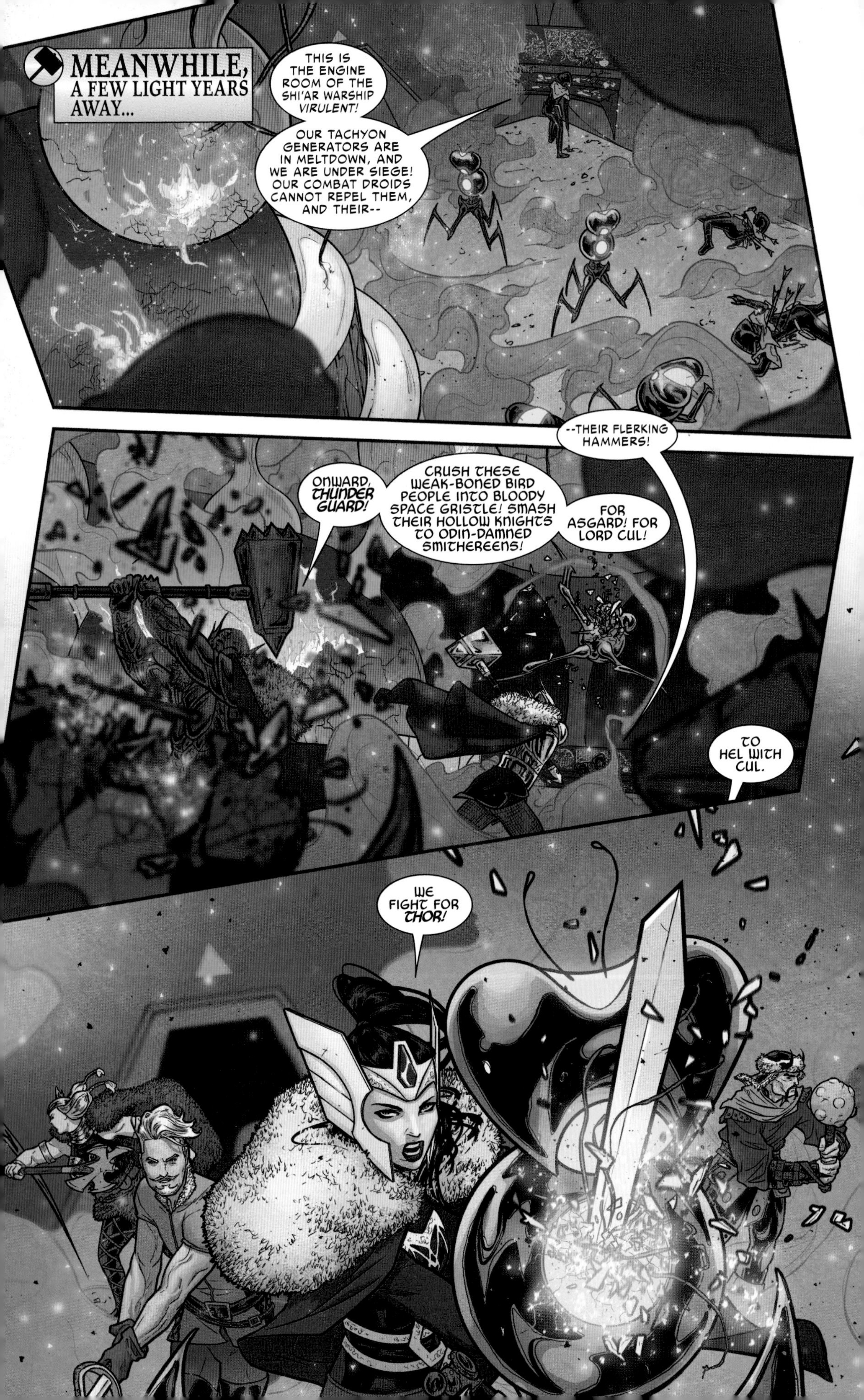
MEANWHILE, A FEW LIGHT YEARS AWAY...
THIS IS THE ENGINE ROOM OF THE SHI'AR WARSHIP *VIRULENT!*
OUR TACHYON GENERATORS ARE IN MELTDOWN, AND WE ARE UNDER SIEGE! OUR COMBAT DROIDS CANNOT REPEL THEM, AND THEIR--
--THEIR FLERKING HAMMERS!
ONWARD, *THUNDER GUARD!*
CRUSH THESE WEAK-BONED BIRD PEOPLE INTO BLOODY SPACE GRISTLE! SMASH THEIR HOLLOW KNIGHTS TO ODIN-DAMNED SMITHEREENS!
FOR ASGARD! FOR LORD CUL!
TO HEL WITH CUL.
WE FIGHT FOR *THOR!*

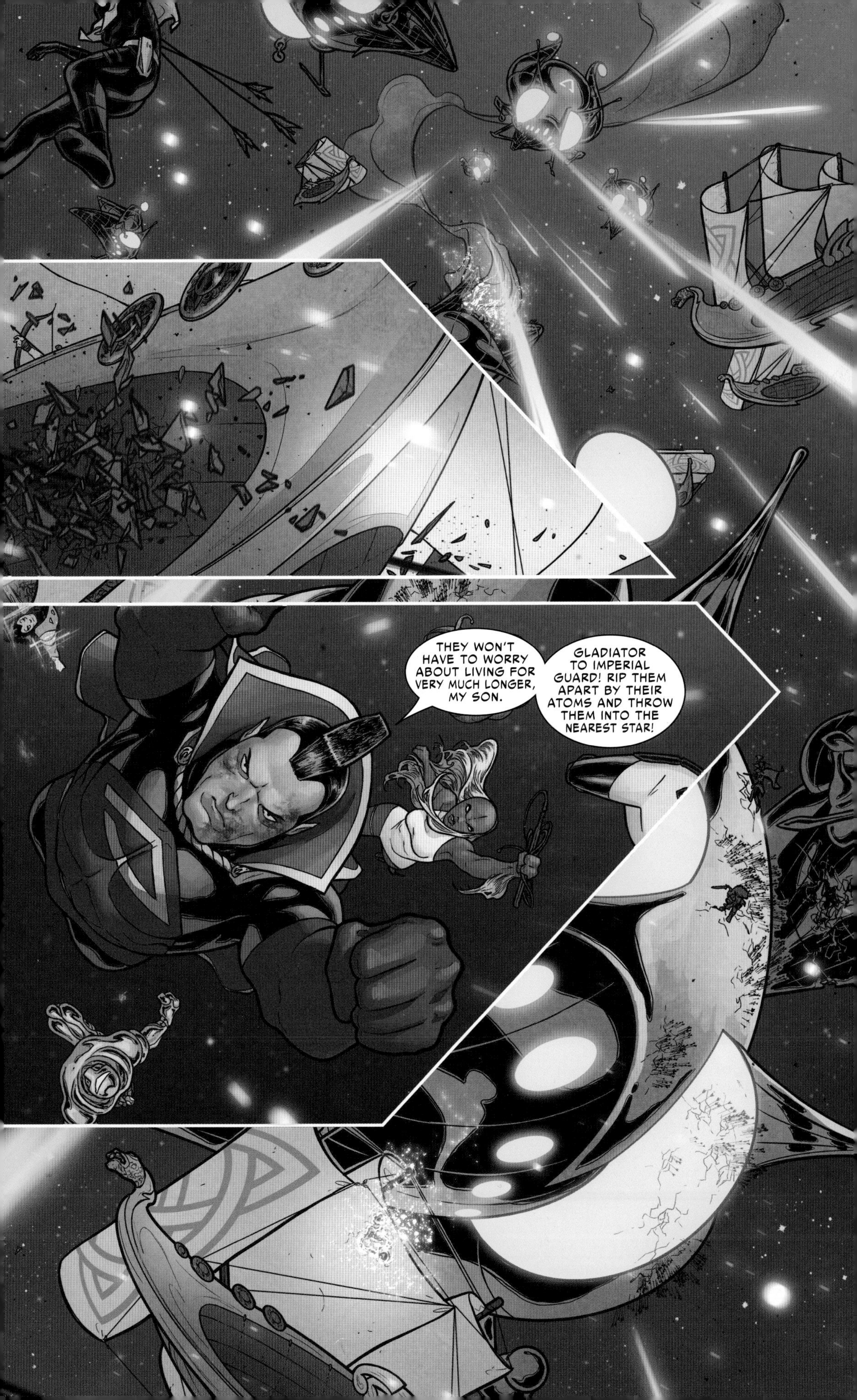
THEY WON'T HAVE TO WORRY ABOUT LIVING FOR VERY MUCH LONGER, MY SON.
GLADIATOR TO IMPERIAL GUARD! RIP THEM APART BY THEIR ATOMS AND THROW THEM INTO THE NEAREST STAR!

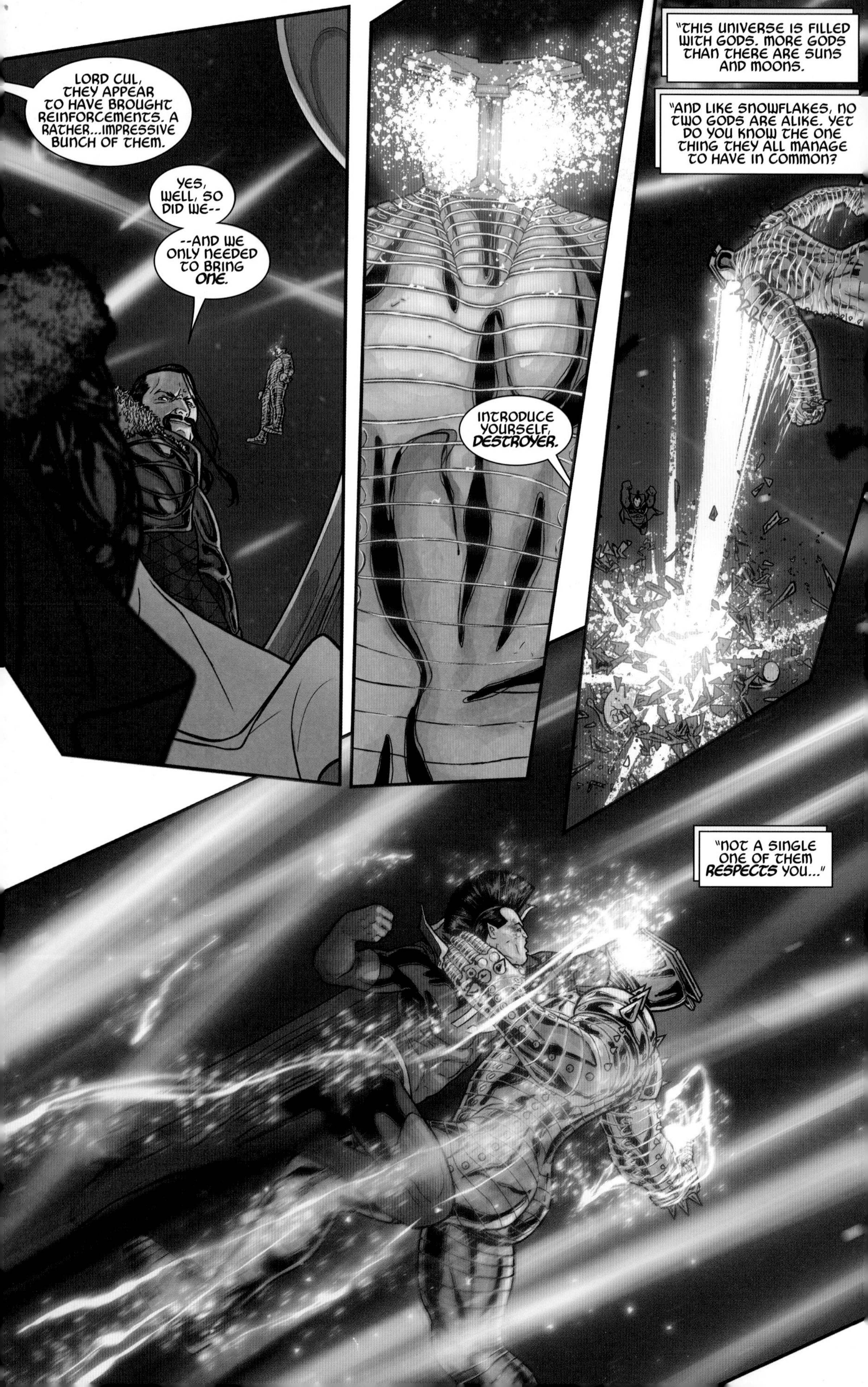
LORD CUL, THEY APPEAR TO HAVE BROUGHT REINFORCEMENTS. A RATHER...IMPRESSIVE BUNCH OF THEM.
YES, WELL, SO DID WE--
--AND WE ONLY NEEDED TO BRING ONE.
INTRODUCE YOURSELF, DESTROYER.
"THIS UNIVERSE IS FILLED WITH GODS. MORE GODS THAN THERE ARE SUNS AND MOONS.
"AND LIKE SNOWFLAKES, NO TWO GODS ARE ALIKE. YET DO YOU KNOW THE ONE THING THEY ALL MANAGE TO HAVE IN COMMON?
"NOT A SINGLE ONE OF THEM RESPECTS YOU..."

...OR FEARS YOU.

I DARE SAY MOST OF THEM DON'T EVEN KNOW YOU EXIST.

THIS STRANGER SHOWS UP UNINVITED TO SPEAK LIES AND NONSENSE RIGHT HERE IN OUR OWN THRONE ROOM?

I SAY WE LASH HIM TO THE BOW OF A SUPERDESTROYER AND FLY HIM THROUGH THE STARFIELDS UNTIL HIS EYEBALLS EXPLODE.

MY DEAR HUSBAND'S WORDS DO MAKE DRAMATICALLY MORE SENSE THAN YOURS, STRANGER. *OF COURSE* WE ARE FEARED.

ALL BEINGS WITH HALF A THOUGHT IN THEIR HEADS KNOW TO FEAR THE GODS OF THE CONQUERING SHI'AR.

AND WHAT EXACTLY HAVE YOU CONQUERED? A FEW MINOR GALAXIES?

THOSE AMOUNT TO A MERE CLUSTER OF TINY ISLANDS IN THE MIDST OF AN ENDLESS SEA. IN OTHER WORDS, *NEXT TO NOTHING.*

DO YOU REALLY THINK THEY KNOW YOU OUTSIDE THOSE FEW SHI'AR-CONTROLLED SYSTEMS?

IN THE GRAND SCHEME OF THE COSMOS, YOU ARE GODS OF STAGGERING INSIGNIFICANCE.

WHEN WAS THE LAST TIME ANYONE PRAYED TO YOU ON CENTAURI IV? OR IN THE HEART OF THE KREE EMPIRE? OR ON EARTH, WHERE THEY'LL PRAY TO ALMOST ANYONE?

NEVER MIND THE DAMNED STARSHIP! I'LL TEAR OUT HIS EYES MYSELF!

BUT DO YOU KNOW WHO *IS* PRAYED TO, WHEREVER THERE ARE BEINGS WITH TONGUES TO UTTER HOSANNAS?

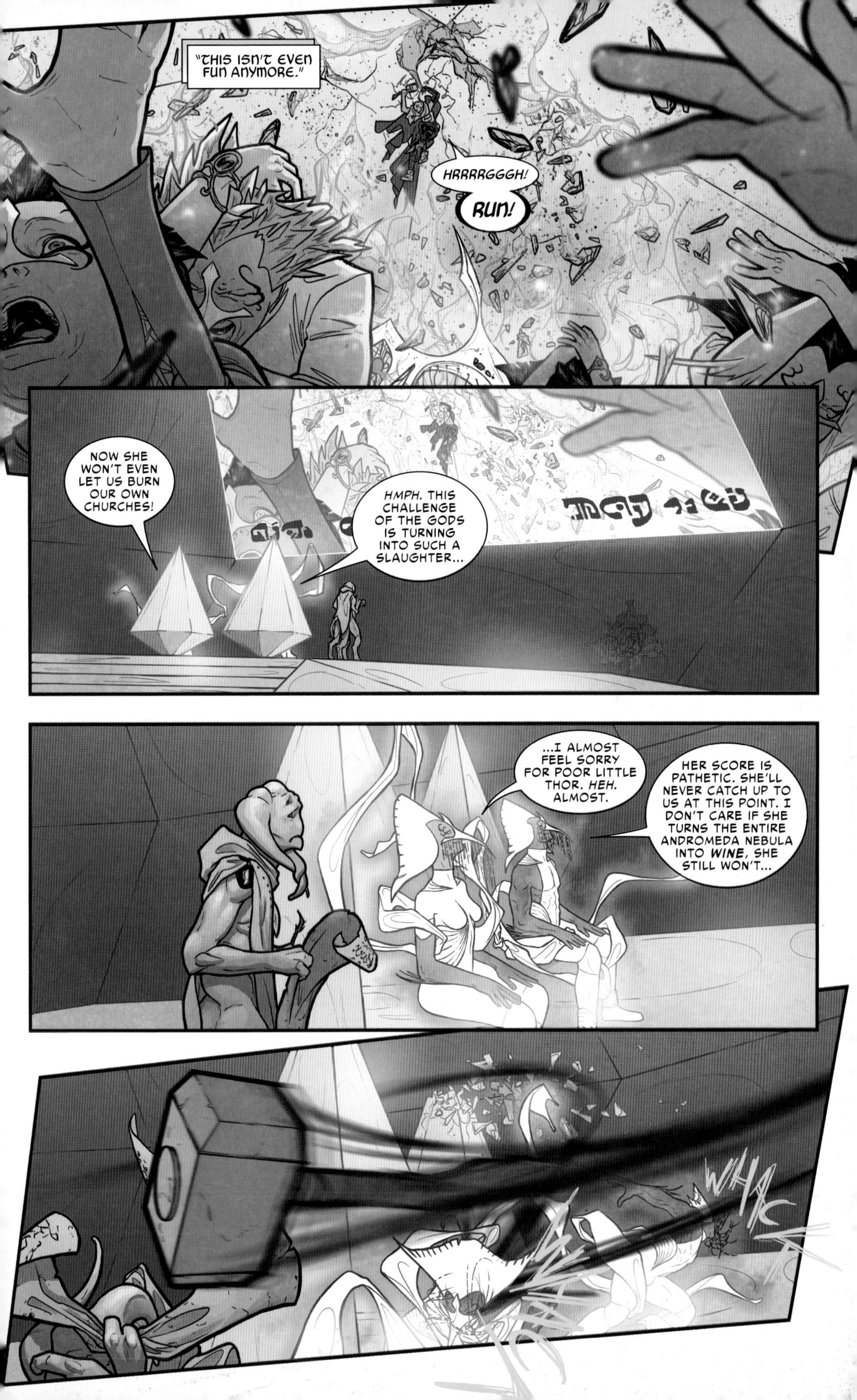
"THIS ISN'T EVEN FUN ANYMORE."
HRRRRGGGH!
RUN!
NOW SHE WON'T EVEN LET US BURN OUR OWN CHURCHES!
HMPH. THIS CHALLENGE OF THE GODS IS TURNING INTO SUCH A SLAUGHTER...
...I ALMOST FEEL SORRY FOR POOR LITTLE THOR. HEH. ALMOST.
HER SCORE IS PATHETIC. SHE'LL NEVER CATCH UP TO US AT THIS POINT. I DON'T CARE IF SHE TURNS THE ENTIRE ANDROMEDA NEBULA INTO WINE, SHE STILL WON'T...
WHACK

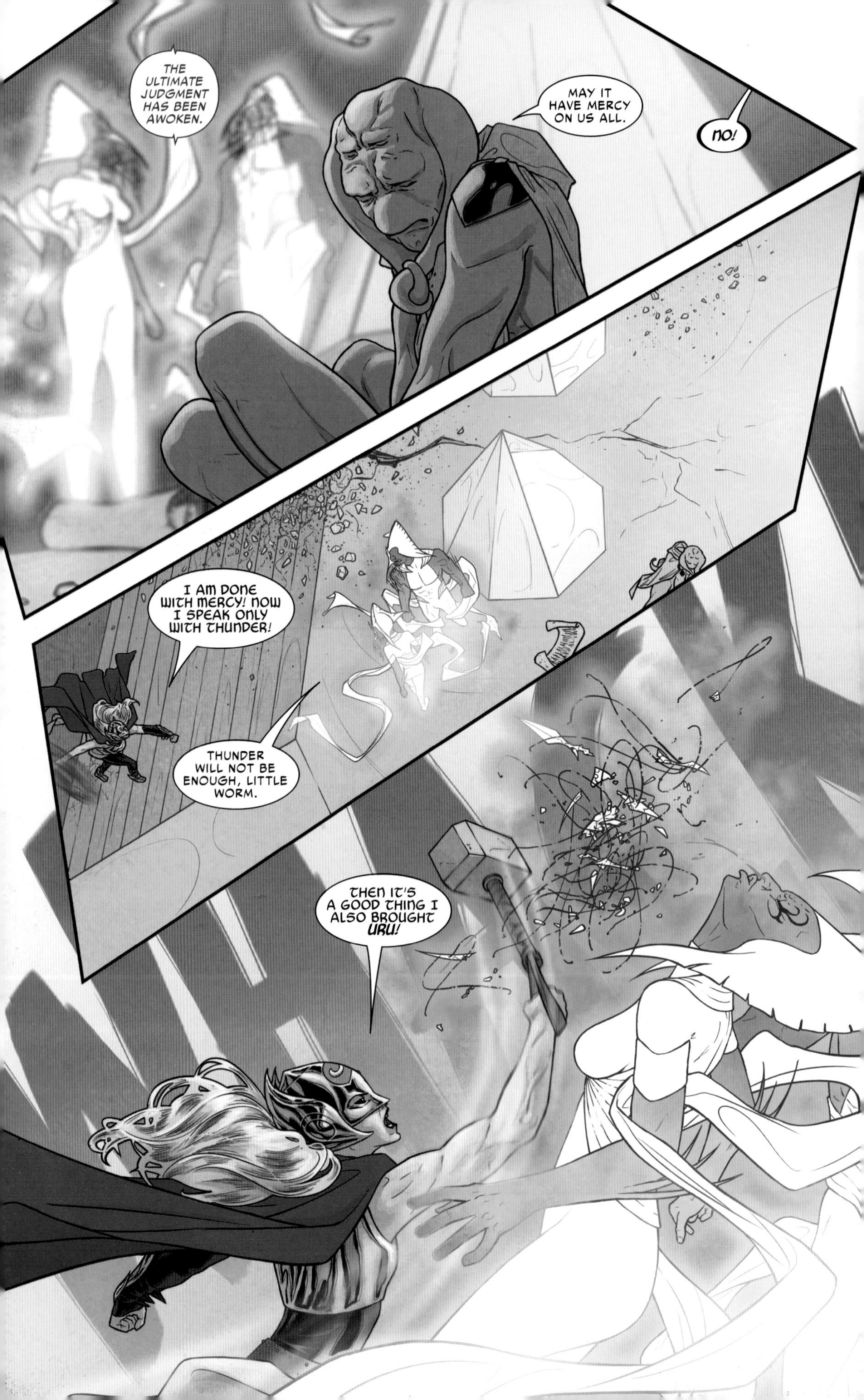
THE ULTIMATE JUDGMENT HAS BEEN AWOKEN.
MAY IT HAVE MERCY ON US ALL.
NO!
I AM DONE WITH MERCY! NOW I SPEAK ONLY WITH THUNDER!
THUNDER WILL NOT BE ENOUGH, LITTLE WORM.
THEN IT'S A GOOD THING I ALSO BROUGHT URU!

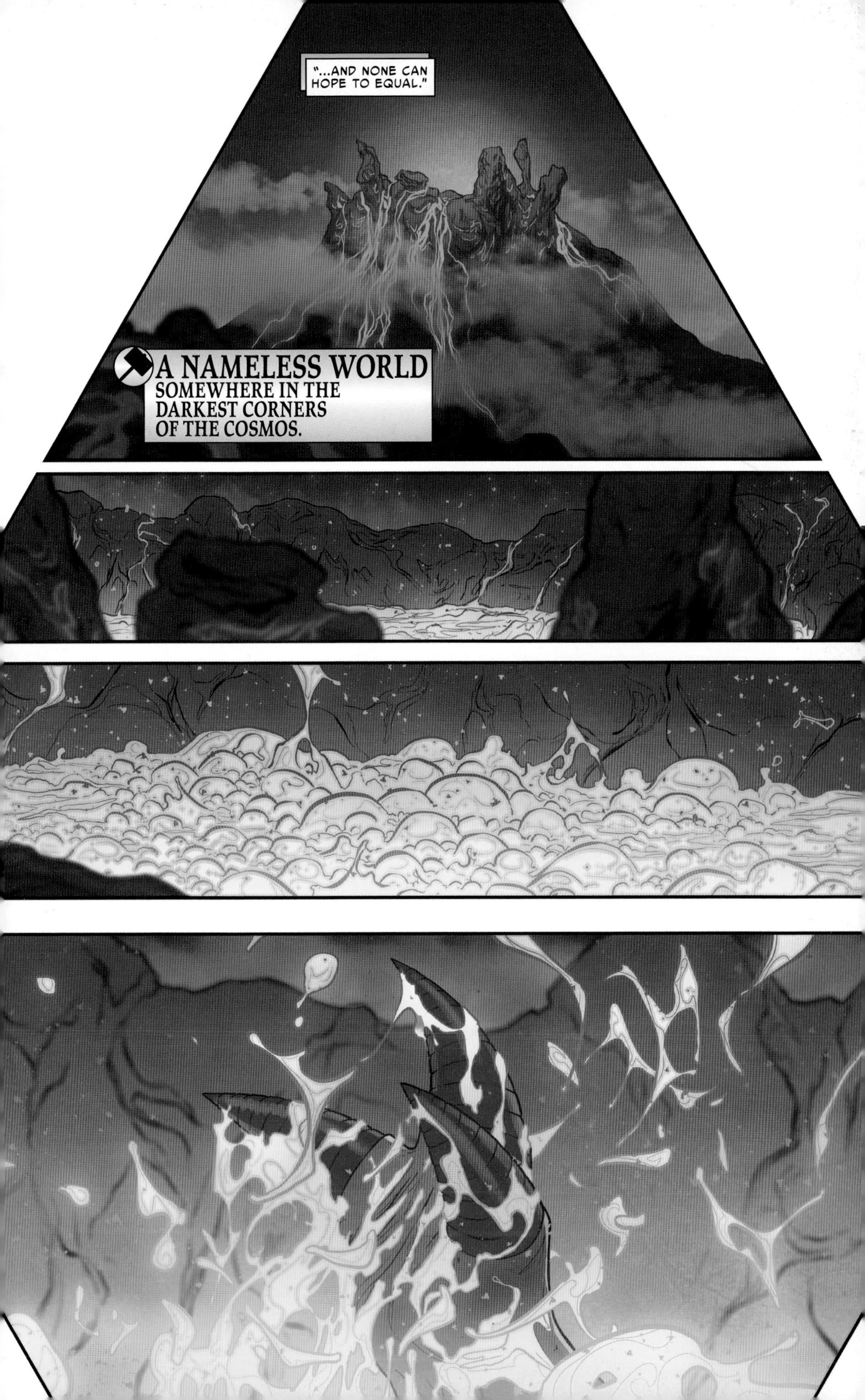
"...AND NONE CAN HOPE TO EQUAL."
A NAMELESS WORLD
SOMEWHERE IN THE DARKEST CORNERS OF THE COSMOS.

The Mighty Thor Variant Cover Gallery

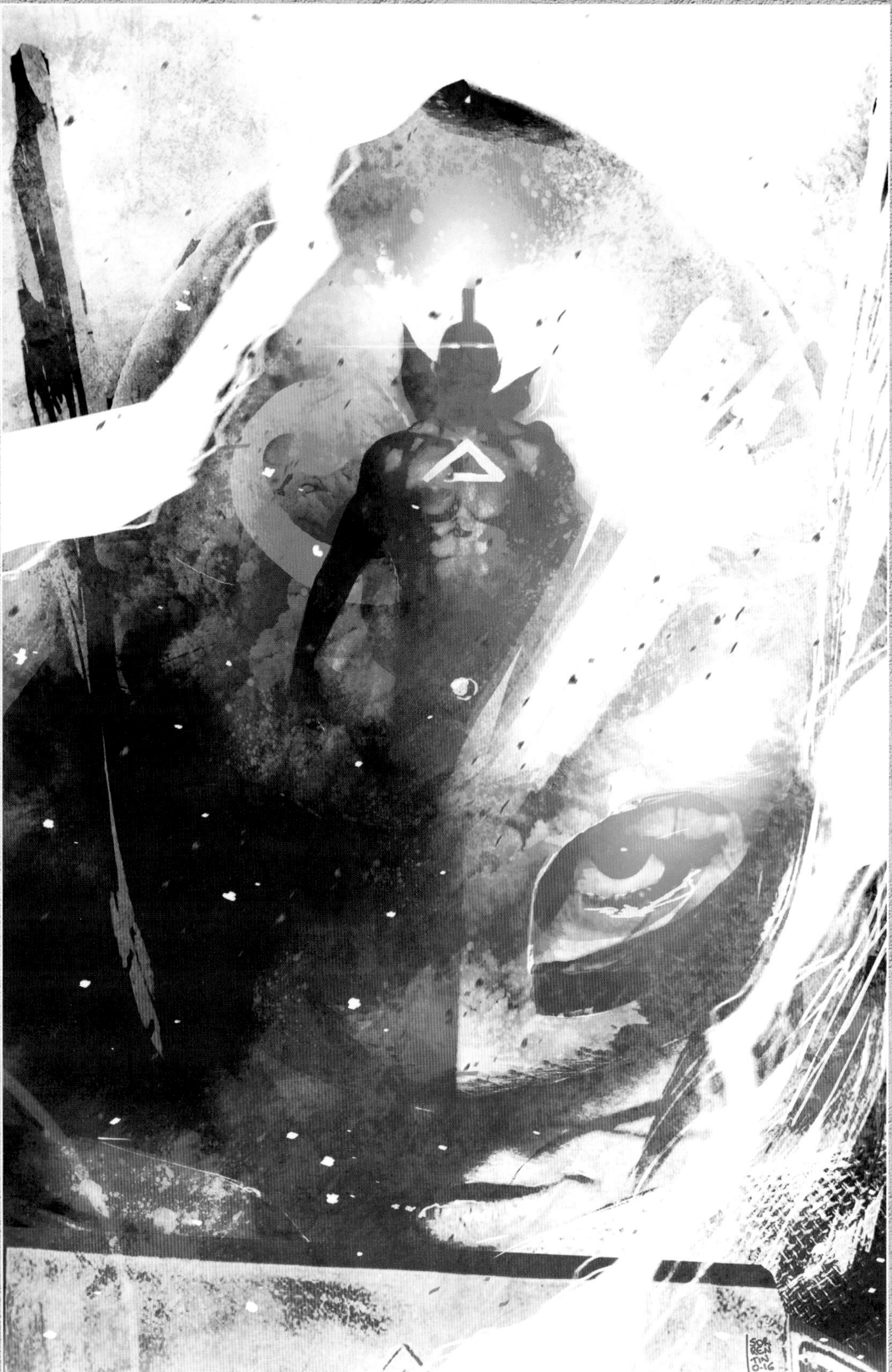

Mighty Thor #15
By Andrea Sorrentino

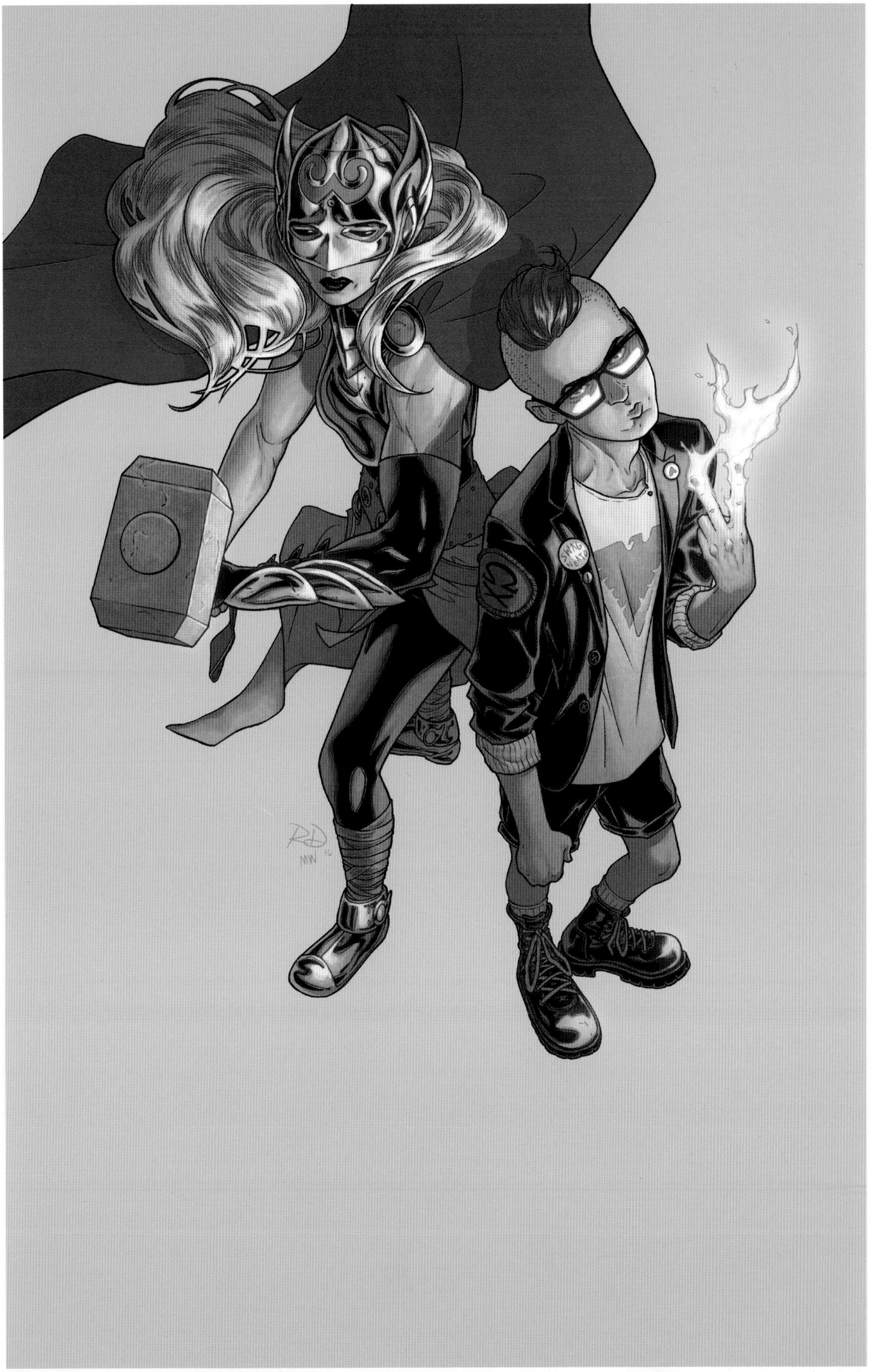

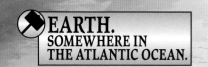

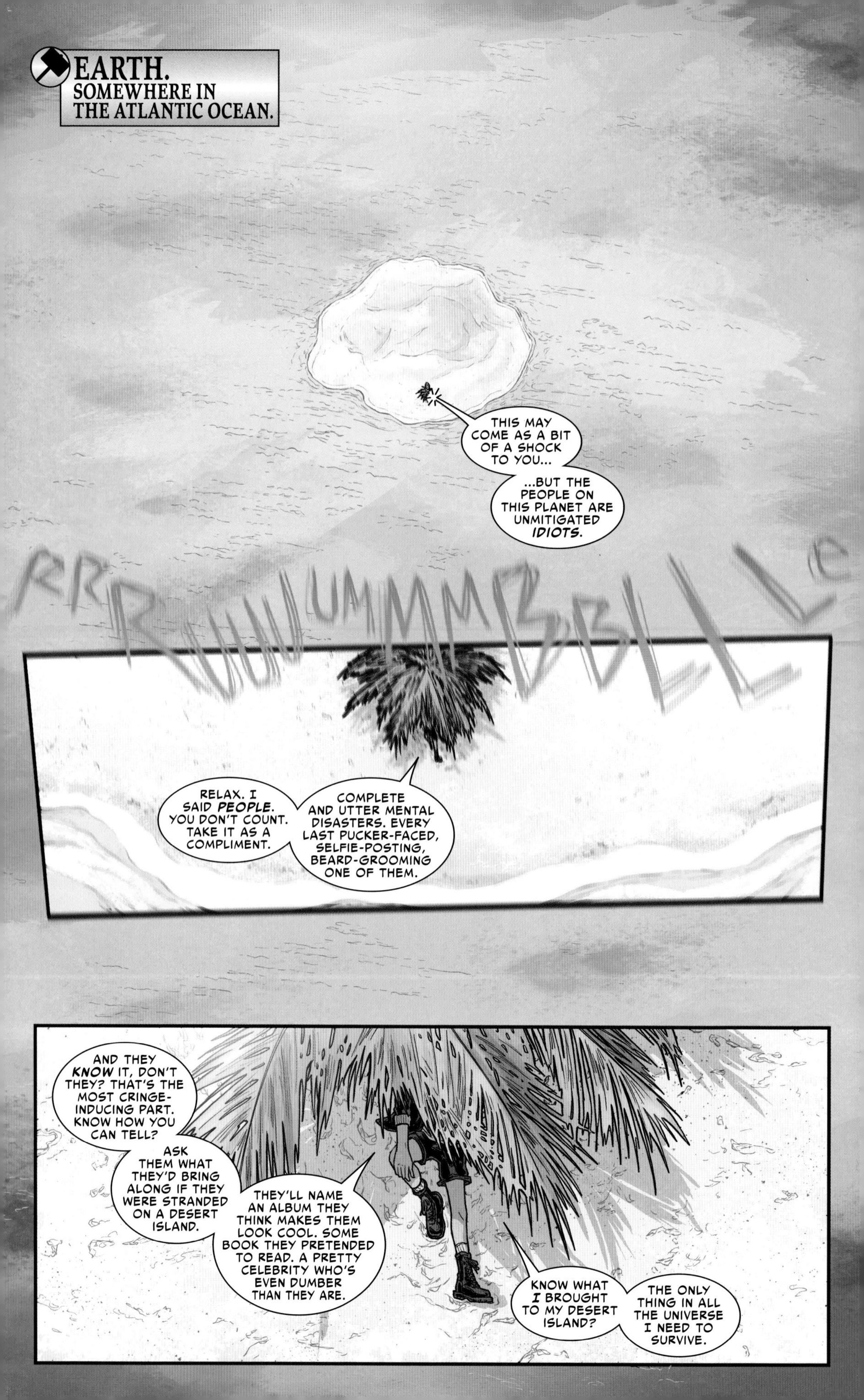
EARTH.
SOMEWHERE IN THE ATLANTIC OCEAN.
THIS MAY COME AS A BIT OF A SHOCK TO YOU...
...BUT THE PEOPLE ON THIS PLANET ARE UNMITIGATED IDIOTS.
RRRUUUUMMMBBLLLE
COMPLETE AND UTTER MENTAL DISASTERS. EVERY LAST PUCKER-FACED, SELFIE-POSTING, BEARD-GROOMING ONE OF THEM.
RELAX. I SAID PEOPLE. YOU DON'T COUNT. TAKE IT AS A COMPLIMENT.
AND THEY KNOW IT, DON'T THEY? THAT'S THE MOST CRINGE-INDUCING PART. KNOW HOW YOU CAN TELL?
ASK THEM WHAT THEY'D BRING ALONG IF THEY WERE STRANDED ON A DESERT ISLAND.
THEY'LL NAME AN ALBUM THEY THINK MAKES THEM LOOK COOL. SOME BOOK THEY PRETENDED TO READ. A PRETTY CELEBRITY WHO'S EVEN DUMBER THAN THEY ARE.
KNOW WHAT I BROUGHT TO MY DESERT ISLAND?
THE ONLY THING IN ALL THE UNIVERSE I NEED TO SURVIVE.

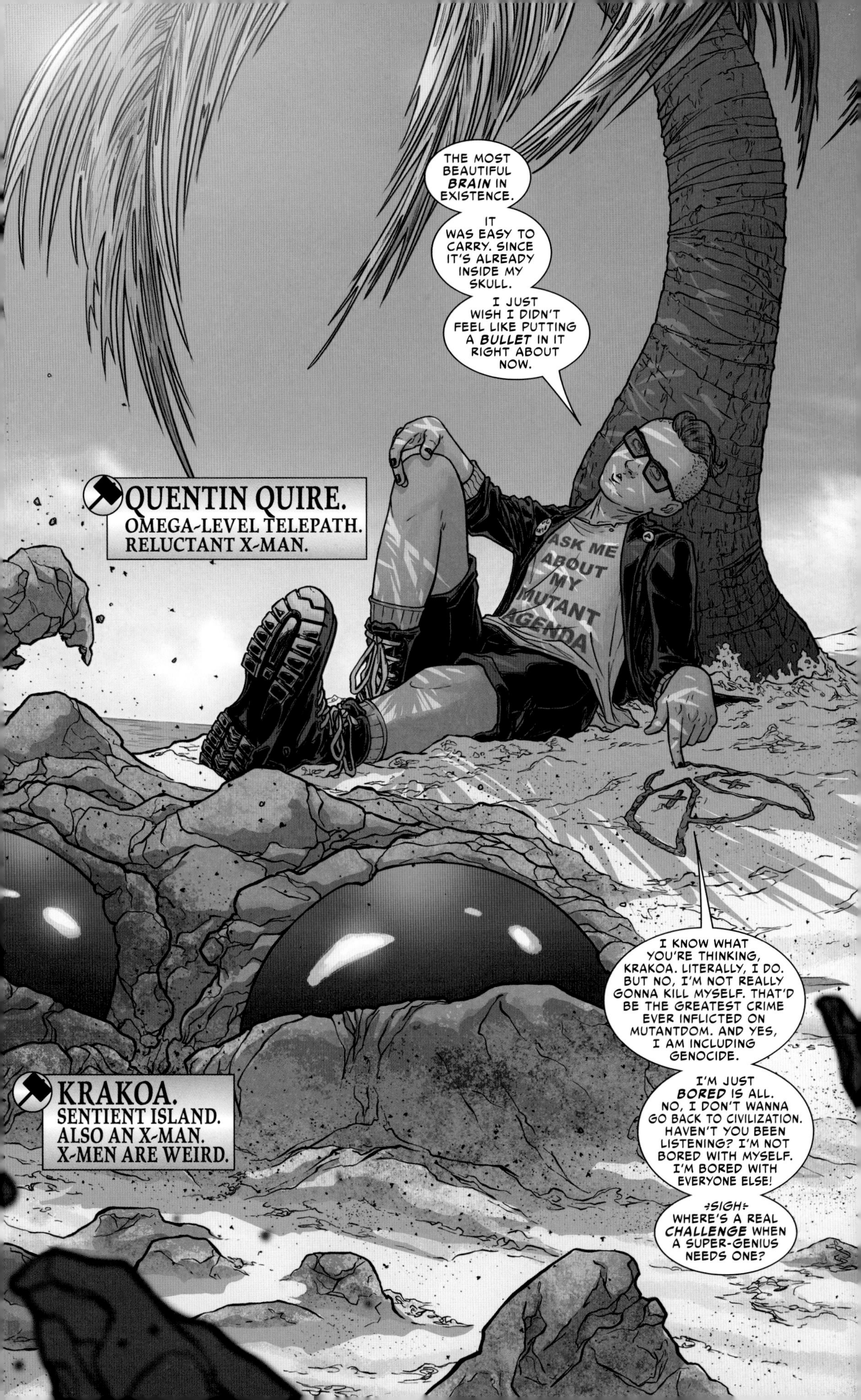

THE MOST BEAUTIFUL BRAIN IN EXISTENCE.
IT WAS EASY TO CARRY. SINCE IT'S ALREADY INSIDE MY SKULL.
I JUST WISH I DIDN'T FEEL LIKE PUTTING A BULLET IN IT RIGHT ABOUT NOW.
QUENTIN QUIRE. OMEGA-LEVEL TELEPATH. RELUCTANT X-MAN.
ASK ME ABOUT MY MUTANT AGENDA
I KNOW WHAT YOU'RE THINKING, KRAKOA. LITERALLY, I DO. BUT NO, I'M NOT REALLY GONNA KILL MYSELF. THAT'D BE THE GREATEST CRIME EVER INFLICTED ON MUTANTDOM. AND YES, I AM INCLUDING GENOCIDE.
KRAKOA. SENTIENT ISLAND. ALSO AN X-MAN. X-MEN ARE WEIRD.
I'M JUST BORED IS ALL. NO, I DON'T WANNA GO BACK TO CIVILIZATION. HAVEN'T YOU BEEN LISTENING? I'M NOT BORED WITH MYSELF. I'M BORED WITH EVERYONE ELSE!
SIGH WHERE'S A REAL CHALLENGE WHEN A SUPER-GENIUS NEEDS ONE?

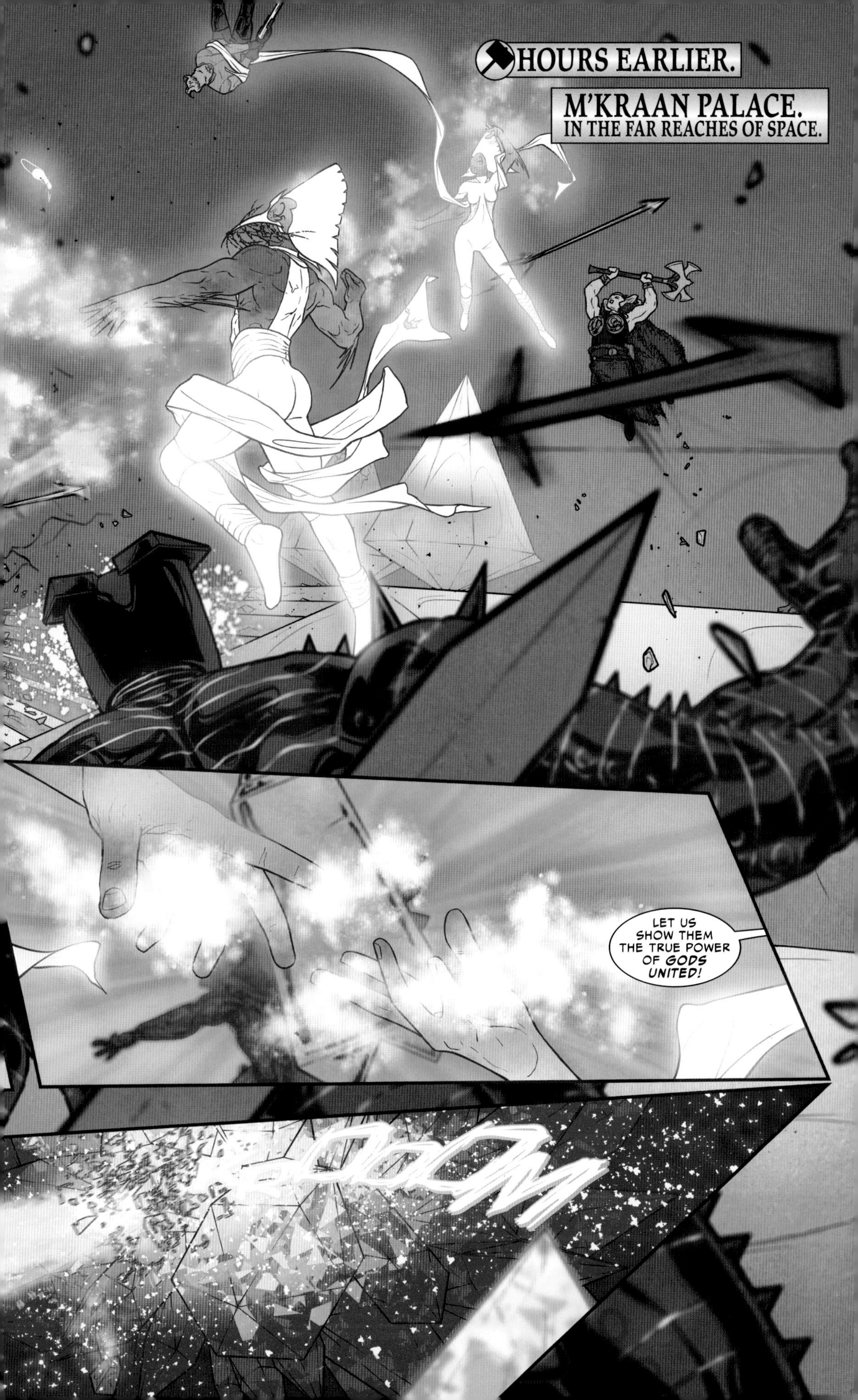
HOURS EARLIER.
M'KRAAN PALACE.
IN THE FAR REACHES OF SPACE.
LET US SHOW THEM THE TRUE POWER OF GODS UNITED!
BOOOOM

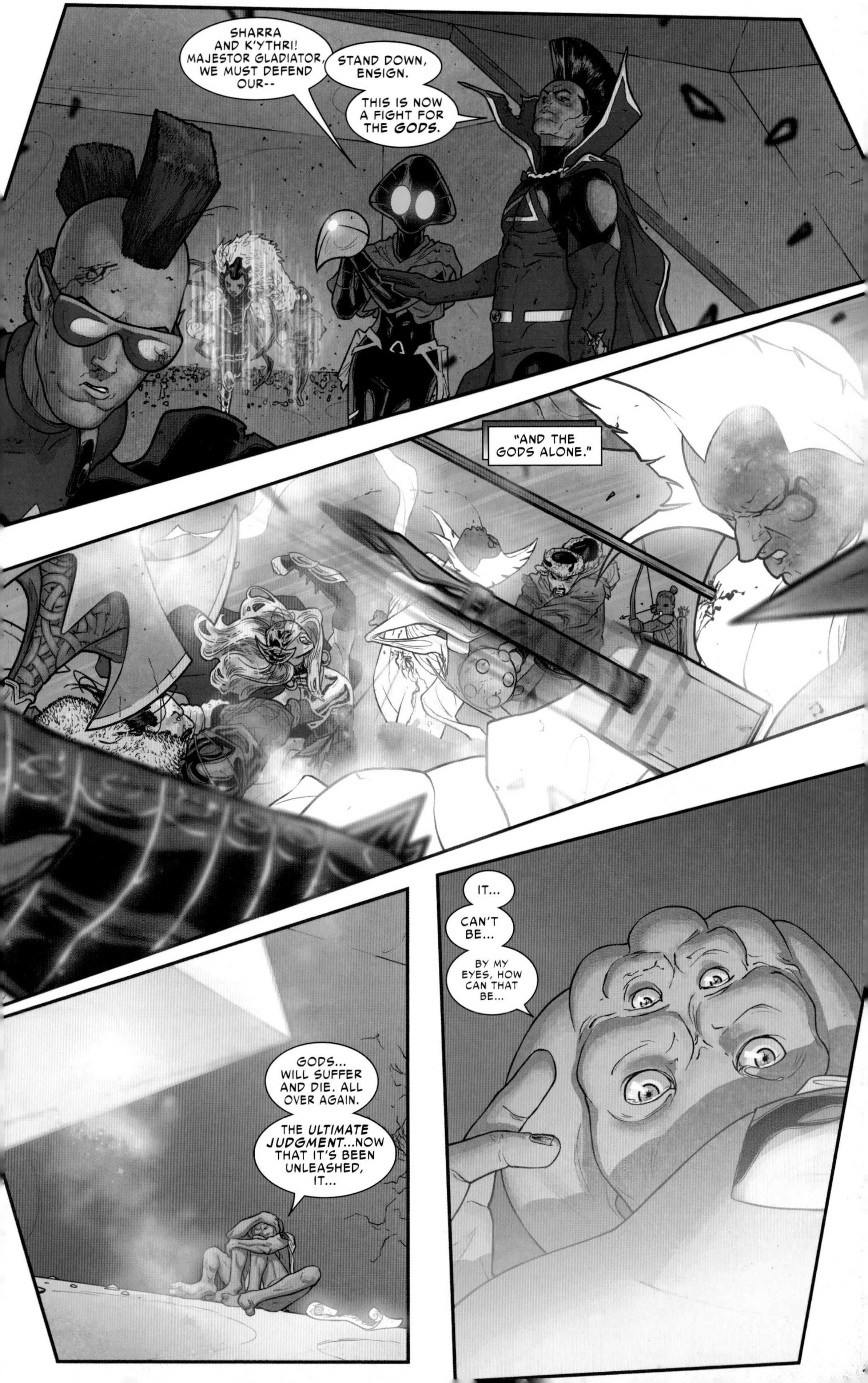
SHARRA AND K'YTHRI! MAJESTOR GLADIATOR, WE MUST DEFEND OUR--
STAND DOWN, ENSIGN.
THIS IS NOW A FIGHT FOR THE *GODS*.
"AND THE GODS ALONE."
IT...
CAN'T BE...
BY MY EYES, HOW CAN THAT BE...
GODS... WILL SUFFER AND DIE. ALL OVER AGAIN.
THE *ULTIMATE JUDGMENT*...NOW THAT IT'S BEEN UNLEASHED, IT...

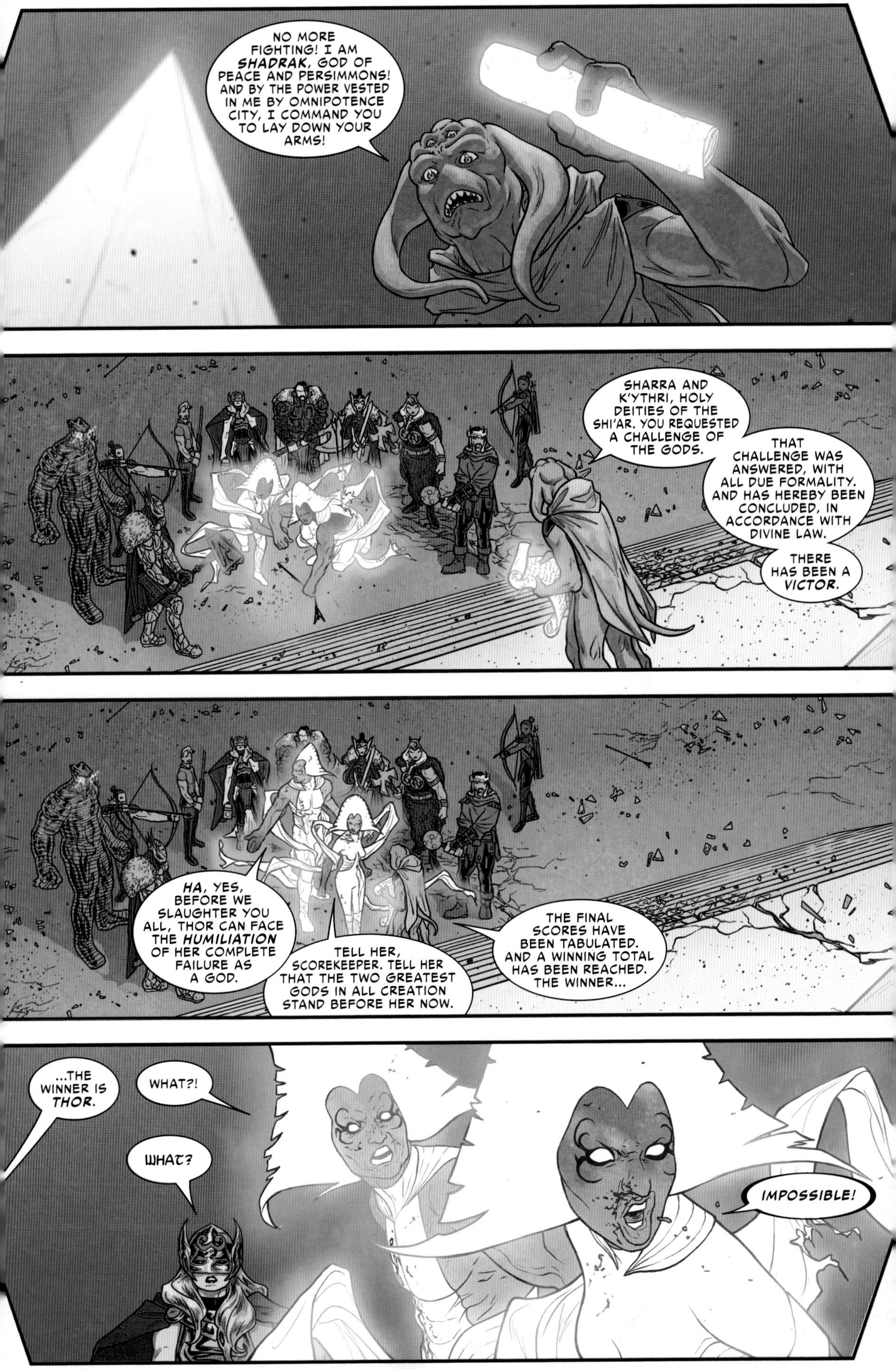
NO MORE FIGHTING! I AM SHADRAK, GOD OF PEACE AND PERSIMMONS! AND BY THE POWER VESTED IN ME BY OMNIPOTENCE CITY, I COMMAND YOU TO LAY DOWN YOUR ARMS!
SHARRA AND K'YTHRI, HOLY DEITIES OF THE SHI'AR. YOU REQUESTED A CHALLENGE OF THE GODS.
THAT CHALLENGE WAS ANSWERED, WITH ALL DUE FORMALITY. AND HAS HEREBY BEEN CONCLUDED, IN ACCORDANCE WITH DIVINE LAW.
THERE HAS BEEN A VICTOR.
HA, YES, BEFORE WE SLAUGHTER YOU ALL, THOR CAN FACE THE HUMILIATION OF HER COMPLETE FAILURE AS A GOD.
TELL HER, SCOREKEEPER. TELL HER THAT THE TWO GREATEST GODS IN ALL CREATION STAND BEFORE HER NOW.
THE FINAL SCORES HAVE BEEN TABULATED. AND A WINNING TOTAL HAS BEEN REACHED. THE WINNER...
...THE WINNER IS THOR.
WHAT?!
WHAT?
IMPOSSIBLE!

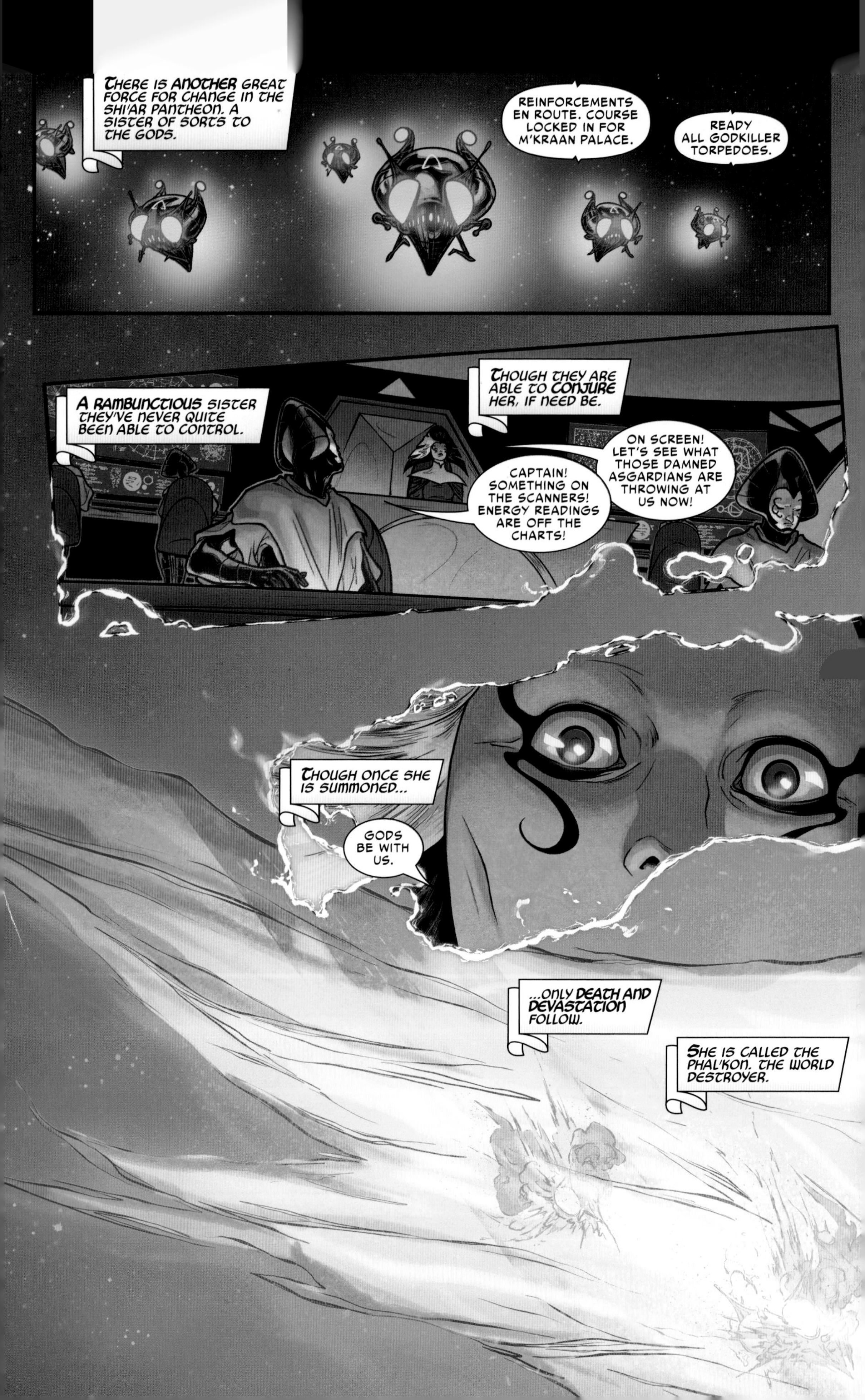

THERE IS ANOTHER GREAT FORCE FOR CHANGE IN THE SHI'AR PANTHEON. A SISTER OF SORTS TO THE GODS.
REINFORCEMENTS EN ROUTE. COURSE LOCKED IN FOR M'KRAAN PALACE.
READY ALL GODKILLER TORPEDOES.
A RAMBUNCTIOUS SISTER THEY'VE NEVER QUITE BEEN ABLE TO CONTROL.
THOUGH THEY ARE ABLE TO CONJURE HER, IF NEED BE.
CAPTAIN! SOMETHING ON THE SCANNERS! ENERGY READINGS ARE OFF THE CHARTS!
ON SCREEN! LET'S SEE WHAT THOSE DAMNED ASGARDIANS ARE THROWING AT US NOW!
THOUGH ONCE SHE IS SUMMONED...
GODS BE WITH US.
...ONLY DEATH AND DEVASTATION FOLLOW.
SHE IS CALLED THE PHAL'KON. THE WORLD DESTROYER.

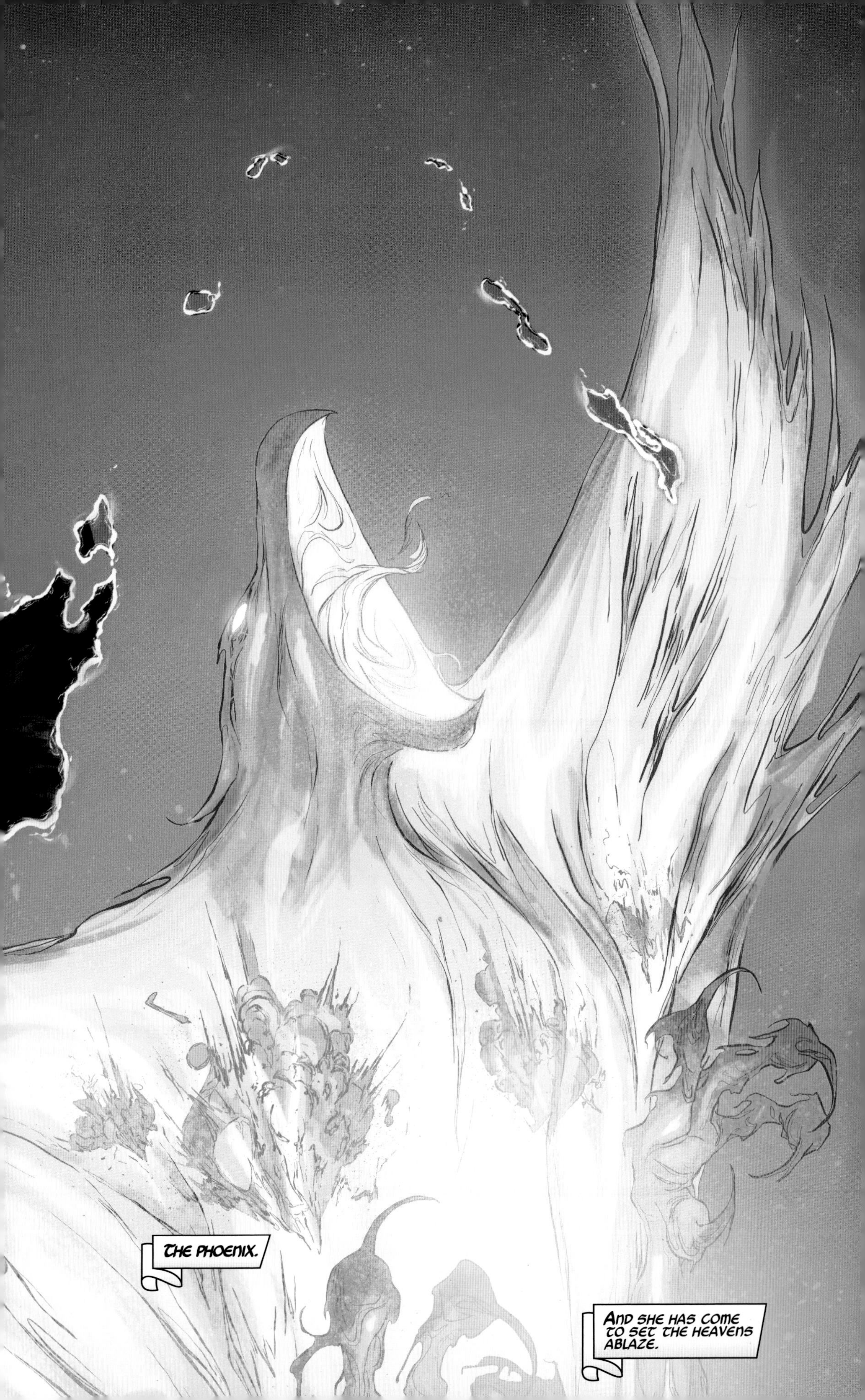
THE PHOENIX.
AND SHE HAS COME TO SET THE HEAVENS ABLAZE.

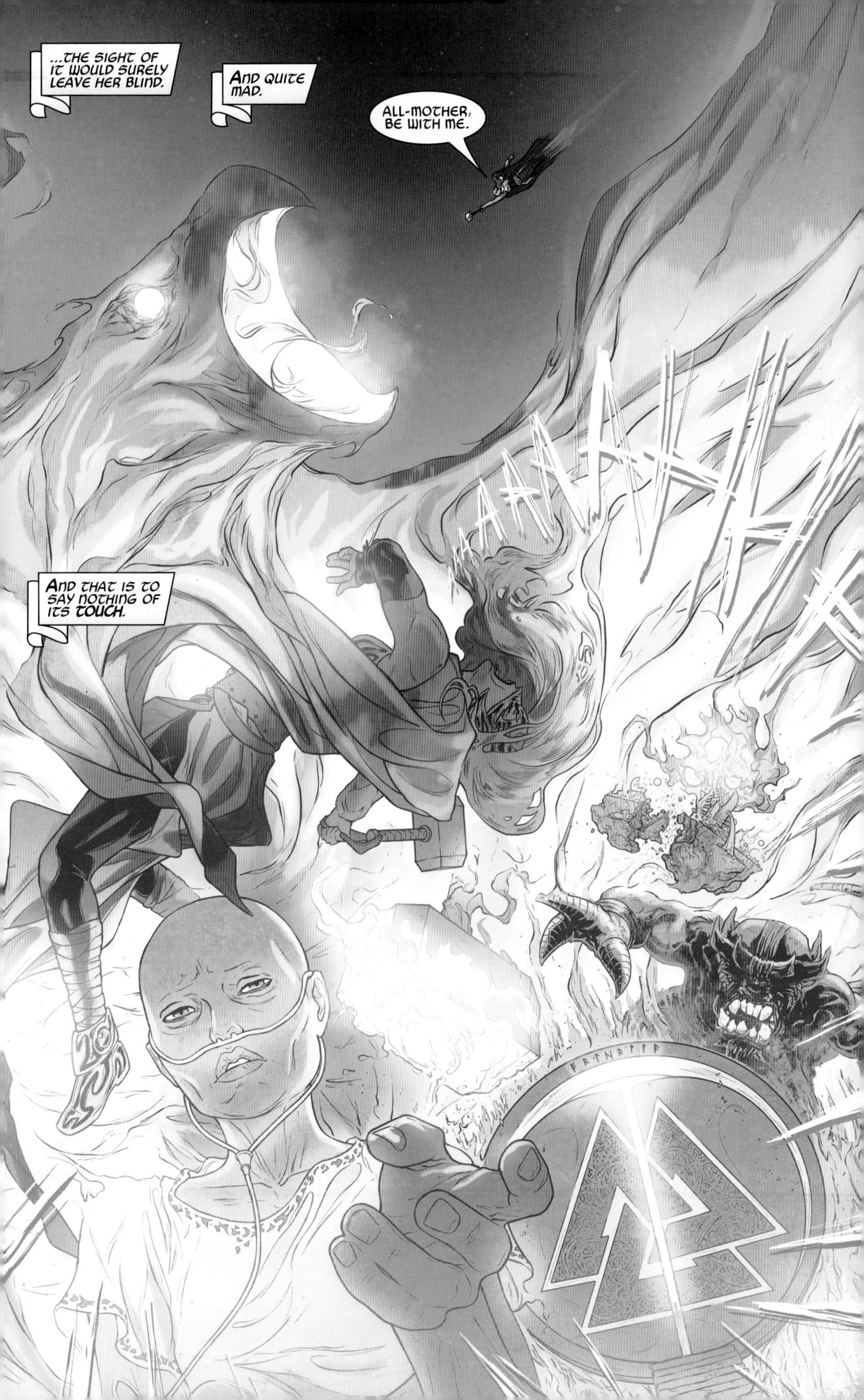
...THE SIGHT OF IT WOULD SURELY LEAVE HER BLIND.
AND QUITE MAD.
ALL-MOTHER, BE WITH ME.
AAAAAAAAHHH
AND THAT IS TO SAY NOTHING OF ITS TOUCH.

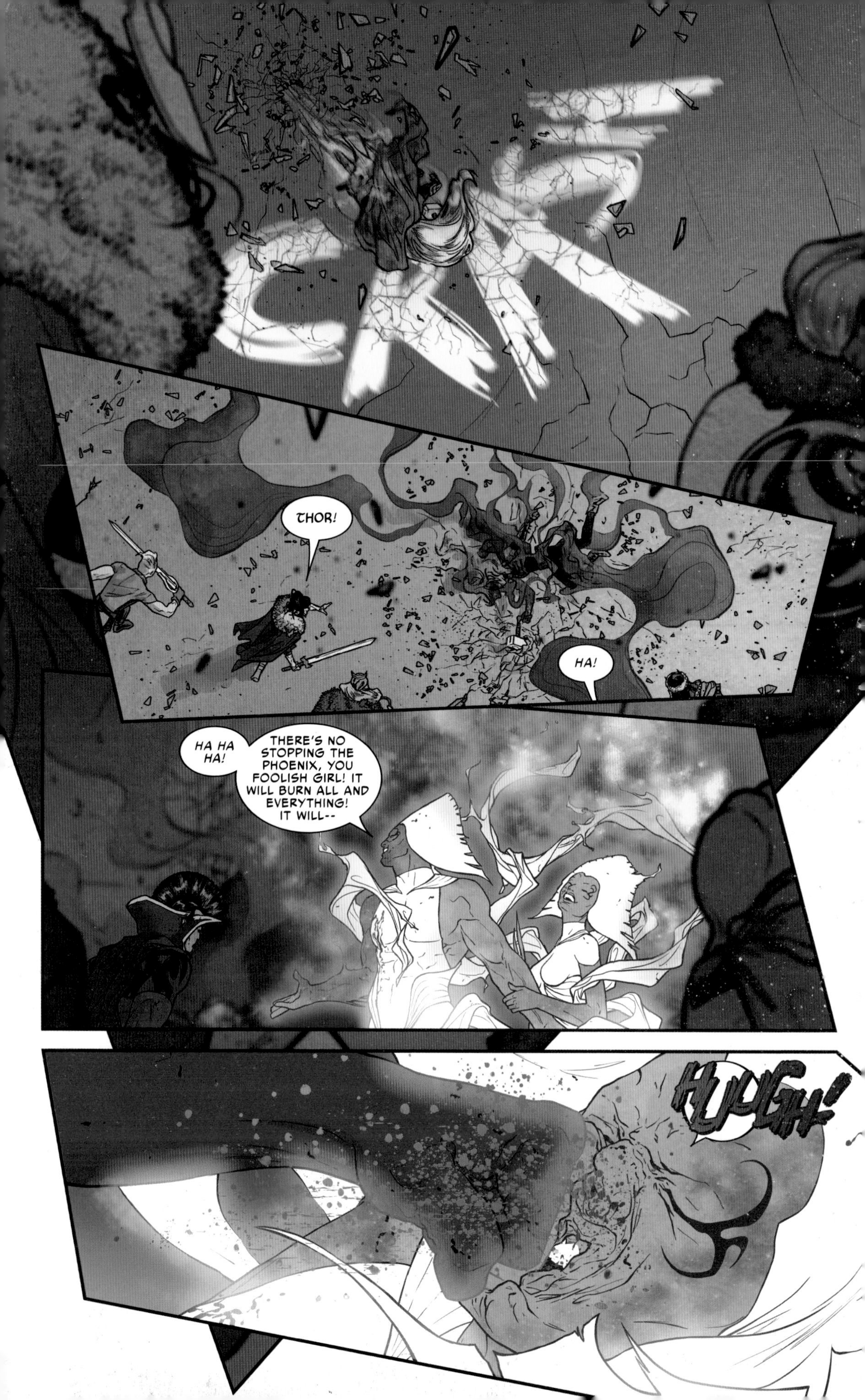
CRAK
THOR!
HA!
HA HA HA!
THERE'S NO STOPPING THE PHOENIX, YOU FOOLISH GIRL! IT WILL BURN ALL AND EVERYTHING! IT WILL--
HUUGH!

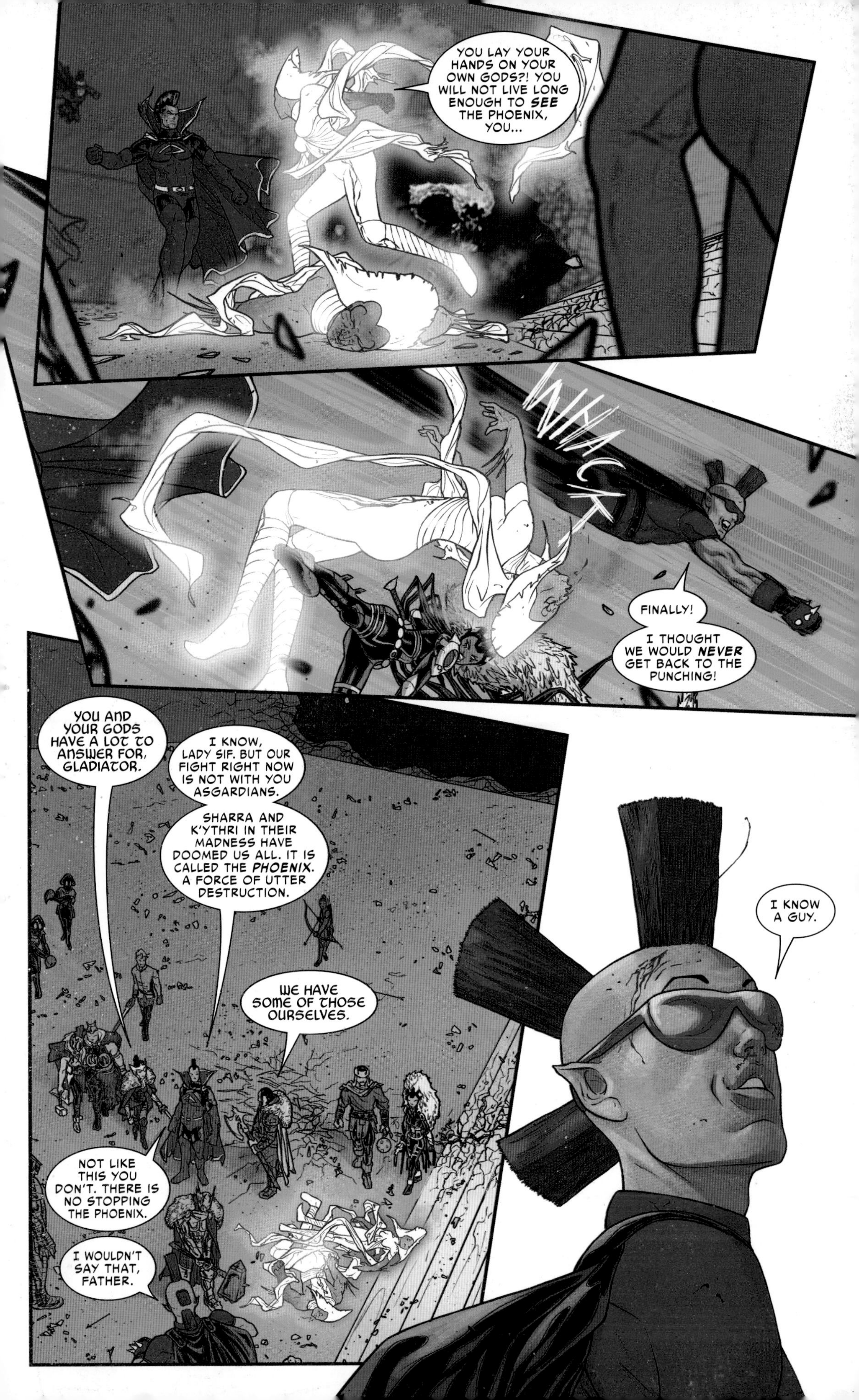

YOU LAY YOUR HANDS ON YOUR OWN GODS?! YOU WILL NOT LIVE LONG ENOUGH TO SEE THE PHOENIX, YOU...
WHACK
FINALLY!
I THOUGHT WE WOULD NEVER GET BACK TO THE PUNCHING!
YOU AND YOUR GODS HAVE A LOT TO ANSWER FOR, GLADIATOR.
I KNOW, LADY SIF. BUT OUR FIGHT RIGHT NOW IS NOT WITH YOU ASGARDIANS.
SHARRA AND K'YTHRI IN THEIR MADNESS HAVE DOOMED US ALL. IT IS CALLED THE PHOENIX. A FORCE OF UTTER DESTRUCTION.
WE HAVE SOME OF THOSE OURSELVES.
NOT LIKE THIS YOU DON'T. THERE IS NO STOPPING THE PHOENIX.
I WOULDN'T SAY THAT, FATHER.
I KNOW A GUY.

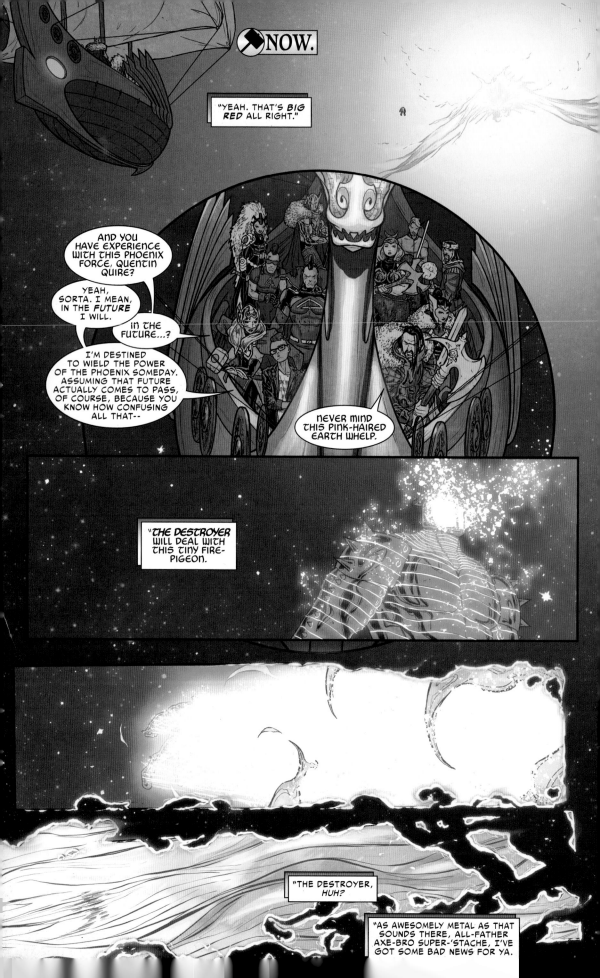

"YEAH. THAT'S *BIG RED* ALL RIGHT."

AND YOU HAVE EXPERIENCE WITH THIS PHOENIX FORCE, QUENTIN QUIRE?

YEAH, SORTA. I MEAN, IN THE *FUTURE* I WILL.

IN THE FUTURE...?

I'M DESTINED TO WIELD THE POWER OF THE PHOENIX SOMEDAY. ASSUMING THAT FUTURE ACTUALLY COMES TO PASS, OF COURSE, BECAUSE YOU KNOW HOW CONFUSING ALL THAT--

NEVER MIND THIS PINK-HAIRED EARTH WHELP.

"*THE DESTROYER* WILL DEAL WITH THIS TINY FIRE-PIGEON.

"THE DESTROYER, HUH?

"AS AWESOMELY METAL AS THAT SOUNDS THERE, ALL-FATHER AXE-BRO SUPER-'STACHE, I'VE GOT SOME BAD NEWS FOR YA.

Mighty Thor #16
By Joe Jusko

MARVEL GRAPHIC NOVEL

MIGHTY THOR #19

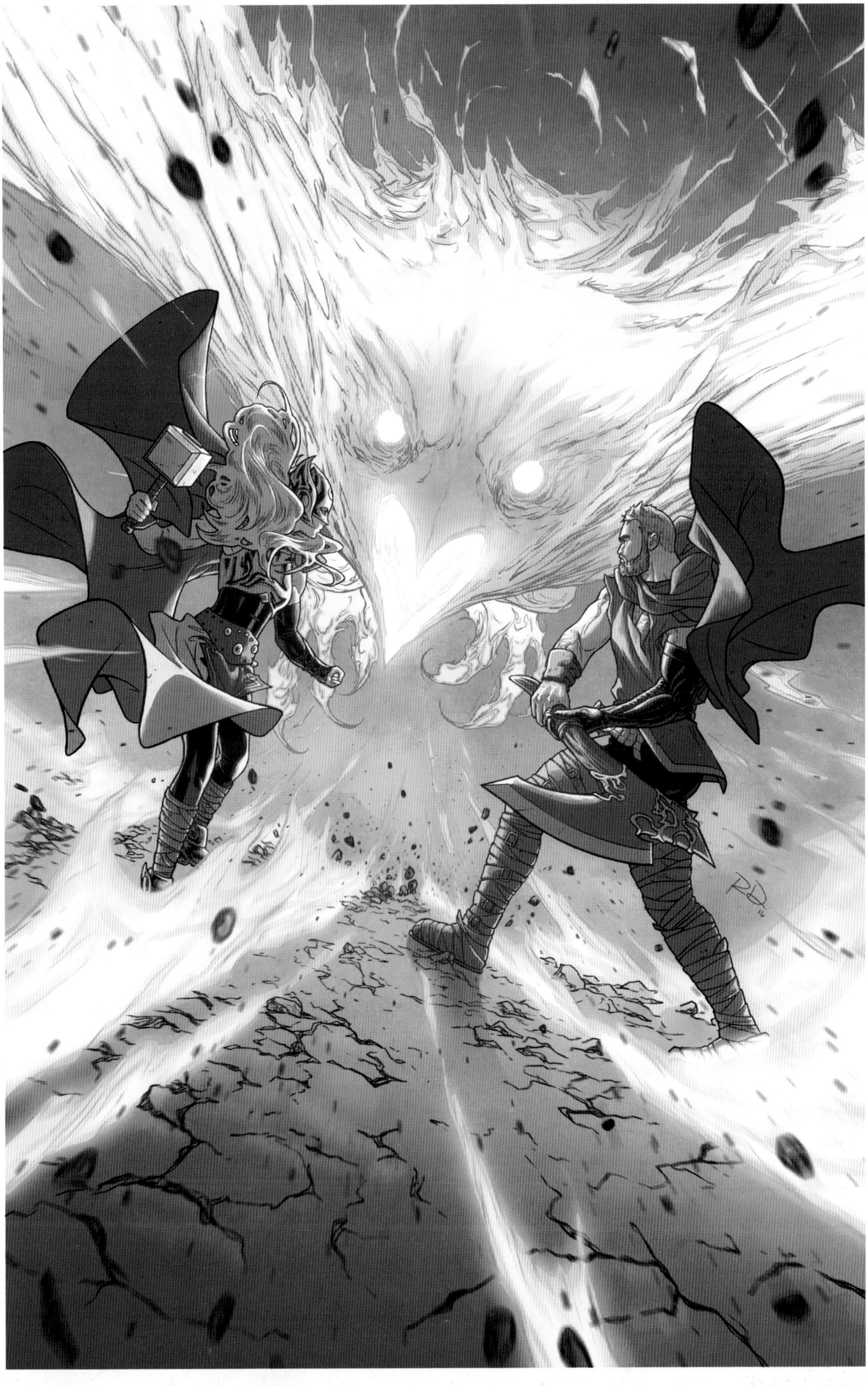

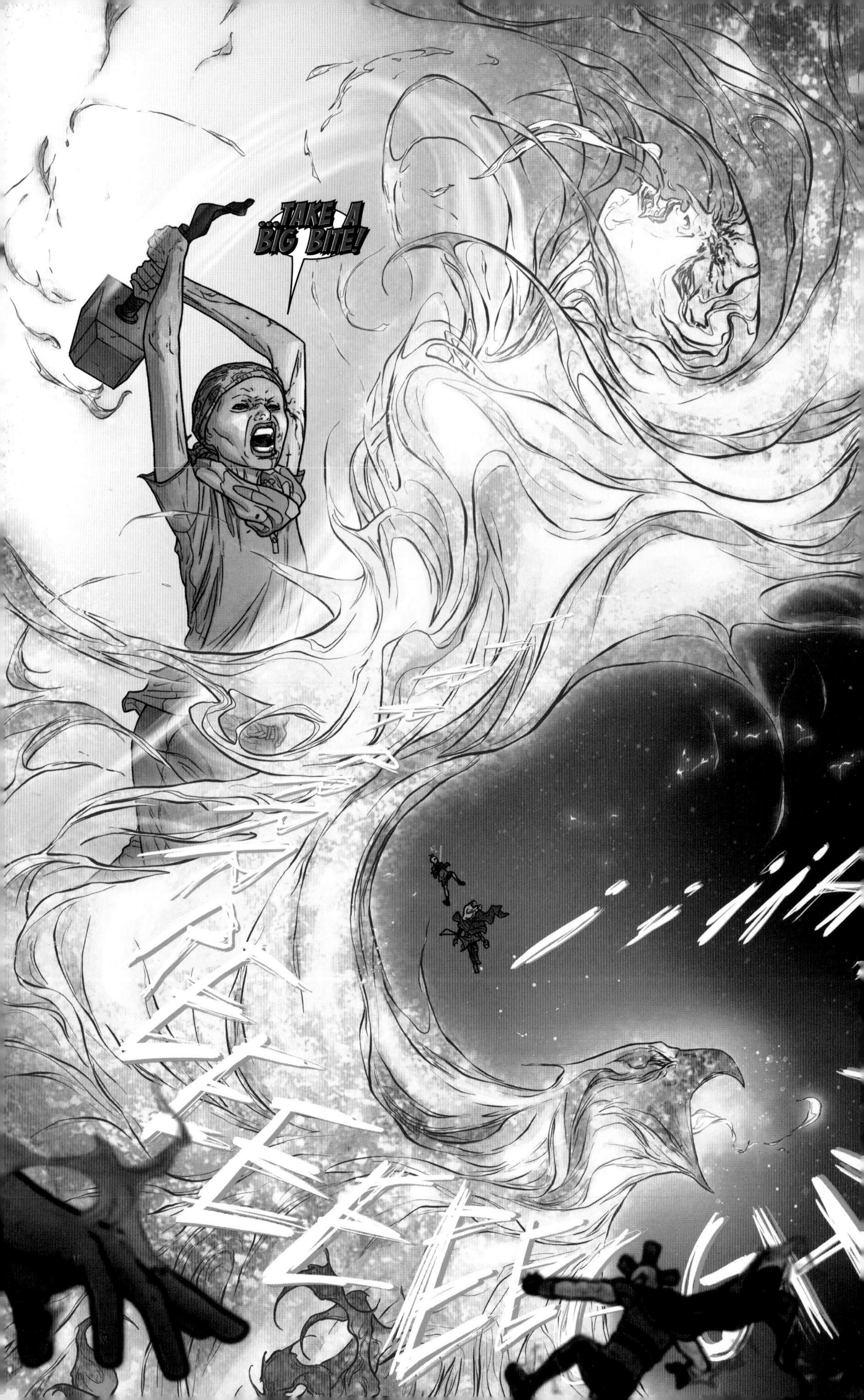
...TAKE A BIG BITE!

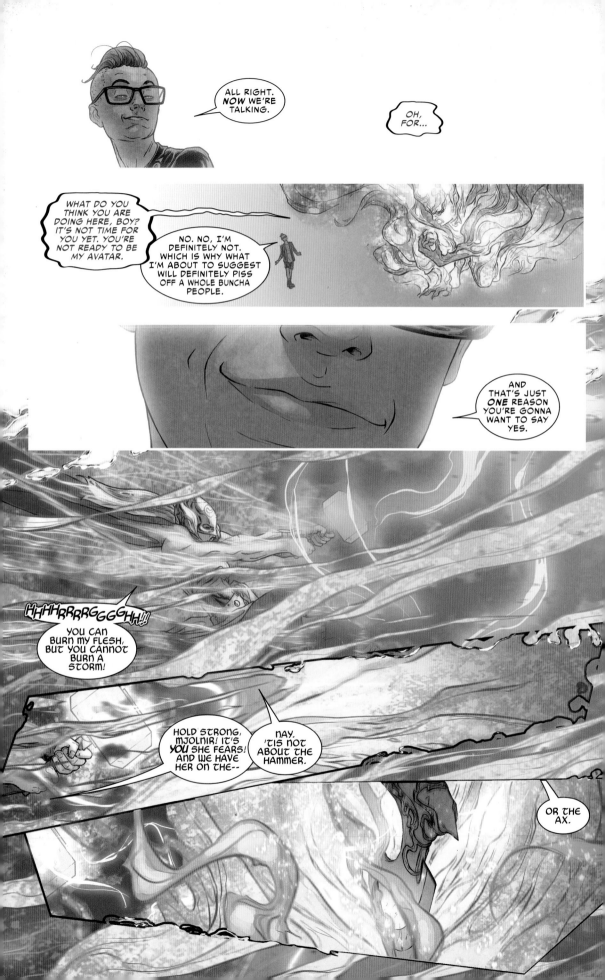

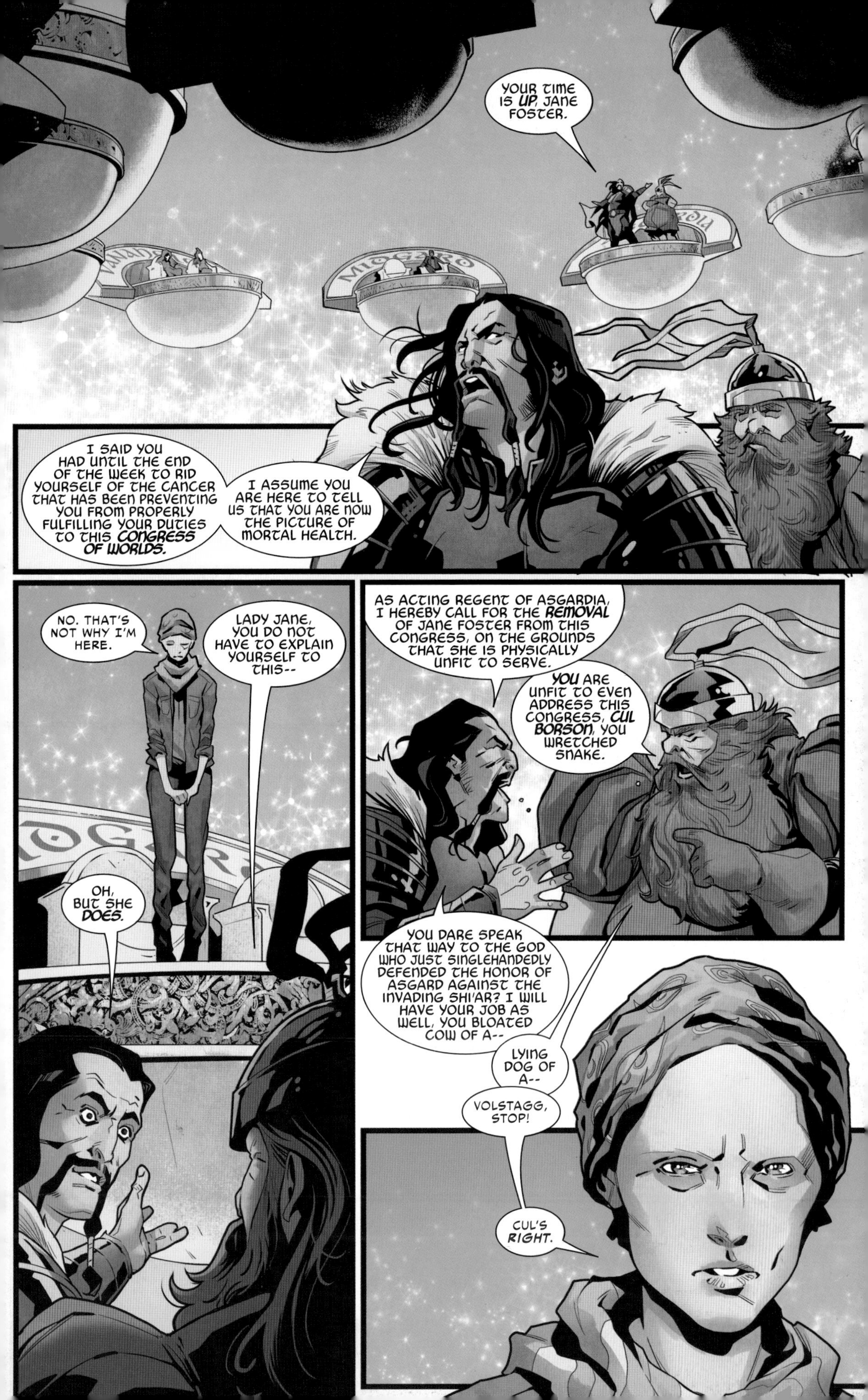

YOUR TIME IS UP, JANE FOSTER.
I SAID YOU HAD UNTIL THE END OF THE WEEK TO RID YOURSELF OF THE CANCER THAT HAS BEEN PREVENTING YOU FROM PROPERLY FULFILLING YOUR DUTIES TO THIS CONGRESS OF WORLDS.
I ASSUME YOU ARE HERE TO TELL US THAT YOU ARE NOW THE PICTURE OF MORTAL HEALTH.
MIDGARD
NO. THAT'S NOT WHY I'M HERE.
LADY JANE, YOU DO NOT HAVE TO EXPLAIN YOURSELF TO THIS--
OH, BUT SHE DOES.
AS ACTING REGENT OF ASGARDIA, I HEREBY CALL FOR THE REMOVAL OF JANE FOSTER FROM THIS CONGRESS, ON THE GROUNDS THAT SHE IS PHYSICALLY UNFIT TO SERVE.
YOU ARE UNFIT TO EVEN ADDRESS THIS CONGRESS, CUL BORSON, YOU WRETCHED SNAKE.
YOU DARE SPEAK THAT WAY TO THE GOD WHO JUST SINGLEHANDEDLY DEFENDED THE HONOR OF ASGARD AGAINST THE INVADING SHI'AR? I WILL HAVE YOUR JOB AS WELL, YOU BLOATED COW OF A--
LYING DOG OF A--
VOLSTAGG, STOP!
CUL'S RIGHT.

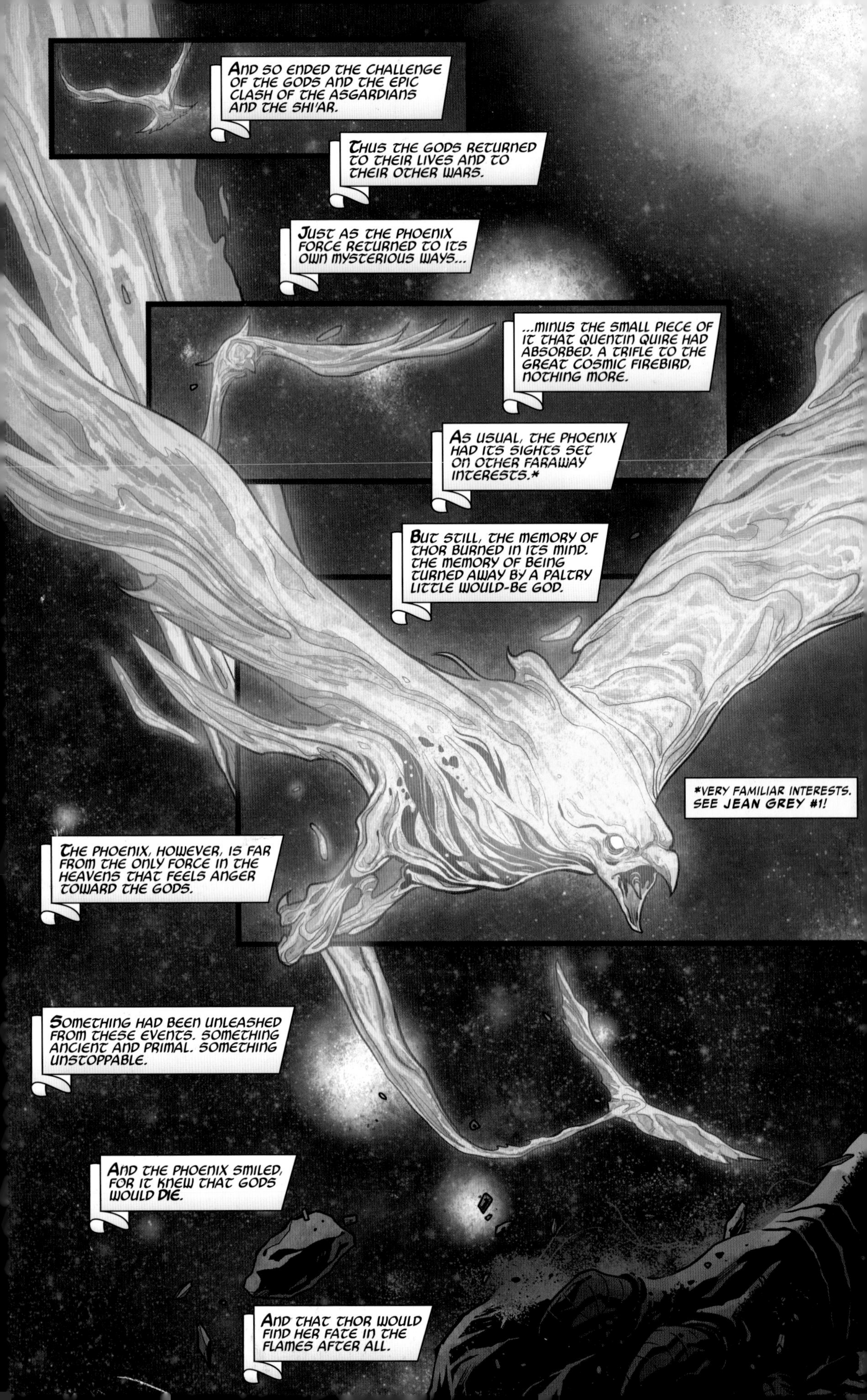
AND SO ENDED THE CHALLENGE OF THE GODS AND THE EPIC CLASH OF THE ASGARDIANS AND THE SHI'AR.
THUS THE GODS RETURNED TO THEIR LIVES AND TO THEIR OTHER WARS.
JUST AS THE PHOENIX FORCE RETURNED TO ITS OWN MYSTERIOUS WAYS...
...MINUS THE SMALL PIECE OF IT THAT QUENTIN QUIRE HAD ABSORBED. A TRIFLE TO THE GREAT COSMIC FIREBIRD, NOTHING MORE.
AS USUAL, THE PHOENIX HAD ITS SIGHTS SET ON OTHER FARAWAY INTERESTS.*
BUT STILL, THE MEMORY OF THOR BURNED IN ITS MIND. THE MEMORY OF BEING TURNED AWAY BY A PALTRY LITTLE WOULD-BE GOD.
*VERY FAMILIAR INTERESTS. SEE JEAN GREY #1!
THE PHOENIX, HOWEVER, IS FAR FROM THE ONLY FORCE IN THE HEAVENS THAT FEELS ANGER TOWARD THE GODS.
SOMETHING HAD BEEN UNLEASHED FROM THESE EVENTS. SOMETHING ANCIENT AND PRIMAL. SOMETHING UNSTOPPABLE.
AND THE PHOENIX SMILED, FOR IT KNEW THAT GODS WOULD DIE.
AND THAT THOR WOULD FIND HER FATE IN THE FLAMES AFTER ALL.

THE RE-FORMED LEAGUE OF REALMS IS MADE UP OF A FEW FAMILIAR FACES AS WELL AS SOME NEW ONES. CHECK OUT THESE AMAZING CHARACTER DESIGNS RUSSELL DAUTERMAN WHIPPED UP FOR TWO OF THE NEW ONES!

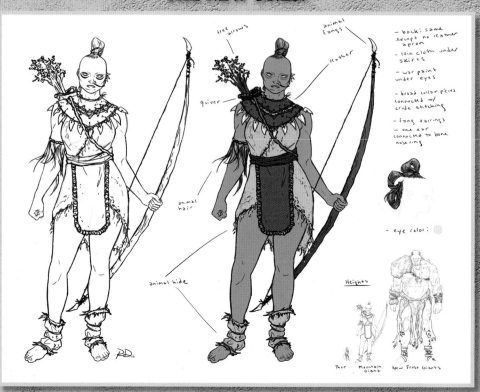

AND SINCE THOR GOT SOME ALL-NEW ALLIES, MALEKITH GOT ONE, TOO: KURSE!

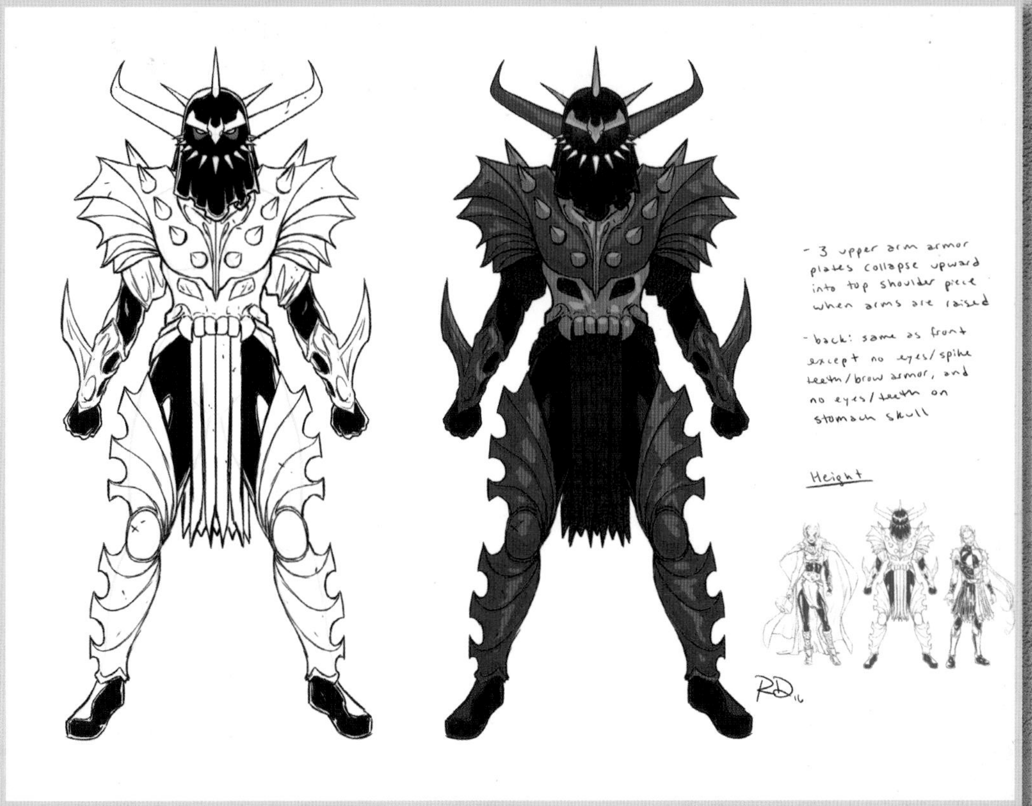
- 3 upper arm armor plates collapse upward into top shoulder piece when arms are raised
- back: same as front except no eyes/spike teeth/brow armor, and no eyes/teeth on stomach skull
Height
RD 16

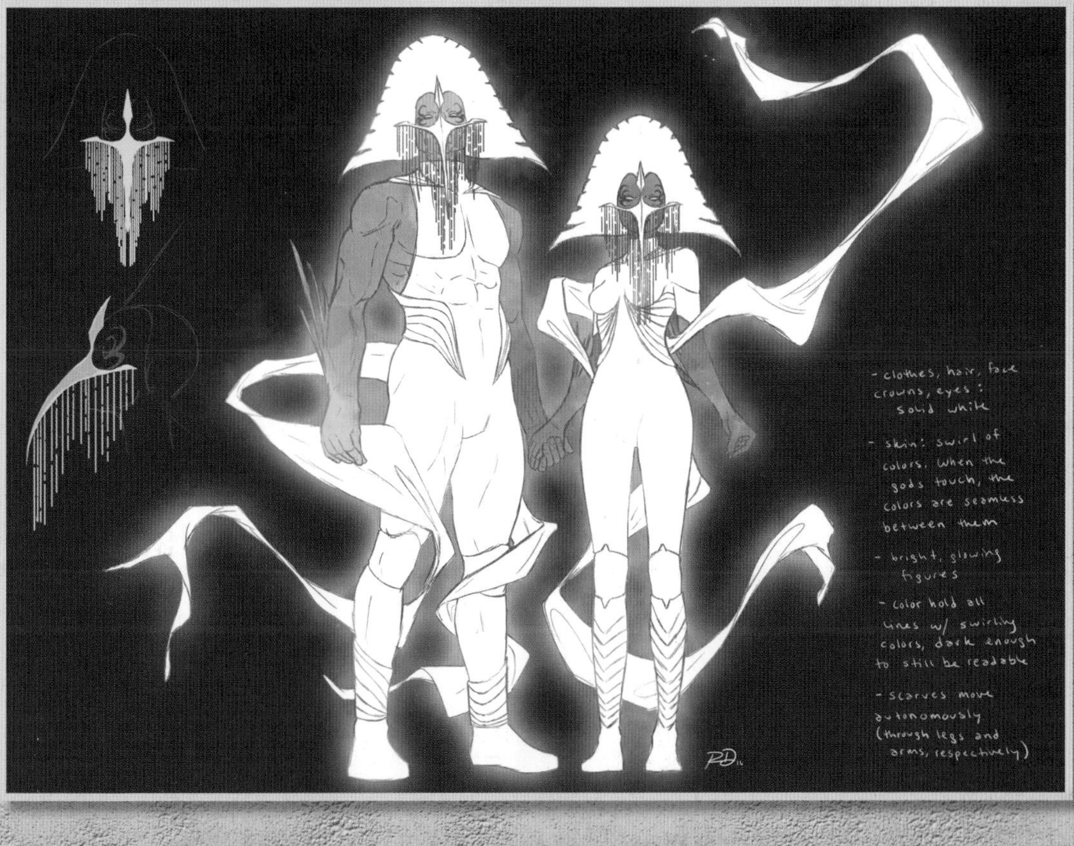
- clothes, hair, face crowns, eyes: solid white
- skin: swirl of colors. When the gods touch, the colors are seamless between them
- bright, glowing figures
- color hold all lines w/ swirling colors, dark enough to still be readable
- scarves move autonomously (through legs and arms, respectively)
RD 16

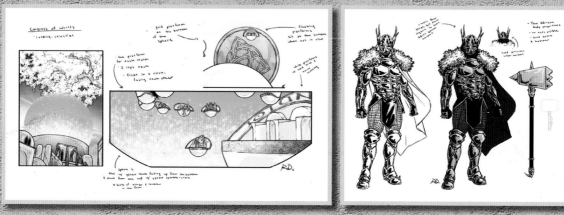